WRITE IT. PUBLISH IT. SELL IT.

M.L. RUSCSAK

Write It. Publish It. Sell It.

Copyright © 2024 Trient Press

All rights reserved. No portion of this publication may be reproduced, distributed, or transmitted in any form or by any means, including photocopying, recording, or other electronic or mechanical methods, without the prior written permission of the publisher. This restriction excludes brief quotations utilized in critical reviews and certain other noncommercial usages as permitted by copyright law. For permission inquiries, direct correspondence to the publisher, marked "Attention: Permissions Coordinator," at the following address:

Trient Press
3375 S Rainbow Blvd
#81710, SMB 13135
Las Vegas, NV 89180

Criminal copyright infringement, including instances without financial gain, is subject to investigation by the FBI and incurs penalties of up to five years in federal imprisonment and a fine of $250,000.

Excepting the original narrative material authored by M.L. Ruscsak, all songs, song titles, and lyrics cited within Write it. Publish it. Sell it.

remain the exclusive property of their respective artists, songwriters, and copyright holders.

Ordering Information:
For quantity sales, Trient Press offers special discounts to corporations, associations, and other organizations. For detailed information, contact the publisher at the address provided above.
For orders by U.S. trade bookstores and wholesalers, please reach out to Trient Press at Tel: (775) 996-3844, or visit www.trientpress.com.

Printed in the United States of America
Publisher's Cataloging-in-Publication Data
Ruscsak, M.L.
Write it. Publish it. Sell it.

Hardcover: **979-8-88990-201-0**

Paperback: ISBN **979-8-88990-202-7**

E-Book: **979-8-88990-203-4**

Introduction to "Write It. Publish It. Sell It."

Welcome to "Write It. Publish It. Sell It.: The Ultimate Publishing Power Move," brought to you by Trient Press as part of our commitment to empowering authors through education. This book is an essential component of our free course for authors, designed to guide you through every stage of the publishing journey. Whether you are an aspiring writer or a seasoned author, this comprehensive guide will provide you with valuable insights and practical strategies to master the art of writing, publishing, and promoting your book.

Write It. Publish It. Sell It.

Table of Contents

Chapter 1: Master the Writing Process Dive into the fundamentals of the writing process. Learn techniques to enhance your creativity, develop compelling characters, and structure your narrative effectively.

Chapter 2: Explore Self-Publishing vs. Traditional or Hybrid Publishing Understand the different publishing paths available to you. Weigh the pros and cons of self-publishing, traditional publishing, and hybrid publishing to make an informed decision about the best route for your book.

Chapter 3: Understanding Marketing vs. Promoting Your Book Discover the nuances between marketing and promoting your book. Learn how to develop a robust marketing strategy and leverage promotional activities to boost your book's visibility and sales.

Chapter 4: Learn What You Should Spend Money On Identify the critical areas where investing money can significantly enhance your book's quality and reach. Learn how to allocate your budget wisely to maximize your return on investment.

Chapter 5: Craft a Compelling Query Letter Master the art of writing a compelling query letter that captures the attention of literary agents and publishers. Learn the key components and techniques to make your query stand out.

Chapter 6: Build and Engage Your Audience Explore effective strategies to build and engage a loyal readership. Learn how to use social media, email newsletters, and community-building activities to connect with your audience.

Chapter 7: Set Real Expectations for Your Author Journey Set realistic and achievable goals for your writing career. Learn how to balance ambition with practicality, and understand the industry challenges and rewards.

Write It. Publish It. Sell It.

Conclusion Reflect on your journey through this book and the course. Summarize the key takeaways and prepare for the next steps in your publishing journey.

Appendices Additional resources, templates, and checklists to support you throughout your writing and publishing process.

About Trient Press and Lexicon Academy

This book and the accompanying course are part of the Lexicon Academy, which offers a variety of free and paid courses designed to support authors in their careers. Among our offerings is the Wealth Builder class, which provides valuable insights into financial planning and wealth management for writers. At Trient Press, we are dedicated to providing high-quality educational resources to help you achieve your publishing goals.

Join us on this journey to transform your writing aspirations into reality. Let's write it, publish it, and sell it together.

Write It. Publish It. Sell It.

Since publishing my first book in 2016, I have been on a journey filled with both triumphs and challenges, one that has constantly enriched my understanding of the publishing world. As an author and publisher, I have had the privilege of belonging to several author groups, where I have observed a recurring theme: new authors and those contemplating publishing their work often grapple with the same questions and uncertainties. It is this collective curiosity and quest for knowledge that inspired me to write "Write It. Publish It. Sell It."

In these circles, the questions range from mastering the intricacies of the writing process to navigating the complex paths of publishing, marketing, and promotion. Each of these questions is a testament to the universal desire to create, share, and succeed. However, many new authors fall into the same traps and face similar setbacks that could have been avoided with the right guidance and information.

My journey has been a continuous learning experience, and through this book, I hope to share the lessons I've gathered along the way. My aim is not just to provide answers, but to offer a roadmap that will help the next generation of authors avoid the pitfalls that many of us have encountered. By doing so, I aspire to foster a community where we rise together—not as competitors, but as colleagues, friends, and most importantly, as a team.

"Write It. Publish It. Sell It." is designed to be more than just a book; it is a companion that mirrors the comprehensive course I have developed. Each chapter is crafted to equip you with practical knowledge and actionable steps, ensuring that you are well-prepared for every stage of your author journey. From mastering your writing craft to making informed decisions about publishing, from understanding the nuances of marketing versus promotion to crafting a compelling query letter, this book covers it all.

Moreover, it is crucial to understand that the path to becoming a successful author does not end with the publication of your book. Building and engaging an audience, setting realistic expectations, and maintaining your motivation are equally vital components of your journey. This book will guide you through these aspects, providing you with the tools you need to achieve your goals.

Let us embark on this journey together. Let us educate and uplift one another, fostering a supportive and collaborative community. Remember, our strength lies not in our individual successes, but in our collective growth and resilience. By sharing our knowledge and experiences, we can create a legacy that empowers future authors to pursue their dreams with confidence and clarity.

Thank you for allowing me to be a part of your journey. Let's make the publishing world a better place, one author at a time.

With gratitude and excitement,

Introduction

The Power of Publishing: Understanding the impact of becoming a published author.

Imagine this: a cozy café, the aroma of freshly brewed coffee in the air, and a group of friends huddled together, animatedly discussing their latest projects. Among them, one friend excitedly shares news of their newly published book. The atmosphere is electric, charged with the thrill of achievement and the anticipation of what comes next.

Becoming a published author is more than just seeing your name on the cover of a book. It is a transformative experience, a milestone that signifies the culmination of countless hours of dedication, creativity, and perseverance. But what exactly does it mean to be a published author, and why is it so powerful?

Publishing a book allows you to share your ideas, stories, and expertise with the world. It's an opportunity to influence, inspire, and connect with readers on a deeply personal level. Think of the books that have shaped your own life—the ones that have made you laugh, cry, think, and grow. Your book has the potential to do the same for others, creating a lasting impact that transcends the pages.

On a practical level, becoming a published author can open doors to new opportunities. It can establish you as an authority in your field, enhance your professional reputation, and even lead to speaking engagements, media appearances, and other avenues to expand your reach. In the digital age, where content is abundant but meaningful connections are rare, a published book stands out as a testament to your commitment and expertise.

Yet, the journey to publishing is often fraught with challenges. Many aspiring authors find themselves overwhelmed by the myriad steps involved in turning a manuscript into a published book. The process can feel like navigating a labyrinth, filled with unexpected twists and daunting obstacles. But remember, every great author once stood where you are now, facing the same uncertainties and fears.

Publishing your work is not just about achieving personal success; it's about contributing to a larger literary and cultural landscape. Your unique voice and perspective add to the rich tapestry of human experience, offering readers new insights and understanding. In this sense, publishing is a powerful act of sharing and connection, one that bridges gaps and builds communities.

As you embark on this journey, know that you are not alone. This book is here to guide you, offering clear, actionable advice and practical examples to help you navigate the publishing process. Together, we'll explore each step, from mastering the writing process to marketing your finished book. Along the way, we'll draw on stories and lessons from successful authors, providing you with the tools and inspiration you need to succeed.

The power of publishing lies not just in the act of sharing your work, but in the transformative journey that brings you there. It's about growing as a writer, overcoming challenges, and ultimately, realizing your dream of becoming a published author. So, let's embark on this journey together, with the understanding that the path to publishing is not just a means to an end, but a rewarding adventure in its own right.

Welcome to "Write It. Publish It. Sell It.: The Ultimate Publishing Power Move." Let's make your publishing dreams a reality.

Book Overview: An introduction to what will be covered in both the course and the book.

Writing a book is a journey—one that begins with a spark of inspiration and culminates in the thrill of seeing your work published. This journey, however, is filled with numerous steps and decisions, each of which plays a crucial role in your success as an author. In "Write It.

Publish It. Sell It.: The Ultimate Publishing Power Move," we will walk through this journey together, chapter by chapter, ensuring you are equipped with the knowledge and tools you need to navigate each stage effectively.

Imagine our sessions as a series of conversations in that cozy café, where we break down complex topics into digestible, enjoyable discussions. We will laugh, learn, and share stories, making this educational experience as entertaining as it is informative.

Master the Writing Process

In our first section, we'll delve into the heart of what it means to be a writer. We'll explore how to find your unique voice, establish a productive writing routine, and overcome common obstacles like writer's block. Editing and revising your manuscript will also be covered, ensuring your work is polished and ready for the next steps. We'll introduce you to essential tools and resources that can support you throughout the writing process.

Explore Self-Publishing vs. Traditional or Hybrid Publishing

Choosing the right publishing path is one of the most critical decisions you will make. We will dissect the differences between self-publishing, traditional publishing, and hybrid models, weighing their pros and cons. Through real-life case studies, you'll gain insights into how successful authors made their decisions and what you can learn from their experiences. By the end of this section, you'll be better equipped to make an informed choice about your publishing journey.

Understanding Marketing vs. Promoting Your Book

Once your book is written and published, the work doesn't stop there. Marketing and promoting your book are essential for reaching your audience and achieving your goals. We'll cover the fundamentals of marketing, including building your author brand, leveraging social media, and utilizing public relations. You'll learn practical promotion strategies that are both effective and manageable.

Learn What You Should Spend Money On

Budgeting wisely is crucial in the publishing process. This section will help you understand where your money is best spent and where you can save. We'll identify key investments that can enhance the quality and reach of your book and highlight common financial pitfalls to avoid.

Craft a Compelling Query Letter

If you choose the traditional publishing route, a compelling query letter is your ticket to getting noticed. We'll break down the components of a successful query letter, provide examples of what works (and what doesn't), and offer tips on how to personalize your approach for different agents and publishers. Follow-up strategies will also be discussed, ensuring you know what steps to take after sending your queries.

Build and Engage Your Audience

Building a loyal readership is essential for long-term success as an author. This section will guide you through identifying your target audience, engaging with them effectively, and fostering a community around your book. We'll discuss content marketing, community building, and managing reader feedback to continually improve your work and strengthen your connection with your audience.

Set Real Expectations for Your Author Journey

Finally, we will set the stage for your ongoing journey as an author. We'll discuss the realities of the publishing world, the challenges you may face, and the rewards you can expect. Goal setting, measuring success, and maintaining motivation are key topics that will help you navigate your path with confidence and clarity.

Throughout this book, we aim to provide a holistic understanding of the publishing process, blending practical advice with motivational insights and engaging stories. By the end of our journey together, you will have a comprehensive roadmap to guide you from the initial spark of an idea to the successful publication and promotion of your book. Let's embark on this adventure with enthusiasm and determination, ready to make your publishing dreams a reality.

Why This Book?: Explaining the purpose of the book and how it complements the course.

Embarking on the journey of writing and publishing a book can feel like stepping into uncharted territory. The path is filled with challenges and decisions that can often seem overwhelming. This book, "Write It. Publish It. Sell It.: The Ultimate Publishing Power Move," is designed to be your compass, guiding you through every stage of the process with clarity and confidence.

In many ways, this book is an extension of the course, providing a detailed and structured roadmap that you can refer to time and again. Think of it as your trusty guide, packed with practical advice, insightful anecdotes, and actionable steps that will empower you to take control of your publishing journey.

By starting each chapter with engaging anecdotes and case studies, we aim to make complex concepts relatable and easier to understand. Storytelling is a powerful tool, and through real-life examples, we can demystify the intricacies of writing, publishing, and marketing your book. This approach ensures that you are not just learning theoretically but seeing how others have navigated similar challenges.

Write It. Publish It. Sell It.

Maintaining a conversational tone throughout the book, we break down complex information into bite-sized, digestible pieces. This makes the learning process enjoyable and keeps you engaged. The goal is to create an atmosphere where you feel like you're having a friendly chat, making the educational journey as entertaining as it is informative.

Personal stories and reflections are woven into the narrative to provide a relatable and motivational backdrop. We all have moments of doubt and uncertainty, and sharing these experiences fosters a sense of camaraderie and support. You'll see that you are not alone in your struggles and that every successful author has faced similar obstacles.

Clear and practical insights form the backbone of this book. We present structured arguments and practical examples that you can directly apply to your writing and publishing endeavors. This ensures that the advice you receive is not just theoretical but grounded in real-world application, helping you make informed decisions at every turn.

Finally, we weave together the different elements of the publishing process into a cohesive narrative, providing a holistic understanding of what it takes to succeed as an author. By integrating historical and contemporary examples, we add depth and context, enriching your learning experience and broadening your perspective.

"Write It. Publish It. Sell It." is not just a book but a companion on your publishing journey. It complements the course by providing a comprehensive guide that you can revisit at any time, reinforcing what you've learned and offering additional insights to help you succeed. Together, the course and the book form a powerful duo, equipping you with the knowledge, tools, and inspiration to achieve your publishing goals.

This book is a testament to the belief that we can rise together—not as competitors, but as colleagues, friends, and a supportive team. By sharing our collective wisdom and experiences, we create a community where everyone has the opportunity to thrive. Let's embark on this journey with a shared vision of success, learning, and growth.

Chapter 1: Master the Writing Process

Writing a book begins with a single word, but the journey from that first word to a finished manuscript is a multifaceted and often daunting process. The foundation of this journey lies in mastering the writing process itself. This chapter is designed to equip you with the essential techniques and strategies that will transform your ideas into polished prose, ready to captivate readers and withstand the scrutiny of the publishing world.

Finding Your Voice: Techniques for Discovering and Honing Your Unique Writing Style

Every writer has a unique voice—a distinct style that sets their work apart. But finding and honing this voice can be a challenge. Imagine walking into a crowded room where everyone is talking; your goal is to make your voice heard, not by shouting the loudest, but by saying something so compelling that everyone stops to listen. In this section, we'll explore techniques to discover your authentic voice, experimenting with different styles and tones until you find the one that resonates most powerfully with you and your audience.

Developing a Writing Routine: Tips for Creating a Consistent Writing Habit

Consistency is key to progress in any endeavor, and writing is no exception. Establishing a writing routine is like planting a garden: with regular care and attention, your ideas will flourish. We'll discuss practical tips for developing a writing habit that fits into your lifestyle, from setting realistic goals to creating a conducive writing environment. Whether you're a morning person or a night owl, finding a routine that works for you is essential to maintaining momentum and productivity.

Overcoming Writer's Block: Strategies for Staying Productive Even When Inspiration Wanes

Writer's block—the dreaded obstacle that every writer faces at some point. It's like hitting an invisible wall that stops you in your tracks. But fear not; writer's block is not insurmountable. In this section, we'll uncover strategies to overcome these creative roadblocks. From freewriting exercises to changing your writing environment, you'll learn practical methods to keep the words flowing, even when inspiration seems elusive.

Editing and Revising: The Importance of Refining Your Manuscript

Writing the first draft of your book is only the beginning. The real magic happens during the editing and revising stages. Think of your manuscript as a rough diamond; it requires careful cutting and polishing to reveal its true brilliance. We'll delve into the editing process, from self-editing techniques to working with professional editors. You'll discover the importance of multiple drafts, constructive feedback, and the meticulous attention to detail that transforms a good manuscript into a great one.

Tools and Resources: Software and Other Resources to Aid in the Writing Process

In today's digital age, a plethora of tools and resources are available to aid writers. From writing software to organizational tools, these resources can streamline your writing process and enhance your productivity. We'll introduce you to some of the best tools available, explaining how each can support different aspects of your writing journey. Whether you need help with grammar, plotting, or staying focused, there's a tool out there that can make your writing life easier.

Embarking on the writing process is an adventure filled with discovery, growth, and creativity. By mastering these foundational elements, you'll be well-prepared to bring your ideas to life and craft a manuscript that stands out in the crowded literary landscape. Let's dive in and start shaping your story, one word at a time.

Finding Your Voice: Techniques for discovering and honing your unique writing style.

Your voice as a writer is like a fingerprint—entirely unique to you. It encompasses your style, tone, and perspective, distinguishing your work from that of others. But how do you find this voice, and how do you hone it to perfection? In this section, we will explore techniques to help you discover and develop your unique writing style, ensuring that your voice resonates authentically with your readers.

1. Embrace Your Authentic Self

Embracing your authentic self is one of the most liberating and impactful steps you can take as a writer. Your writing voice is a unique reflection of who you are—it embodies your experiences, beliefs, personality, and perspective. By embracing your authenticity, you not only differentiate yourself from other writers but also establish a genuine connection with your readers.

Start by focusing on subjects that ignite your passion. Writing about topics that you care deeply about brings a natural enthusiasm and depth to your work that readers can sense and appreciate. When you write with passion, your voice shines through more clearly and powerfully.

Your natural voice is the way you express yourself when you're not trying to conform to any particular style or expectation. It's how you speak, think, and perceive the world. Embrace this natural voice in your writing. Engage in freewriting exercises where you write continuously without worrying about grammar, structure, or audience. This practice helps you tap into your natural voice without self-censorship.

It's natural to admire other writers and be influenced by their styles, but trying to imitate them can stifle your authenticity. Instead, focus on developing your own unique voice. Read a diverse range of authors to understand different styles and techniques, but when it comes to your writing, stay true to your own voice.

Your life experiences are a rich source of material that can infuse your writing with authenticity. Reflect on your personal stories, challenges, triumphs, and lessons learned. Use your experiences as a foundation for your writing. Personal anecdotes and reflections can add depth and relatability to your work.

Authenticity often requires a level of honesty and vulnerability that can be challenging but incredibly rewarding. Sharing your true thoughts and feelings, even the uncomfortable ones, creates a deeper connection with your readers. Don't shy away from exploring difficult or personal topics. Readers appreciate honesty and the courage to tackle real issues.

Your perspective is shaped by your background, culture, and individual experiences. Embrace what makes your viewpoint unique and use it to enrich your writing. Incorporate elements from your cultural background or personal history into your work. These details add authenticity and depth.

Authenticity in writing fosters a genuine connection with readers. When readers sense that you are being true to yourself, they are more likely to connect with and trust your voice. Interact with your readers in a genuine way. Share your writing process, struggles, and successes with them. This openness builds a loyal and supportive readership.

By embracing your authentic self, you unlock the full potential of your writing voice. Authenticity not only sets you apart from other writers but also creates a meaningful and lasting connection with your readers. It's this genuine connection that turns casual readers into dedicated fans, eagerly awaiting your next piece of work. So, write with honesty, passion, and confidence—your authentic voice is your greatest asset.

2. Experiment with Different Styles and Genres

To find your voice, it's helpful to experiment with various writing styles and genres. Trying your hand at different forms of writing can uncover hidden facets of your voice that you might not have discovered otherwise. Dive into fiction, non-fiction, poetry, and even more niche forms like essays, blogs, or short stories. Each style and genre brings out different aspects of your creativity and expression.

When you explore fiction, you might discover a knack for creating compelling characters and intricate plots. Writing non-fiction could reveal your ability to convey facts and ideas clearly and engagingly. Poetry might help you tap into a more lyrical and emotional side of your writing, while essays can refine your skills in presenting arguments and personal reflections.

Don't be afraid to step outside your comfort zone. Write a thriller if you usually stick to romance, or try your hand at science fiction if your comfort zone is historical fiction. You might be surprised by how different genres influence your voice and expand your versatility as a writer. Pay attention to which styles feel most comfortable and which ones allow you to express yourself most effectively.

Experimentation is also a way to keep your writing fresh and exciting. It prevents you from becoming too rigid or formulaic in your approach. The more you explore, the more tools you add to your writer's toolkit, enriching your overall craft.

Through this process, you'll likely find that certain styles and genres resonate more with your natural voice. This doesn't mean you have to stick to one type of writing forever, but it does give you a foundation to build upon. The key is to remain open and flexible, allowing your voice to evolve and grow with each new writing experience.

In summary, experimenting with different styles and genres is a journey of discovery. It's about finding out what works best for you and where your strengths lie. This journey not only helps you find your authentic voice but also makes you a more adaptable and skilled writer. So, embrace the adventure, try new things, and watch as your unique voice emerges and flourishes.

3. Read Widely and Analytically

Reading widely exposes you to different voices and styles, helping you understand what resonates with you as a reader and why. As you immerse yourself in a variety of books, take the time to analyze the works of authors you admire. Notice their sentence structures, tone, pacing, and how they convey emotion. Reflect on what you like and dislike, and think about how you can incorporate those elements into your own writing.

When you read a beautifully crafted sentence or a particularly moving passage, take a moment to dissect it. Ask yourself what makes it effective. Is it the choice of words, the rhythm of the prose, or the vivid imagery? By breaking down these elements, you gain insights into the techniques that resonate with you and can start to integrate them into your own style.

Pay attention to different genres and forms as well. How does a mystery novel build suspense compared to a literary fiction novel? What makes a poem's language so evocative? This analytical reading not only broadens your understanding of various writing styles but also helps you identify the techniques that best express your voice.

Reflect on your findings and experiment with incorporating them into your writing. If you admire an author's ability to create tension, try to emulate that in your own work, but with your unique twist. If a particular narrative style captures your interest, explore how it might fit into your storytelling. The goal is not to copy but to learn and adapt, making those elements your own.

This process of reading and analyzing is continuous. As your writing evolves, so will your preferences and influences. Keep challenging yourself with new authors and genres, and let your voice develop naturally through this ongoing exploration. By staying curious and open to learning, you'll continue to refine and strengthen your authentic writing voice.

4. Write Regularly and Reflect

Consistency is crucial in discovering your voice. Writing regularly, even if it's just a few hundred words a day, helps you develop a rhythm and flow that are uniquely yours. The act of writing frequently allows your natural voice to emerge more effortlessly over time.

As you write, take time to reflect on your work. Consider what aspects of your writing you enjoy and what parts feel forced or unnatural. This reflection can be incredibly insightful. Keeping a writing journal can be particularly beneficial for this purpose. Document your thoughts on your writing process, your progress, and the evolution of your style. Note the days when the words flow easily and those when they don't, and try to understand why.

Reflecting on your writing helps you become more aware of your voice and how it develops over time. You might start to notice patterns in your writing—certain themes or styles that consistently appear. This awareness allows you to consciously nurture the elements that resonate with you and refine those that don't.

In your journal, consider also writing about your goals and aspirations as a writer. What do you hope to achieve with your writing? What messages or stories are you passionate about sharing? This self-reflection keeps you grounded in your purpose and continually guides your development as a writer.

Over time, these consistent writing and reflection practices will help you hone a voice that is unmistakably yours. You'll find that your writing becomes more fluid and confident, and your unique style will become more pronounced. Remember, the journey to discovering your voice is ongoing, and every word you write brings you closer to that authentic expression.

By committing to regular writing and thoughtful reflection, you lay a solid foundation for your writing career. Your voice will continue to evolve, and with each piece you create, you'll strengthen your connection to your authentic self. Keep writing, stay consistent, and embrace the journey of discovering and refining your unique writing voice.

5. Seek Feedback and Be Open to Criticism

Imagine you're at a lively writer's workshop, the kind where everyone's buzzing with ideas and eager to share. You've just read a chapter of your manuscript, and now it's time for feedback. The room is quiet for a moment, then fills with a mix of praise and constructive criticism. It's a bit nerve-wracking, right? But here's the thing: this feedback is pure gold for your growth as a writer.

When you share your work with others, especially in writing groups or workshops, you get a variety of perspectives. This isn't just about people patting you on the back; it's about understanding how your writing resonates with readers and what you might need to tweak. Think of it as getting a fresh pair of eyes on your work, spotting things you might have missed.

Now, let's be real—hearing criticism can be tough. You've put your heart and soul into your writing, and it's not easy to hear that something doesn't quite work. But remember, constructive criticism is incredibly valuable. It can highlight areas where you can improve, like a character's motivation that isn't clear or a plot twist that needs more buildup. These insights help you refine your work and make it stronger.

However, it's crucial to balance this feedback with your vision. Not every piece of advice will fit your style or goals. Some might even suggest changes that don't align with what you want for your story. Take J.K. Rowling, for instance. She faced numerous rejections and critiques before Harry Potter was published. If she had changed her unique style to fit every piece of feedback, we might not have the magical world of Hogwarts as we know it.

So, how do you navigate this? Start by joining writing groups or workshops where you can regularly share your work. These communities are supportive and offer diverse perspectives that can really help you grow. When you seek feedback, be specific about what you need. Are you looking for help with character development, plot structure, or overall tone? Clear questions will guide your reviewers and give you targeted feedback.

Take time to reflect on the feedback you receive. Think about how it aligns with your vision for your work. Not every suggestion will be relevant, so it's important to filter out what doesn't fit and focus on what will genuinely enhance your writing. Use criticism to polish your voice, not to change it fundamentally. Your voice is what makes your writing unique, and feedback should help you refine it, not dilute it.

Think of your writing journey like a sculptor working on a piece of marble. Each piece of feedback is a chisel stroke, gradually revealing the masterpiece within. This process might be slow and sometimes frustrating, but with each critique, your work becomes clearer and more refined.

Remember those moments when you received feedback that truly transformed your writing? Reflect on those experiences and use them as motivation. Sharing these personal stories can illustrate the importance of staying open to criticism while maintaining your artistic integrity.

By embracing feedback and using it constructively, you'll not only improve your writing but also build resilience and confidence in your craft. This openness to critique, balanced with a steadfast commitment to your voice, will guide you through the ups and downs of writing and publishing.

So, embrace this journey with an open heart and mind, and you'll find that each piece of feedback is a stepping stone towards becoming the writer you're meant to be.

6. Emphasize Your Strengths

As you gain confidence in your writing, it's time to start playing to your strengths. Think about the elements of your writing that receive the most positive feedback or the parts you personally enjoy the most. Maybe you have a knack for witty dialogue that makes your characters come alive and your readers laugh. Or perhaps your descriptive passages are so vivid that they transport readers to another world. Whatever your strengths are, it's time to let them shine.

Highlighting your strengths is more than just focusing on what you're good at; it's about building a distinctive style that sets your work apart. Take those witty dialogues and use them to make your characters unforgettable. Let your evocative descriptions paint scenes so vividly that readers feel like they're right there with your characters. When you emphasize your strengths, you create a unique voice that becomes the hallmark of your writing.

Think of it this way: Every writer has a toolbox filled with different skills. Some tools might be sharper or more polished than others, and that's okay. The key is to use your best tools—the ones that feel natural and powerful to you. As you write more and more, these strengths will become the defining features of your voice.

Let's say you're great at creating suspense. Lean into that. Build tension in your stories, keep your readers on the edge of their seats, and make them eagerly turn the pages to find out what happens next. Or maybe you excel at crafting complex, relatable characters. Dive deep into character development, explore their inner worlds, and let your readers connect with them on a profound level.

Over time, as you continue to highlight your strengths, you'll notice that your voice becomes more defined and recognizable. It's like an artist developing a signature style. Your readers will start to know what to expect from your work and will be drawn to it because of your unique strengths.

Don't shy away from showcasing what you do best. Embrace it, refine it, and let it define your writing. By emphasizing your strengths, you're not just improving your work; you're creating a distinctive, compelling voice that will set you apart in the literary world. So go ahead, play to your strengths, and watch as your writing blossoms into something truly special.

7. Let Go of Perfectionism

Let's talk about perfectionism. It's something that can really get in the way of your creativity and the development of your unique voice. The truth is, striving for perfection can be paralyzing. You might find yourself stuck on a single sentence, trying to make it flawless, instead of letting your ideas flow freely.

Here's the thing: your first drafts don't need to be perfect. In fact, they shouldn't be. They're just the starting point, the raw material from which you'll craft your final piece. Allow yourself to write imperfectly. Let your thoughts and ideas spill onto the page without worrying too much about grammar, style, or coherence. This is the stage where you explore, experiment, and discover your voice.

Imagine a painter working on a canvas. The first strokes of paint might be rough, unrefined, even chaotic. But these initial marks are essential—they form the foundation of the final masterpiece. Your writing process is no different. Embrace the messiness. Allow your drafts to be messy, knowing that you'll have plenty of opportunities to refine and polish them later.

Remember, perfectionism can stifle your creativity. It can make you hesitant to try new things or take risks in your writing. But when you let go of the need to be perfect, you open yourself up to endless possibilities. You give yourself the freedom to experiment, to make mistakes, and to learn from them. This is how your voice will evolve and improve over time.

Think about some of the greatest authors you admire. They didn't achieve their unique voices by being perfect from the start. They wrote, rewrote, and kept refining their work. They allowed themselves to produce less-than-perfect drafts, understanding that perfection is an unrealistic goal.

So, let go of perfectionism. Give yourself permission to write imperfectly. Embrace the process, with all its messiness and imperfections. Focus on expressing your genuine thoughts and ideas. Over time, with practice and persistence, your voice will become stronger and more distinctive. Remember, it's not about being perfect; it's about being authentic and true to yourself.

8. Stay Patient and Persistent

Finding your voice as a writer is a journey, and like any worthwhile journey, it requires patience and persistence. It's not going to happen overnight, and that's perfectly okay. Trust the process and allow yourself the time and space to grow. Remember, every writer's path is unique, and there's no set timeline for discovering your voice.

Think about it like planting a garden. You don't expect the seeds to sprout into full-grown plants immediately. You water them, give them sunlight, and patiently wait for them to grow. Writing is much the same. Each word, sentence, and draft is like a seed. With time and care, these seeds will grow into something beautiful and uniquely yours.

Celebrate your progress, no matter how small it may seem. Did you write a paragraph that really captures the emotion you were aiming for? That's a win! Did you finally figure out a tricky plot point? Another win!

These small victories are important milestones on your journey. They show that you're moving forward, even if it feels slow at times.

Staying committed to your craft means showing up, even on days when you don't feel particularly inspired. It means writing regularly, revising diligently, and continually learning. Some days will be easier than others, but every bit of effort you put in contributes to your growth as a writer.

Think of famous authors who took years to find their voice. For instance, Harper Lee spent a decade working on "To Kill a Mockingbird," revising and refining her story until it became the classic we know today. Her patience and persistence paid off, and her unique voice shone through.

So, stay patient and persistent. Trust that with each word you write, you're getting closer to finding your voice. Embrace the ups and downs of the writing process and keep pushing forward. Your voice is there, waiting to be discovered and developed. Keep nurturing it, and in time, it will emerge stronger and clearer than ever. Remember, this journey is about growth, not perfection, and every step you take brings you closer to becoming the writer you're meant to be.

9. Reflect on Your Journey

Let's take a moment to reflect on your writing journey. It's important to periodically pause and look back at where you started and how far you've come. Grab a cup of your favorite coffee or tea, find a cozy spot, and pull out some of your earlier works. Compare them to what you're writing now. Notice the changes and the evolution of your voice. Can you see the growth? Take pride in that.

Reflecting on your journey isn't just about spotting improvements. It's about appreciating your development and acknowledging the effort you've put in. Remember those days when writing felt like a struggle? Or the moments when you received feedback that initially stung but ultimately made your work better? These are all part of your growth as a writer.

Reflection helps you stay motivated. It's easy to get caught up in the daily grind of writing and forget how much you've achieved. By looking back, you remind yourself of your progress and reignite your passion for the craft. Celebrate your milestones, no matter how small they might seem. Each step forward is a victory worth acknowledging.

Think of reflection as a way to connect the dots of your journey. It gives you a clearer picture of your development and helps you understand how your voice has evolved. Maybe you've become more confident in your dialogue, or perhaps your descriptions have become more vivid and immersive. Whatever the case, reflecting on these changes shows you that your hard work is paying off.

In this journey, remember to embrace your authentic self. Experiment with different styles and genres to see what feels right. Read widely to draw inspiration from other writers. Write regularly to keep honing your skills. Seek feedback to gain new perspectives and refine your voice. Emphasize your strengths, letting them shine through your work. Let go of perfectionism and allow yourself to write freely. Stay patient and persistent, trusting that your voice will continue to develop over time.

By doing all these things and taking the time to reflect on your journey, you will discover and hone a writing voice that is unmistakably your own. Your unique voice is your greatest asset as a writer. It's what makes your work stand out and resonate deeply with your readers. So, keep writing, keep reflecting, and keep growing. Your journey is just as important as the destination, and every step you take brings you closer to becoming the writer you're meant to be.

Developing a Writing Routine: Tips for creating a consistent writing habit.

A consistent writing routine is the backbone of a successful writing career. It transforms writing from an occasional activity into a disciplined practice, ensuring steady progress on your manuscript. Establishing a writing routine can seem daunting, but with the right strategies, you can create a habit that fits seamlessly into your daily life. Here are some tips to help you develop a writing routine that works for you.

1. Set Clear Goals

Let's talk about setting clear goals for your writing. It's one of the best ways to give yourself a sense of direction and purpose. Without goals, it's easy to feel lost or unmotivated. But with clear, achievable objectives, you'll know exactly what you're working towards, and that can make a huge difference in your productivity and satisfaction as a writer.

Start by thinking about what you want to achieve. Do you want to complete a certain number of words per day? Maybe finishing a chapter each week sounds more manageable. Or perhaps you want to dedicate a specific amount of time to writing each day. Whatever your goals are, make sure they're realistic and attainable. Setting goals that are too ambitious can be discouraging, while goals that are too easy won't push you to grow.

Once you've set your goals, write them down. There's something powerful about putting your intentions on paper. It makes them feel more concrete and holds you accountable. Keep these written goals in a place where you can see them regularly. Maybe it's a sticky note on your computer monitor or a page in your planner. Having a constant reminder of what you're working towards can help keep you focused and motivated.

Let's say you decide to write 500 words a day. It might not sound like a lot, but over time, those words add up. By the end of the week, you'll have 3,500 words. By the end of the month, you'll have around 15,000 words. It's the consistent effort that pays off. And when you reach your daily goal, take a moment to celebrate. Each small achievement is a step closer to your larger objective.

Clear goals also help you manage your time better. If you know you need to write 500 words a day, you can plan your schedule around that. Maybe you set aside an hour in the morning before work, or perhaps you carve out some time in the evening after dinner. Whatever works best for you, having a set goal makes it easier to prioritize your writing.

Remember, goals can be flexible. Life happens, and sometimes you might not hit your target. That's okay. The important thing is to stay committed and get back on track as soon as you can. Adjust your goals if needed, but don't give up on them. Persistence is key.

Setting clear goals is about more than just hitting a word count or finishing a chapter. It's about building habits and creating a routine that supports your writing. It's about staying motivated and giving yourself a roadmap to follow. And as you achieve each goal, you'll build confidence and momentum, making it easier to keep moving forward.

So, take a moment to set your goals. Make them clear, make them achievable, and write them down. Keep them visible as a constant reminder of what you're working towards. With clear goals guiding you, you'll find it easier to stay focused, motivated, and on track with your writing journey.

2. Establish a Writing Schedule

Let's talk about establishing a writing schedule. Consistency is key to developing a strong writing habit, and having a set schedule can make all the difference. The idea is to fit writing into your daily routine in a way that feels natural and sustainable.

Write It. Publish It. Sell It.

First, think about when you're most alert and creative. Everyone has different peak times for productivity. For some, it's early in the morning when the world is still quiet and fresh. For others, it might be during lunch breaks, providing a nice mental escape from the day's tasks. And then there are the night owls who find their best ideas flowing late at night when the hustle and bustle have died down.

Once you identify your ideal writing time, commit to it. It doesn't have to be a huge block of time. Even 30 minutes a day can make a significant impact. The important thing is to be consistent. Write at the same time each day, and it will soon become a natural part of your routine.

Imagine your writing time as a daily appointment with yourself. Just like you wouldn't cancel a meeting with a colleague or a friend, treat your writing time with the same level of importance. This commitment reinforces the habit and signals to your brain that this is a priority.

Let's say you choose to write early in the morning. Set your alarm a bit earlier, grab a cup of coffee or tea, and settle into a cozy spot where you won't be disturbed. Those first few minutes might feel a bit groggy, but as you stick to it, you'll find that your mind starts to anticipate and prepare for this creative time.

Or, if lunchtime works better, find a quiet place away from your usual work environment. Use this break to shift your focus and immerse yourself in your writing. It's a great way to refresh your mind and come back to your other tasks feeling recharged.

For night owls, carving out that time in the evening can be a wonderful way to wind down. Settle in with a cup of herbal tea and let the calmness of the night inspire your words. This can also be a fantastic way to process the events of the day and channel them into your writing.

Consistency is what turns writing from a task into a habit. Over time, you'll find that writing at your scheduled time becomes second nature.

The words will come more easily, and you'll feel a sense of accomplishment from sticking to your routine.

Think about how runners train for a marathon. They don't start with the full distance. They build up their stamina with regular, consistent runs. Writing is much the same. By committing to a regular schedule, you're building your writing stamina. Each session adds up, and before you know it, you'll have a significant body of work.

So, establish your writing schedule. Find that time of day when you're most alert and creative, and make a commitment to yourself. Whether it's morning, midday, or night, those consistent writing sessions will help you develop a natural and sustainable writing habit. Over time, writing will become an integral and effortless part of your day, bringing you closer to achieving your writing goals.

3. Create a Dedicated Writing Space

Let's chat about the importance of having a dedicated writing space. This can significantly enhance your productivity and creativity. Think of it as creating a personal sanctuary where your ideas can flow freely without any interruptions.

Start by choosing a quiet and comfortable place where you can write without distractions. It doesn't have to be a whole room—just a corner of your home where you can set up your writing haven. The key is to make this space solely for writing, so your brain knows it's time to get creative whenever you sit down there.

Imagine your perfect writing spot. Maybe it's by a window where you can glance outside for a bit of inspiration, or perhaps it's a cozy nook with a comfy chair that invites you to settle in and get to work. Make sure the seating is comfortable enough for you to sit for extended periods without getting sore or fidgety.

Lighting is crucial too. Good lighting can make a world of difference. Natural light is fantastic if you can get it, but a good desk lamp can work wonders as well. The idea is to reduce eye strain and create a bright, welcoming atmosphere.

Next, think about the little touches that make the space inviting and conducive to creativity. Add some inspiring quotes or artwork that motivates you. Maybe it's a favorite literary quote, a piece of art that stirs your imagination, or even a vision board with your writing goals and dreams.

Keep your writing tools handy and organized. Whether you prefer writing by hand or typing, having everything you need within arm's reach can help maintain your flow. A clutter-free space can also help you stay focused, so consider adding some storage solutions to keep things tidy.

Personalize your space to make it feel truly yours. Maybe you have a favorite mug for your coffee or tea that you always use while writing. Perhaps there's a particular scent, like a candle or essential oil, that helps you relax and concentrate. These small details can create a comfortable and familiar environment that's conducive to productivity.

Remember, the goal is to create a space that signals to your brain that it's time to write whenever you sit down. This dedicated writing space becomes a mental cue, telling your brain to switch into writing mode. Over time, you'll find that just being in this space can help spark creativity and focus.

Imagine you've had a busy day, but as soon as you step into your writing space, you feel a shift. The surroundings are familiar and welcoming, and your mind starts to settle into the rhythm of writing. This dedicated area can become a powerful tool in your writing arsenal, helping you maintain consistency and productivity.

So, take some time to set up your dedicated writing space. Make it quiet, comfortable, and inviting. Fill it with things that inspire you and make you feel at ease. With a designated space for writing, you'll find it easier to slip into the creative mindset and make the most of your writing time.

4. Minimize Distractions

Distractions are the arch-nemesis of productivity, especially when it comes to writing. When it's time to write, creating a distraction-free environment can make a huge difference in how focused and productive you are.

First things first: turn off notifications. Those constant pings and dings from your phone and computer can be incredibly disruptive. Put your phone on silent or, better yet, in another room. If you need to keep it nearby, use the "Do Not Disturb" mode to silence non-essential notifications. The same goes for your computer. Close any unnecessary tabs and apps that might tempt you to stray from your writing.

Next, let others know that you're unavailable during your writing time. If you live with family or roommates, a simple conversation can go a long way. Let them know when you'll be writing and ask for their support in minimizing interruptions. You could even put up a sign on your door or desk to remind them that you're in the middle of a writing session.

Consider using tools like website blockers. These can be lifesavers when you find yourself habitually checking social media, news sites, or other distractions. There are several apps and browser extensions available that can block access to specific sites during your writing time. By removing the temptation, you can stay focused on your work.

Creating a distraction-free environment isn't just about eliminating external interruptions. It's also about managing internal distractions. Have you ever sat down to write and suddenly remembered a dozen other things you need to do? Keep a notepad next to you. When a distracting thought pops up, jot it down and promise yourself you'll deal with it later. This way, you can clear your mind and get back to writing.

Think about the physical environment too. A clean, organized space can help you stay focused. Make sure you have everything you need within reach—your notes, a glass of water, whatever it is that keeps you comfortable and productive. If you're someone who gets distracted by noise, consider using noise-canceling headphones or listening to instrumental music to help you concentrate.

Imagine you're about to start a writing session. You've silenced your phone, closed all unnecessary tabs on your computer, and let everyone know you're unavailable. Your desk is tidy, your notes are ready, and you have a cup of your favorite beverage by your side. You sit down, take a deep breath, and dive into your writing with a clear mind and a focused attitude.

By minimizing distractions, you create an environment where you can truly concentrate and make the most of your writing time. It's all about setting yourself up for success. The fewer distractions you have, the more you can immerse yourself in your work and let your creativity flow.

So, the next time you're ready to write, take a few minutes to eliminate those distractions. Turn off notifications, close unnecessary tabs, let others know you're busy, and maybe even use a website blocker. Creating this distraction-free environment will help you stay focused, making your writing sessions more productive and enjoyable.

5. Warm Up with Writing Prompts

Sometimes, getting started is the hardest part of writing. You sit down, ready to work, but the blank page just stares back at you. This is where writing prompts can be incredibly helpful. They act as a warm-up, getting your creative juices flowing and helping you ease into a productive writing session.

Think of writing prompts as a way to stretch your creative muscles. Spend a few minutes writing on a random prompt before diving into your main project. This exercise can help overcome that initial resistance and make the transition to your primary writing smoother.

Prompts can be simple or complex. For instance, you might start with something straightforward like describing a scene or a character. What does a bustling marketplace look like? Who is the mysterious figure standing in the shadows? Or, you could choose a more complex prompt, like exploring a what-if scenario related to your story. What if your protagonist suddenly discovered they could time travel? How would that change their journey?

These warm-up exercises don't have to be perfect or polished. The goal is to get words flowing and ideas sparking. You might even discover new angles or elements to incorporate into your main project. Plus, it's a great way to experiment with different styles and voices without the pressure of it being part of your finished work.

Let's say you've chosen a prompt about describing a thunderstorm from a character's perspective. You spend a few minutes capturing the sound of the rain, the flash of lightning, and the character's emotions. As you write, you find yourself getting into the groove. The words start coming more easily, and before you know it, you're ready to switch gears and tackle your main project with renewed energy.

Using prompts can also help you push through writer's block. When you're stuck on a particular scene or chapter, a prompt can provide a fresh starting point, helping you break free from the mental logjam. It's like taking a detour to find a clearer path back to your main route.

So, the next time you find yourself struggling to start, give writing prompts a try. Spend a few minutes warming up with a random prompt. Whether it's a simple description or a complex what-if scenario, this exercise can help you overcome that initial hurdle and dive into your main project with greater ease and creativity. Warm up, get those words flowing, and watch as your writing sessions become more productive and enjoyable.

6. Set Realistic Expectations

It's important to set realistic expectations for your writing sessions. Understand that not every day will be equally productive, and that's okay. Some days you'll write pages, while others you might struggle with a single paragraph. The key is to keep showing up and putting in the effort, regardless of how much you accomplish in each session. Celebrate small victories and progress, no matter how incremental.

When it comes to writing, setting realistic expectations is crucial. Not every writing session is going to be a home run, and that's perfectly fine. Some days you'll find yourself in the zone, churning out pages of brilliant prose. Other days, you might spend an hour wrestling with a single sentence. The important thing is to keep showing up and putting in the effort, no matter how much—or how little—you accomplish.

It's easy to get frustrated when you're not hitting your word count or when the words just aren't flowing. But remember, writing is a process, and it's not always a linear one. There will be ups and downs, peaks of productivity, and valleys where everything feels like a struggle. Setting realistic expectations can help you stay motivated and avoid burnout.

Think of it like any other long-term commitment, like training for a marathon. You wouldn't expect to run 10 miles every day right from the start. Some days you might do a long run, while other days are for short jogs or rest. Writing is the same. Allow yourself to have those varied days. What matters is the consistency and the persistence to keep going.

Celebrate your small victories. Did you finally nail that tricky dialogue? Great! Did you manage to outline a new chapter? Fantastic! Each step forward, no matter how small, is progress. Recognizing these small wins can boost your morale and keep you motivated.

Let's say you sit down to write and only manage a couple of paragraphs. It's easy to feel like you haven't accomplished much, but think about it this way: those paragraphs are progress. They're words that didn't exist before. They're a step closer to your goal.

It's also helpful to remember that writing isn't just about putting words on the page. Thinking through plot points, developing characters in your mind, or even daydreaming about your story are all valuable parts of the process. Give yourself credit for these less tangible forms of progress.

On days when you feel like you're not getting anywhere, remind yourself of the bigger picture. Every word, every sentence, every idea contributes to your overall progress. It's all part of the journey. Keep showing up, keep putting in the effort, and trust that it will pay off in the long run.

So, set realistic expectations for yourself. Understand that there will be productive days and less productive ones. Embrace the process and celebrate the small victories. Writing is a marathon, not a sprint, and every step you take is bringing you closer to your goal. Keep going, stay patient, and enjoy the journey.

7. Track Your Progress

Tracking your progress can be a fantastic motivator. Think of it as keeping a journal of your writing journey, a place where you record your daily word count, the time you spent writing, and any breakthroughs or challenges you encountered. This practice not only provides a sense of accomplishment but also helps you identify patterns in your productivity.

Imagine you're keeping a writing journal. Each day, you jot down a few notes about your writing session: how many words you wrote, how long you spent writing, and how you felt during the process. Maybe you had a breakthrough with a tricky plot point, or perhaps you struggled to find the right words. By capturing these details, you create a tangible record of your progress.

Write It. Publish It. Sell It.

You could also use a tracking app if you prefer digital tools. There are plenty of apps designed for writers that allow you to log your word count, set goals, and even track your writing streaks. These apps can provide visual progress charts, which can be incredibly satisfying to see. Watching your word count grow day by day can be a powerful incentive to keep going.

Reviewing your progress regularly can be eye-opening. You might notice that you're more productive at certain times of the day or that you write more when you're in a particular mood. Identifying these patterns can help you optimize your writing routine. For example, if you find that you write best in the mornings, you can try to schedule your writing sessions earlier in the day.

Tracking your progress also allows you to celebrate your achievements. When you look back at your journal or app and see how much you've written over the past weeks or months, it's a great boost to your motivation. Even on days when it feels like you're not making much headway, reviewing your progress can remind you of how far you've come.

Additionally, tracking helps you stay accountable. When you record your daily writing activity, you're more likely to stick to your goals. It's like having a gentle nudge that encourages you to keep going, even when you're not feeling particularly inspired.

Let's say you're halfway through your manuscript. By looking back at your progress, you can see the days when you were especially productive and the times when you struggled. This insight can help you adjust your approach. Maybe you realize you need more frequent breaks, or perhaps you find that setting smaller, more manageable goals works better for you.

In essence, tracking your progress is about staying connected to your writing journey. It's a way to celebrate your efforts, learn from your experiences, and continually refine your process. Whether you prefer a handwritten journal or a digital app, the key is to consistently record your writing activities and reflect on them.

So, start tracking your progress today. Keep a journal, use a tracking app, or even create a simple spreadsheet. Note down your daily word count, the time spent writing, and any significant moments from your sessions. As you review your progress, you'll gain valuable insights, a sense of accomplishment, and the motivation to keep moving forward on your writing journey.

8. Develop a Pre-Writing Ritual

Developing a pre-writing ritual can be a game-changer for your productivity. This ritual serves as a signal to your brain that it's time to shift gears and focus on writing. It helps create a mental transition from your everyday activities to your writing mindset, making it easier to get started and stay focused.

Think about what could become your pre-writing ritual. It doesn't have to be complicated or time-consuming. Maybe you start by making a cup of your favorite tea or coffee. The simple act of brewing your drink can become a calming, grounding practice that tells your brain it's time to write.

Music can also be a powerful part of your ritual. Create a playlist of songs that inspire you or help you concentrate. Listening to the same playlist every time you sit down to write can create a Pavlovian response, where your brain starts associating those tunes with writing mode. Over time, just hearing the first few notes can help you switch into a creative mindset.

Some people find that spending a few minutes meditating or doing a brief mindfulness exercise helps them focus. This could be as simple as closing your eyes, taking a few deep breaths, and setting an intention for your writing session. This practice can clear your mind of distractions and help you approach your writing with a calm, centered mindset.

You might also consider incorporating some light stretching or movement into your ritual. Sitting down to write after a few minutes of gentle exercise can help wake up your body and mind, making it easier to stay alert and focused during your writing session.

Let's say your pre-writing ritual involves lighting a candle and spending five minutes journaling about your day. The act of lighting the candle becomes a signal that it's time to write, and the journaling helps clear your mind of any lingering thoughts or worries. By the time you start working on your main project, you're already in a more focused and creative headspace.

The key is consistency. Perform your ritual before every writing session, and over time, it will become a powerful cue for your brain. You'll start to notice that it's easier to get into the flow of writing because your mind is conditioned to know that it's time to create.

Experiment with different activities to see what works best for you. Maybe it's a combination of several small actions, like making tea, listening to a specific song, and spending a minute in quiet reflection. Whatever your ritual looks like, the goal is to create a routine that helps you transition smoothly into your writing time.

Developing a pre-writing ritual not only makes it easier to get started but also helps you stay focused and productive. It's about creating a dedicated space in your day for writing, where your mind and body are prepared to dive into your creative work. So, find a ritual that resonates with you, practice it consistently, and watch how it transforms your writing sessions.

9. Stay Flexible and Adaptable

While consistency is important in developing a writing habit, it's equally crucial to remain flexible and adaptable. Life is unpredictable, and there will inevitably be days when your routine gets disrupted. The key is not to be too hard on yourself if you miss a writing session or need to adjust your schedule. Adaptability ensures that you can get back on track without feeling discouraged.

Imagine you've planned a perfect writing session, but suddenly something comes up—an unexpected meeting, a family obligation, or simply a day where you're not feeling your best. It's easy to get frustrated and feel like you've fallen off the wagon. But here's the thing: missing a day or needing to shift your schedule isn't the end of the world. It's just a bump in the road.

The goal is long-term consistency, not perfection. Understand that your writing journey is a marathon, not a sprint. There will be good days and not-so-good days, and that's perfectly okay. What matters is your overall commitment to your writing practice.

Let's say you usually write in the mornings, but today you have an early appointment. Instead of skipping your writing session entirely, look for another time in the day when you can squeeze in even a few minutes of writing. Maybe it's during lunch or before you go to bed. Being adaptable allows you to maintain your writing habit, even if it's in a modified form.

Sometimes, flexibility might mean adjusting your expectations. If you're having a particularly busy week, set smaller, more manageable goals for your writing. Instead of aiming for 1,000 words a day, maybe you aim for 300. The important thing is to keep the momentum going, even if it's at a slower pace.

Think of adaptability as a safety net. It catches you when life throws you off balance and helps you land back on your feet. When you approach your writing practice with a flexible mindset, you're more resilient and less likely to feel defeated by setbacks.

Also, give yourself permission to rest when needed. If you're feeling burnt out or overwhelmed, taking a break can be the best thing for your creativity. Allowing yourself a day off to recharge can actually make your writing sessions more productive in the long run.

Remember, the aim is to cultivate a sustainable writing habit that fits into the ebb and flow of your life. Flexibility and adaptability are crucial components of this. They ensure that you can navigate life's unpredictability without losing sight of your writing goals.

So, embrace flexibility in your writing routine. Be kind to yourself when things don't go as planned and find ways to adapt. Whether it's shifting your writing time, adjusting your goals, or taking a needed break, staying adaptable keeps you on the path of long-term consistency. After all, it's the persistent, adaptable writer who reaches the finish line, not the one who demands perfection from every single day.

10. Seek Accountability and Support

Having someone to hold you accountable can significantly boost your commitment to your writing routine. Join a writing group, find a writing buddy, or share your goals with a trusted friend or family member. Regular check-ins and encouragement from others can help keep you motivated and on track. Additionally, participating in writing challenges or workshops can provide external deadlines and a supportive community.

By setting clear goals, establishing a consistent schedule, creating a dedicated writing space, minimizing distractions, warming up with prompts, setting realistic expectations, tracking progress, developing a pre-writing ritual, staying flexible, and seeking accountability, you can develop a writing routine that fosters creativity and productivity. Remember, the key to success is persistence and patience. Over time, your writing routine will become a natural and integral part of your daily life, paving the way for steady progress and growth as a writer.

Overcoming Writer's Block: Strategies for staying productive even when inspiration wanes.

Writer's block is a common obstacle that every writer encounters at some point. It's that frustrating moment when words seem to dry up, ideas become elusive, and the blank page feels more intimidating than ever. However, writer's block is not an insurmountable barrier. By employing various strategies, you can break through these creative blocks and maintain your productivity. Here are some effective techniques to help you stay productive even when inspiration wanes.

1. Change Your Environment

Have you ever felt like you're staring at the same four walls and your creativity just isn't flowing? Sometimes, a change of scenery can do wonders for your writing. If you usually write at home, why not shake things up a bit? Try taking your laptop or notebook to a cozy café, a quiet library, or a peaceful park. The new environment can stimulate your senses and spark fresh ideas.

Think about it—when you're in a new place, your brain is exposed to different sights, sounds, and smells. These new stimuli can trigger inspiration and help you see your story from a fresh perspective. Imagine sitting in a bustling café, the hum of conversations around you, the aroma of freshly brewed coffee filling the air. Or picture yourself in a serene park, surrounded by the rustling of leaves and the chirping of birds. These experiences can provide a new backdrop for your thoughts and ideas.

Even if you can't get out of the house, a small change can make a big difference. Try moving to a different room. If you usually write at a desk, maybe try sitting on the couch or even the floor. Rearranging your writing space can also help. Declutter your desk, add some plants, or put up new artwork. Sometimes, just shifting your environment a bit can help reignite your creativity.

Remember, our brains love novelty. When we change our surroundings, we break out of our routines and allow our minds to think differently. It's like hitting the refresh button. You might find that a new environment helps you overcome writer's block or brings a fresh wave of creativity to your project.

Here's an idea: make a list of places you'd like to try writing. Maybe it's a charming bookstore café, a scenic overlook, or even a friend's patio. Schedule some writing sessions in these new spots and see how it affects your creativity. You might be surprised at how much a change in scenery can inspire you.

Another tip is to use these different environments to match the mood of what you're writing. Working on a tense, dramatic scene? A busy, energetic café might help you channel that intensity. Writing a peaceful, reflective passage? A quiet park could be the perfect setting. Let the environment enhance your writing process.

Changing your environment isn't just about finding inspiration; it's also about making writing more enjoyable. It can turn a routine writing session into an adventure. So, next time you're feeling stuck or uninspired, grab your writing tools and head somewhere new. Embrace the change, and watch your creativity flourish.

In conclusion, don't underestimate the power of a change of scenery. Whether it's a new location or simply a different setup at home, altering your environment can stimulate your senses, spark fresh ideas, and reignite your creativity. Give it a try—you might find that it's exactly what you needed to get those words flowing again.

2. Freewriting

Have you ever found yourself staring at a blank page, unable to get any words down? Writer's block can be frustrating, but there's a powerful technique that can help you break through it: freewriting. It's a simple yet effective way to get your creative juices flowing and bypass that pesky internal editor.

Here's how it works: Set a timer for 10-15 minutes and just write continuously. Don't worry about grammar, punctuation, or whether what you're writing makes sense. The goal is to let your thoughts flow freely onto the page without any self-censorship.

Think of it as a brain dump. You're giving yourself permission to write whatever comes to mind, no matter how random or disjointed it may seem. This can help you unlock new ideas and often leads to surprising and inspiring results.

For example, let's say you're stuck on a scene in your novel. Set your timer and start writing about anything related to that scene. You might begin with descriptions of the setting, snippets of dialogue, or even your character's thoughts and feelings. As you write, you might stumble upon a new plot twist or a deeper understanding of your character's motivations.

Freewriting can also be a great warm-up exercise before you dive into your main writing project. It helps loosen up your mind and gets you into the flow of writing. You might even discover that some of the freewriting material can be polished and incorporated into your work.

Don't worry if your freewriting session seems chaotic or unstructured. That's part of the process. The beauty of freewriting is that it allows you to explore your thoughts without the pressure of perfection. You might end up with a mix of brilliant insights and nonsensical ramblings, and that's okay. The important thing is that you're writing and generating ideas.

Here's a tip: keep a dedicated freewriting notebook or document. This way, you can look back at your freewriting sessions and see how your ideas have evolved. Sometimes, an idea that didn't seem useful at first can spark inspiration later on.

If you're new to freewriting, start with a prompt to get you going. It could be a question like, "What if my main character discovered a hidden talent?" or a simple phrase like, "In the middle of the storm…" Let the prompt guide your thoughts, but don't feel constrained by it. The point is to keep writing without stopping to think too much.

Freewriting can also be a stress-reliever. When you're feeling overwhelmed or stuck, taking a few minutes to freewrite can clear your mind and help you regain focus. It's a way to process your thoughts and emotions, which can be particularly helpful during challenging writing sessions.

So, the next time you're facing writer's block or just need a creativity boost, give freewriting a try. Set your timer, let go of any self-criticism, and let your thoughts spill onto the page. You might be surprised at the fresh ideas and inspiration that emerge from this simple exercise. Freewriting is all about unlocking your creativity and giving yourself the freedom to explore new possibilities.

By incorporating freewriting into your routine, you can overcome writer's block, discover new ideas, and enjoy the process of writing more fully. It's a versatile tool that every writer can benefit from, so don't hesitate to make it a regular part of your creative practice.

3. Use Writing Prompts

Writing prompts are fantastic tools to kickstart your creativity. They provide a starting point that can help you get past the initial hurdle of writer's block and get those words flowing. Whether you're looking for inspiration or need a creative nudge, prompts can be a game-changer.

Imagine this: you're staring at a blank page, unsure where to begin. Sometimes, all you need is a spark—a little push to get your imagination going. That's where writing prompts come in. They offer a specific scenario, theme, or question that you can build upon, making the daunting task of starting much easier.

Finding and Choosing Prompts

There are countless writing prompts available online, covering a wide range of genres and topics. Websites, blogs, and writing communities often share daily or weekly prompts to inspire writers. You can also find books filled with prompts tailored to different writing styles and genres.

When choosing a prompt, look for one that piques your interest or challenges you to think differently. It might be a single word, a phrase, a question, or a detailed scenario. The key is to find something that resonates with you and sparks your curiosity.

For example, if you're working on a fantasy novel, a prompt like "Write about a character who discovers they have magical powers on their birthday" might be just what you need to explore new plot twists or character development. If you're writing a romance, a prompt like "Two strangers meet at a masquerade ball" could ignite a fresh scene or subplot.

Creating Your Own Prompts

You can also create your own prompts based on themes, characters, or scenarios relevant to your current project. Think about the aspects of your story that you want to explore further. Maybe there's a secondary character you'd like to flesh out, or a plot point that needs more depth.

For instance, if your story involves a mystery, you might create a prompt like, "Write a scene where your protagonist discovers a hidden room in an old mansion." This can help you dive deeper into your story and uncover new layers you hadn't considered before.

Using Prompts as Writing Exercises

Treat writing prompts as exercises to flex your creative muscles. Set a timer for 10-15 minutes and write continuously, focusing solely on the prompt. Don't worry about perfection—just let your ideas flow. This practice can help you break free from writer's block and warm up your writing skills.

Here's a fun idea: turn using prompts into a game. Write several prompts on slips of paper and put them in a jar. Whenever you need inspiration, draw one at random and challenge yourself to write a short piece based on it. This element of surprise can add excitement to your writing routine.

Integrating Prompts into Your Work

Sometimes, the pieces you write from prompts can be directly integrated into your main project. Other times, they might spark new ideas or directions you hadn't previously considered. Even if a prompt doesn't fit perfectly into your current work, it can still help you explore different angles and enhance your overall creativity.

For example, let's say you're writing a sci-fi novel and use a prompt like, "Describe a day in the life of a futuristic city." This exercise might not only help you build the world of your novel but also inspire new plot developments or character arcs.

Sharing and Discussing Prompts

Don't underestimate the power of sharing prompts with other writers. Join a writing group or community where you can exchange prompts and discuss the pieces you create. Feedback from fellow writers can provide new perspectives and insights, further enriching your writing process.

Conclusion

Writing prompts are versatile and valuable tools for any writer. They can kickstart your creativity, help you overcome writer's block, and lead to surprising and inspiring results. Whether you find prompts online or create your own, incorporating them into your writing routine can make the process more enjoyable and productive.

So, the next time you're feeling stuck or just need a boost, turn to writing prompts. Let them guide you, challenge you, and open up new possibilities in your writing. You might be amazed at where these simple starting points can take you.

4. Set Small, Achievable Goals

When writer's block strikes, the thought of writing an entire chapter or hitting a significant word count can feel overwhelming. It's easy to become paralyzed by the sheer size of the task ahead. That's why it's important to set small, manageable goals that are easier to achieve. By focusing on bite-sized pieces of your project, you can build momentum and gradually make substantial writing progress.

Why Small Goals Matter

Imagine you're at the base of a mountain, looking up at the peak. The climb seems daunting and nearly impossible. But if you focus on reaching the next ledge, then the next, and so on, each small step becomes more manageable, and before you know it, you're halfway up. Writing works in much the same way.

Setting small goals takes the pressure off. Instead of worrying about finishing an entire chapter, you can concentrate on writing a single paragraph, describing a character, or even just crafting a compelling sentence. These small achievements can boost your confidence and keep you moving forward.

Examples of Small Goals

Here are some examples of small, achievable writing goals:

1. **Write One Paragraph**: Focus on a single, well-crafted paragraph. This could be part of your current scene or a standalone piece to get your creative juices flowing.
2. **Describe a Character**: Spend a few minutes detailing one of your characters. What do they look like? What are their quirks? How do they speak and move?
3. **Craft a Sentence**: Challenge yourself to write a powerful, compelling sentence. It could be the opening line of your chapter or a poignant moment in your story.
4. **Set a Timer**: Write for just 10-15 minutes. This short burst of focused writing can help you overcome inertia and get words on the page.
5. **Outline a Scene**: Instead of writing the scene, outline its main events and key dialogues. This helps structure your thoughts and makes writing the scene later much easier.

Building Momentum

Each small goal you achieve builds momentum. It's like stacking small victories, one on top of the other. You might start with just a sentence, but then you find you've written a paragraph. Before long, that paragraph turns into a page, and pages turn into chapters.

Let's say you start with the goal of writing a single paragraph about your protagonist's morning routine. As you write, you might get into the flow and find yourself continuing on to describe their interactions at work or a pivotal moment in their day. That initial small goal was just the spark you needed to ignite a longer writing session.

Celebrating Small Successes

It's important to celebrate these small successes. Each completed goal, no matter how minor it may seem, is a step forward. Give yourself credit for each achievement. This positive reinforcement can make a big difference in maintaining motivation and combating writer's block.

Consider keeping a writing journal where you track your goals and accomplishments. At the end of the day, jot down what you've achieved, no matter how small. Over time, you'll see a record of progress that can be incredibly motivating.

Adjusting Goals to Fit Your Needs

Remember, small goals are flexible. If you find that writing a paragraph is too easy, aim for two. If crafting a sentence feels too daunting, break it down further into brainstorming descriptive words or phrases. The key is to adjust your goals to fit your current needs and capabilities.

Using Small Goals to Tackle Big Projects

Even large writing projects can be tackled with small goals. If you're working on a novel, break it down into chapters, then scenes, and then individual moments within those scenes. Each small goal brings you closer to completing the larger project.

Conclusion

When writer's block looms, setting small, achievable goals can make a world of difference. By breaking down your writing into manageable pieces, you can reduce overwhelm and build momentum. Focus on one paragraph, one character description, or even one sentence at a time. Celebrate your small successes and watch as they accumulate into significant progress. Remember, every journey starts with a single step, and each small goal is a step closer to finishing your writing project.

5. Read and Recharge

When you're struggling with writer's block, sometimes the best thing you can do is take a step back and immerse yourself in someone else's words. Reading can be an excellent way to overcome writer's block. Taking a break from your writing and diving into a good book, a captivating poem, an insightful article, or even an engaging blog post can work wonders for your creativity.

Why Reading Helps

Think of reading as a way to recharge your creative batteries. When you're deep in your own writing, it's easy to get tunnel vision and feel stuck. Reading allows you to step out of your head and experience new ideas, styles, and perspectives. It can remind you why you love storytelling and how impactful well-written words can be.

What to Read

Choose something that inspires you. It doesn't have to be directly related to what you're writing. Sometimes, the most unexpected sources can provide the best inspiration. Here are a few suggestions:

1. **Novels**: Read a book in your favorite genre or try something completely different. Notice how the author builds characters, creates tension, or describes settings.
2. **Poetry**: Poems can offer a fresh perspective and spark new ideas with their unique use of language and imagery.
3. **Articles and Essays**: Find articles or essays on topics that interest you. These can provide new insights and ideas that might find their way into your writing.

4. **Blog Posts**: Explore blog posts from writers you admire. Their experiences and tips might resonate with you and give you the push you need to get back to your own writing.

Finding Inspiration

As you read, pay attention to what resonates with you. Maybe it's a beautifully crafted sentence, a surprising plot twist, or a character that feels incredibly real. These moments can inspire you and give you ideas for your own work. Jot down any thoughts or ideas that come to mind. You might be surprised at how reading someone else's work can spark your own creativity.

The Benefits of a Break

Taking a break to read isn't just about finding inspiration; it's also about giving yourself a mental rest. Constantly pushing yourself to write without a break can lead to burnout. Allowing yourself time to enjoy a good book or an interesting article can reduce stress and help you return to your writing with a fresh perspective.

Reconnecting with Your Love for Writing

Reading can also remind you why you love writing in the first place. The way an author weaves a story, the power of a well-placed word, the emotions a piece of writing can evoke—these are the reasons you became a writer. Reconnecting with these elements can reignite your passion and motivate you to get back to your own writing.

Creating a Reading Routine

Incorporate regular reading into your routine. Even setting aside 15-20 minutes a day to read can make a significant difference. It keeps your mind engaged and exposes you to different writing styles and techniques. Plus, it's a great way to relax and enjoy the craft of writing from a different angle.

Conclusion

When writer's block strikes, sometimes the best solution is to take a break and recharge by reading. Whether it's a novel, a poem, an article, or a blog post, immersing yourself in someone else's words can provide new ideas and perspectives, and remind you why you love storytelling. So, grab a book, find a cozy spot, and let yourself get lost in another world. You'll likely return to your own writing feeling refreshed, inspired, and ready to create.

6. Engage in a Different Creative Activity

Sometimes, the best way to overcome writer's block is to step away from writing altogether and engage in a different creative activity. When you're stuck, forcing yourself to write can sometimes make the block even worse. Instead, try shifting your focus to something else that stimulates your creativity.

Think about activities that you enjoy and that allow your mind to relax and wander. Drawing, painting, playing music, or even cooking can be excellent ways to give your brain a break from writing. These activities stimulate different parts of your brain and can help you approach your writing with a fresh perspective.

Imagine picking up a sketchpad and doodling freely, without any pressure to create something perfect. Or playing a musical instrument, letting the melodies flow without worrying about hitting the right notes. Maybe you enjoy cooking—experimenting with new recipes and flavors can be a wonderful way to engage your senses and creativity.

Engaging in these different creative activities can provide a much-needed mental break. They reduce the pressure you might be feeling about writing and allow your ideas to percolate in the background. Often, stepping away from the problem gives your subconscious time to work on it, leading to breakthroughs when you least expect them.

For instance, you might find that while you're painting, a solution to a plot problem in your story suddenly becomes clear. Or while you're playing guitar, you might think of a perfect line of dialogue for your character. These moments of insight often come when you're not actively trying to force them.

Additionally, engaging in a different creative activity can be incredibly rejuvenating. It reminds you that creativity isn't limited to just writing. Exploring other forms of art can renew your passion and inspire new ideas that you can bring back to your writing.

So, next time you're facing writer's block, don't just sit at your desk and struggle. Step away and do something else creative. Draw, paint, play music, or cook. Allow yourself to enjoy these activities without any pressure. You'll likely return to your writing feeling refreshed, inspired, and ready to tackle it with a new perspective.

7. Establish a Writing Ritual

Creating a writing ritual can be a powerful tool to signal to your brain that it's time to write, making it easier to overcome writer's block. A ritual helps establish a sense of routine and familiarity, easing you into a productive writing state.

Think about simple, enjoyable activities that you can incorporate into your writing routine. Your ritual could be lighting a candle, listening to a specific playlist, or drinking a cup of tea before you start writing. The key is to choose actions that are calming and that you enjoy, making the transition into writing more pleasant.

Imagine sitting down at your desk, lighting a scented candle, and taking a moment to enjoy its aroma. Maybe you put on your favorite writing playlist—music that inspires you and helps you focus. Or perhaps you brew a cup of your favorite tea, savoring its warmth and flavor as you prepare to dive into your work.

These small, consistent actions can create a mental shift, signaling to your brain that it's time to move from everyday activities to writing mode. Over time, your brain starts to associate these rituals with the act of writing, making it easier to get into the flow.

For instance, if you always listen to a particular playlist when you write, just hearing the first few notes can help you switch gears and get into a creative mindset. Similarly, the act of brewing a cup of tea can become a soothing routine that prepares your mind for the writing process.

Consistency is key. Try to perform your ritual before each writing session, whether it's in the morning, during lunch breaks, or late at night. The more you practice your ritual, the more effective it becomes in signaling to your brain that it's time to write.

In addition to helping you overcome writer's block, a writing ritual can also make your writing sessions more enjoyable. It adds an element of routine and comfort to your creative process, reducing stress and making it something you look forward to.

So, think about what actions you can incorporate into your writing ritual. Whether it's lighting a candle, listening to music, or drinking tea, find what works best for you. Establishing a writing ritual can make it easier to start writing and help you maintain a consistent, productive writing routine.

8. Embrace the Imperfection

Perfectionism can be a significant contributor to writer's block. The fear of writing something imperfect can prevent you from writing anything at all. It's important to embrace the idea that first drafts are meant to be rough and imperfect. Allow yourself to write without judgment or self-criticism.

Imagine you're sitting down to write, and instead of worrying about every word being perfect, you give yourself permission to write freely. First drafts are all about getting your ideas down on paper. They don't need to be polished or perfect—they just need to exist.

Think of your first draft as a lump of clay. It's not beautiful yet, but it has potential. Your job is to mold and shape it during the editing and revising process. That's where the real polishing happens. Allowing yourself to write imperfectly takes the pressure off and helps you get past the initial hurdle of starting.

Perfectionism can paralyze you, making you second-guess every word and sentence. But remember, you can't edit a blank page. Writing something—anything—gives you material to work with. Embracing imperfection means accepting that your first draft will have flaws, but that's okay. It's all part of the process.

Think about famous authors and their rough drafts. Even the most celebrated writers didn't create masterpieces in one go. They wrote imperfect drafts and then revised them, often multiple times, to create the final polished version. Your writing journey is no different.

Try setting a timer for a short writing session and commit to writing without stopping or editing yourself. Let the words flow, no matter how messy they might seem. You might be surprised at the ideas and creativity that emerge when you turn off your inner critic.

Another helpful approach is to separate writing and editing into distinct stages. When you're writing, focus solely on getting your thoughts down. Save the editing for later. This way, you can fully engage in the creative process without the constant interruption of self-criticism.

Embracing imperfection also means being kind to yourself. Writing is a challenging and often unpredictable process. Some days, the words will come easily; other days, they won't. That's normal. What matters is that you keep going, even when it feels difficult.

Celebrate small victories and progress, no matter how incremental. Every word you write brings you closer to your goal. By allowing yourself to write imperfectly, you free yourself from the constraints of perfectionism and open up to the joy of creativity.

So, the next time you sit down to write, remember to embrace the imperfection. Let go of the need to get everything right on the first try. Write freely and without judgment. The real magic happens in the editing and revising stages. Your first draft is just the beginning of the journey, and it's okay if it's rough around the edges. What's important is that you're writing.

9. Take Breaks and Practice Self-Care

Sometimes, writer's block is a sign that you need a break. Pushing yourself too hard can lead to burnout, which only makes it harder to write. When you feel stuck, it's important to step away from your writing and engage in activities that relax and rejuvenate you.

Taking a break doesn't mean you're giving up. It's actually an essential part of maintaining long-term productivity and creativity. Think of it as hitting the refresh button for your mind.

Ways to Recharge

Go for a Walk: A change of scenery and some fresh air can work wonders. Walking helps clear your mind and can often lead to unexpected bursts of inspiration. Plus, the physical activity is good for your health.

Practice Mindfulness or Meditation: Mindfulness exercises and meditation can help reduce stress and improve your focus. Even just a few minutes of deep breathing or a guided meditation can help reset your mind and alleviate the pressure you might be feeling.

Exercise: Physical activity is a great way to relieve tension and boost your mood. Whether it's yoga, running, or a simple home workout, exercise helps release endorphins that can improve your mental state and enhance your creativity.

Spend Time with Loved Ones: Connecting with family and friends can provide emotional support and a much-needed distraction. Sometimes, a good conversation or shared laughter is all you need to feel recharged.

The Importance of Self-Care

Taking care of your mental and physical well-being is crucial for maintaining your creativity and productivity over the long term. Self-care isn't just about indulging in activities you enjoy; it's about ensuring that you're in a good place, both mentally and physically, to continue your creative work.

Imagine you're a well of creative energy. If you keep drawing from the well without replenishing it, eventually it will run dry. Taking breaks and practicing self-care helps keep that well full, ensuring you have the energy and inspiration you need to write.

Making Breaks a Part of Your Routine

Incorporate regular breaks into your writing routine. You might set a timer to remind yourself to step away every hour or so. Use that time to stretch, move around, or simply relax. These short breaks can prevent burnout and keep your mind fresh.

It's also helpful to have a go-to list of self-care activities that you enjoy. This way, when you feel stuck or overwhelmed, you can easily choose an activity that helps you recharge. Whether it's reading a book, listening to music, or indulging in a hobby, having these activities planned can make it easier to take a break when you need one.

Recognizing the Signs

Pay attention to your body and mind. If you're feeling fatigued, stressed, or frustrated, it might be time for a break. Ignoring these signs can lead to deeper burnout, making it even harder to get back to your writing. Listen to yourself and give yourself permission to rest.

Conclusion

Remember, taking breaks and practicing self-care are not luxuries—they're necessities for sustaining your creativity and productivity. Stepping away from your writing to engage in relaxing and rejuvenating activities can help you return with a clearer mind and renewed energy. So, next time you hit a block, try going for a walk, practicing mindfulness, exercising, or spending time with loved ones. Your well-being is crucial for your long-term success as a writer.

10. Reflect and Reconnect with Your Why

When you're struggling with writer's block, it can be incredibly helpful to take a step back and reflect on why you started writing in the first place. Sometimes, in the midst of deadlines, critiques, and the daily grind, it's easy to lose sight of the passion and purpose that initially drove you to pick up the pen.

Take a moment to ask yourself: Why do I write? What stories am I passionate about telling? What impact do I hope to make with my words? These questions can help you reconnect with your core motivations and reignite your inspiration.

Remember Your Passion: Think back to the moment you decided you wanted to be a writer. Was it a book that changed your life? A story you felt compelled to tell? Reflecting on these memories can remind you of the joy and excitement that writing once brought you.

Reflect on Your Goals: Consider the goals you had when you first started writing. Maybe you wanted to inspire others, share your unique perspective, or simply entertain. Revisiting these goals can help you see the bigger picture and understand that each writing session, no matter how difficult, is a step towards achieving them.

Visualize the Impact: Imagine the impact your finished work could have on readers. Picture someone being moved by your story, finding solace in your words, or being inspired to see the world differently. This visualization can provide a powerful boost of motivation, reminding you that your writing has the potential to make a difference.

Reconnect with Your Stories: Spend some time thinking about the stories you want to tell. Write down your ideas, revisit old notes, or simply daydream about your characters and plot. Reconnecting with the creative aspects of your work can spark new ideas and reignite your enthusiasm.

Write a Letter to Yourself: Consider writing a letter to your future self, explaining why you write and what you hope to achieve. This exercise can be a powerful reminder of your motivations and can serve as a source of encouragement during tough times.

By reflecting on your reasons for writing, you can gain a renewed sense of purpose. This deeper connection to your "why" can help you push through writer's block and keep going, even when the process feels challenging.

Conclusion

When writer's block strikes, taking the time to reflect and reconnect with your "why" can be incredibly powerful. Remind yourself of the passion and purpose that first drew you to writing. Think about the stories you want to tell and the impact you hope to make. This reflection can reignite your inspiration and give you the drive to push through the block, helping you continue on your writing journey with renewed enthusiasm and clarity.

11. Break Down Your Project

Breaking down your writing project into smaller, more manageable tasks can make it less intimidating. Create an outline or a to-do list that breaks your project into specific sections or chapters. Focus on completing one section at a time. This approach helps you maintain a sense of progress and achievement, even if you're only working on a small part of the overall project.

12. Seek Support from Other Writers

Connecting with other writers who understand the challenges of writer's block can be incredibly supportive. Join a writing group, attend workshops, or participate in online forums. Sharing your struggles and receiving encouragement from fellow writers can help you feel less isolated and more motivated to keep writing.

Overcoming writer's block requires a combination of patience, persistence, and creative strategies. By changing your environment, freewriting, using prompts, setting small goals, reading, engaging in other creative activities, establishing rituals, embracing imperfection, taking breaks, reflecting on your motivations, breaking down your project, and seeking support, you can break through the barriers and keep your writing momentum going. Remember, writer's block is a temporary hurdle, not a permanent roadblock. With the right approach, you can overcome it and continue to make progress on your writing journey.

Editing and Revising: The importance of refining your manuscript.

Writing the first draft of your manuscript is a significant achievement, but the journey doesn't end there. The true artistry of writing often lies in the process of editing and revising. This stage is where you refine your ideas, polish your prose, and transform your rough draft into a compelling and cohesive piece of work. Editing and revising are crucial steps that can elevate your manuscript from good to great. Here's why these processes are essential and how to approach them effectively.

1. Enhancing Clarity and Coherence

The first draft of a manuscript often feels like a raw and unfiltered outpouring of ideas. And that's exactly what it should be—an uninhibited capture of your thoughts and emotions. But once you've got those initial words down, the next crucial step is to enhance clarity and coherence for your readers. This is where editing and revising come into play.

Think of your first draft as a block of marble. The essence of your story or argument is there, but it needs to be chiseled and shaped to reveal its true form. Editing helps you organize your ideas logically, ensuring that your narrative flows smoothly and your arguments are well-structured. This process transforms your initial outpouring into a clear, coherent, and engaging manuscript.

Start by reading through your draft with fresh eyes. Look for areas where your thoughts may have strayed or where your ideas jump around without clear connections. These are the spots that need attention. Your goal is to create a seamless flow, guiding your readers effortlessly from one point to the next.

For instance, if you're writing a novel, check that your plot developments are logically sequenced and that each scene naturally leads to the next. If you're working on a non-fiction piece, ensure that your arguments build on each other in a logical progression, making it easy for readers to follow and understand your points.

Next, focus on clarity. Sometimes, in the heat of the writing moment, we can be too close to our own work to see where things might be confusing or ambiguous. Pay attention to passages where you've received feedback that readers didn't quite get what you meant. These are your cues to clarify.

Write It. Publish It. Sell It.

Consider simplifying complex sentences and breaking down dense paragraphs. Use precise language and avoid jargon unless it's necessary and well-explained. The clearer your writing, the more accessible it will be to a wider audience. Remember, you're not just writing for yourself; you're writing to communicate with others.

Eliminating ambiguity is another key part of this process. Ambiguous statements can leave readers puzzled and disrupt the flow of your narrative or argument. Be specific in your descriptions and definitive in your assertions. If something can be interpreted in multiple ways, revise it until your intended meaning is unmistakably clear.

Revising also involves tightening your prose. Look for repetitive phrases or unnecessary words that don't add value to your manuscript. Cutting these out can make your writing more powerful and direct. Each word should serve a purpose, contributing to the overall clarity and coherence of your piece.

Finally, don't underestimate the power of feedback. Share your revised draft with a trusted friend, writing group, or beta reader. They can offer fresh perspectives and point out areas that might still be unclear or disjointed. Use their insights to further refine your manuscript.

In summary, while the first draft is all about capturing your raw ideas, the editing and revising stages are where you shape those ideas into a polished, clear, and coherent manuscript. Organize your thoughts logically, clarify confusing passages, and eliminate ambiguity. By doing so, you make your work more accessible and engaging for your readers, ensuring that your message shines through brilliantly.

2. Improving Language and Style

Editing and revising your manuscript aren't just about fixing errors; they're golden opportunities to refine your language and enhance your writing style. This stage is where you can really polish your work, making it shine and ensuring it resonates with your readers.

Start by eliminating unnecessary words. It's easy to get caught up in the flow of writing and end up with sentences that are a bit too wordy. Look for places where you can simplify your language without losing meaning. For instance, instead of saying "due to the fact that," you can simply say "because." Trimming the fat from your prose makes it cleaner and more impactful.

Varying your sentence structures is another key aspect. If all your sentences follow the same pattern, your writing can become monotonous. Mix things up with a combination of short, punchy sentences and longer, more complex ones. This variation keeps your readers engaged and adds a pleasing rhythm to your writing.

Choosing precise vocabulary is crucial. The right words can convey your ideas more effectively and vividly. Avoid vague language and opt for words that paint a clear picture in your reader's mind. For example, instead of saying "walked quickly," you might say "rushed" or "hurried." Each word you choose should serve a specific purpose and contribute to the overall clarity and tone of your work.

Pay attention to the rhythm and tone of your prose. The way your sentences flow can greatly affect the reader's experience. Read your work aloud to get a sense of its natural rhythm. Does it feel choppy or smooth? Does the tone align with the mood and theme of your story or argument? Adjust as needed to ensure that your writing feels cohesive and harmonious.

This stage is also about finding and highlighting your unique voice. Your voice is what sets your writing apart from others, and it should come through consistently across your manuscript. Think about what makes your perspective distinct and ensure that it's reflected in your style. Whether it's a touch of humor, a lyrical quality, or a straightforward clarity, your voice should shine through in every sentence.

For instance, if you're writing a suspenseful novel, your language might be terse and direct, building tension with every word. On the other hand, a reflective memoir might have a more leisurely, contemplative pace, with rich descriptions and thoughtful insights. Whatever your style, make sure it fits the content and enhances the reader's experience.

Improving your language and style isn't about making your writing sound more complicated; it's about making it more effective and engaging. It's about crafting sentences that resonate, choosing words that evoke the right emotions, and creating a rhythm that keeps your readers hooked.

Finally, don't be afraid to experiment. Revising is the perfect time to try out different phrasings, structures, and stylistic elements. See what works best and what feels most authentic to you. Remember, your unique voice is your greatest asset as a writer.

So, dive into the editing and revising process with an eye for improving language and style. Eliminate unnecessary words, vary your sentence structures, choose precise vocabulary, and pay attention to rhythm and tone. Let your unique voice shine through, making your manuscript not just a piece of writing, but a work of art that captivates and moves your readers.

3. Correcting Grammar and Punctuation

Let's dive into the nitty-gritty of correcting grammar and punctuation. Grammatical errors and punctuation mistakes can be major distractions for readers and can even undermine your credibility as a writer. The editing stage is your chance to meticulously check for these errors and correct them, ensuring that your work is polished and professional.

Start by using grammar-checking tools. Programs like Grammarly or the built-in checkers in word processors can catch a lot of mistakes, from misplaced commas to incorrect verb tenses. However, don't rely solely on these tools. They're helpful, but they're not infallible. A manual review of your manuscript is essential to catch errors that automated tools might miss or misunderstand.

Consider reading your manuscript aloud. This technique can be incredibly effective for catching awkward phrasings, missing words, and punctuation mistakes. When you read aloud, you're more likely to notice if something doesn't sound quite right. Your ears can catch errors that your eyes might overlook, especially after you've been staring at the same text for a long time.

Pay special attention to common trouble spots. For instance, check that your subject-verb agreement is consistent, ensure that pronouns clearly refer to the correct nouns, and verify that your verb tenses are consistent. Look out for misplaced or dangling modifiers, which can create confusion or unintended meanings.

Punctuation is just as important. Proper use of commas, periods, semicolons, and other punctuation marks can clarify meaning and improve the readability of your text. For example, a well-placed comma can change the meaning of a sentence entirely: "Let's eat, Grandma!" versus "Let's eat Grandma!" Little details like these matter.

Think about the overall structure of your sentences and paragraphs. Are your sentences too long and convoluted, making them hard to follow? Or are they too choppy, disrupting the flow of your narrative? Aim for a balance that maintains clarity and keeps the reader engaged.

Another useful strategy is to take breaks between editing sessions. Your brain can become desensitized to mistakes if you've been working on the same piece for too long. Coming back to your manuscript with fresh eyes after a break can help you see errors more clearly.

It can also be helpful to get a second pair of eyes on your work. Having someone else review your manuscript can provide a new perspective and catch errors you might have missed. This could be a trusted friend, a writing group, or even a professional editor.

Remember, proper grammar and punctuation are fundamental to professional writing. They help ensure that your ideas are communicated clearly and effectively. While the creative aspects of writing are vital, the technical side cannot be overlooked. Good grammar and punctuation can significantly impact how your work is received, making it more enjoyable and easier to read.

So, take the time to carefully review your manuscript for grammatical and punctuation errors. Use tools to assist you, read your work aloud, and consider getting feedback from others. By ensuring your writing is technically sound, you enhance your credibility and make a stronger impression on your readers.

4. Strengthening Character and Plot Development

For fiction writers, editing and revising are crucial steps in deepening character development and strengthening plotlines. This stage is where you can truly enhance the emotional depth and narrative complexity of your story, making it more compelling for readers.

Start by revisiting your characters. Take a closer look at their motivations, conflicts, and growth throughout the story. Are their actions consistent with their established personalities and backgrounds? Do their decisions make sense given their goals and challenges? Ensuring that your characters are believable and relatable is key to keeping readers engaged.

Consider your protagonist's journey. How have they changed from the beginning to the end of the story? What obstacles have they faced, and how have they grown as a result? Make sure that their development is clear and impactful. If their transformation feels rushed or unconvincing, take the time to flesh out their experiences and reactions.

Similarly, examine your supporting characters. Do they have their own arcs, or are they simply there to serve the protagonist's story? Well-developed supporting characters can add richness to your narrative and make the world of your story feel more real and dynamic. Ensure that each character has a distinct voice and purpose within the plot.

Next, turn your attention to the plot. Look for any inconsistencies or plot holes that need addressing. Is the sequence of events logical and coherent? Are there any gaps in the storyline that could confuse readers? Tightening the plot and ensuring that all elements are connected and make sense is essential for a smooth and satisfying narrative.

Pay particular attention to pacing. Does your story move too quickly in some parts and drag in others? Striking the right balance can keep readers hooked from start to finish. Consider whether each scene advances the plot or develops the characters. If a scene doesn't serve a clear purpose, it might need to be revised or cut.

Think about the stakes and tension in your story. Are the conflicts compelling and meaningful? Do they escalate in a way that keeps readers on the edge of their seats? Each conflict should push your characters to their limits and force them to grow and adapt. The resolution should feel earned and satisfying, providing a sense of closure.

This stage is also an opportunity to enhance the emotional depth of your story. Are the emotional beats resonating with readers? Do the characters' relationships feel authentic and impactful? Adding layers of emotion can make your story more engaging and memorable.

One effective technique is to map out your characters' arcs and plot points visually. This can help you see the overall structure of your story and identify any areas that need strengthening. You can use tools like index cards, storyboards, or software designed for writers to organize your thoughts and track changes.

Don't be afraid to make significant revisions. Sometimes strengthening your story means making tough decisions, like cutting a beloved scene or reworking a character's arc. Keep the bigger picture in mind and focus on what will make your story the best it can be.

Lastly, seek feedback from others. Beta readers, writing groups, or professional editors can provide valuable insights into your character and plot development. They can point out areas that might not be working as well as you think and offer suggestions for improvement.

Strengthening character and plot development is about creating a cohesive and compelling narrative that resonates with readers. By revisiting and refining these elements during the editing and revising stages, you can elevate your story to new heights, making it more engaging and impactful.

So, dive deep into your characters and plot. Revisit motivations, conflicts, and growth. Address inconsistencies and enhance emotional depth. This process will make your story not only more coherent but also more captivating for your readers.

5. Eliminating Redundancies and Repetition

Redundancies and repetition can really bog down your manuscript and dilute its impact. During the revision process, it's essential to identify and remove any repetitive ideas, phrases, or descriptions. This streamlining enhances readability and keeps your readers engaged from start to finish.

Start by reading through your manuscript with a critical eye. Look for sections where you've repeated the same idea or description. Sometimes, in the flow of writing, we reiterate points to emphasize them, but too much repetition can make the text feel cumbersome and redundant. For instance, if you've described a character's nervousness multiple times using different words, see if you can combine those descriptions into one powerful image.

Pay attention to phrases you tend to overuse. Every writer has their favorite words or phrases that creep in more often than they should. Maybe you find yourself using "suddenly" or "just" in almost every paragraph. These small redundancies can add up and make your writing feel repetitive. Highlight these overused phrases and find ways to vary your language.

Another area to scrutinize is your descriptions. Descriptive writing is wonderful for creating vivid images, but repeating the same descriptions can bore your readers. If you've described a sunset in three different ways across your manuscript, choose the one that best captures the scene and cut the rest. Each description should serve to enhance the narrative, not bog it down.

Consider the overall structure of your manuscript as well. Are there entire sections or chapters that repeat the same information or themes? Sometimes in the process of drafting, we circle back to the same points multiple times. While this can be useful for reinforcing key ideas, it can also be overdone. Ensure that each section of your manuscript adds something new to the narrative or argument.

Streamlining your manuscript isn't just about cutting out words. It's about ensuring that each word, sentence, and paragraph serves a purpose and contributes to the overall narrative or argument. When every element of your writing is intentional, it makes for a more compelling and engaging read.

Let's say you've written a scene where a character reflects on their past. If you've already covered this background information earlier in the story, consider how necessary it is to repeat it here. Can you reference it more subtly, or weave it into the dialogue or action instead? Keeping the information fresh and integrated into the flow of the narrative helps maintain reader interest.

Reading your manuscript aloud can be incredibly helpful for spotting redundancies and repetition. Hearing your words can make repetitive phrases and ideas stand out more clearly. You might notice that you've used the same adjective multiple times in a short span, or that two paragraphs convey the same information. When you hear it, it's easier to recognize and eliminate unnecessary repetition.

Finally, don't hesitate to get feedback from others. Beta readers or writing groups can provide a fresh perspective and catch redundancies that you might have missed. They can point out where your narrative drags or where you've repeated yourself, giving you valuable insights for your revisions.

In conclusion, eliminating redundancies and repetition is about making your manuscript as tight and engaging as possible. By carefully reviewing your work and cutting out unnecessary repetition, you can enhance the readability and impact of your writing. Each word should pull its weight, contributing to a cohesive and compelling narrative that keeps readers hooked.

So, take the time to trim the excess. Identify and remove repetitive ideas, phrases, and descriptions. Streamline your manuscript to ensure that every word serves a purpose, and watch as your writing becomes more powerful and engaging.

6. Incorporating Feedback

Receiving feedback from others is an invaluable part of the editing and revising process. Sharing your manuscript with trusted peers, beta readers, or professional editors can provide you with constructive criticism that helps elevate your work. Being open to their suggestions and willing to make changes can significantly improve your manuscript.

Start by selecting a group of people whose opinions you trust and who understand your goals as a writer. This could be fellow writers, avid readers, or professionals in the publishing industry. Each of these perspectives can offer unique insights into different aspects of your manuscript.

When you receive feedback, approach it with an open mind. It can be tough to hear critiques about something you've poured your heart into, but remember that the goal is to make your manuscript the best it can be. Constructive criticism is not a personal attack; it's a tool for growth.

One effective way to handle feedback is to look for common themes or repeated comments. If multiple readers point out the same issue, it's likely something worth addressing. Maybe several people felt a character's motivation was unclear, or a plot point was confusing. These recurring points are invaluable in guiding your revisions.

On the other hand, not all feedback will resonate with you or align with your vision for the manuscript. That's okay. The key is to discern which suggestions will truly enhance your work and which might lead you astray. It's important to stay true to your voice and story while being open to improvements.

When you decide to incorporate feedback, start by making a plan. Identify the major areas for revision and prioritize them. Maybe you need to deepen a character's arc, clarify a plot twist, or tighten up the pacing. Having a clear plan helps you tackle revisions systematically rather than feeling overwhelmed by all the changes at once.

Let's say one of your beta readers felt that the climax of your story was rushed. This feedback is valuable because it points to a specific part of the narrative that needs more development. Take the time to expand this section, adding details and tension to make the climax more satisfying and impactful.

Incorporating feedback also allows you to see your manuscript from different perspectives. You might be so close to your work that you miss certain issues or opportunities for improvement. Fresh eyes can spot inconsistencies, plot holes, or areas where the narrative drags. This external perspective is crucial for refining your manuscript.

Consider keeping a feedback journal where you note down all the suggestions and your thoughts on them. This can help you track changes and remember why you made certain revisions. It also provides a record of your manuscript's evolution, which can be motivating and insightful.

When you've incorporated the feedback and revised your manuscript, it's a good idea to share it again with a few readers to ensure the changes have had the desired effect. This iterative process of feedback and revision can be time-consuming but immensely rewarding.

Remember, the goal of incorporating feedback is not just to fix problems but to make your manuscript the best it can be. It's about enhancing your story, enriching your characters, and ensuring that your narrative resonates with readers.

So, embrace the feedback process. Share your manuscript with trusted peers, beta readers, or professional editors. Be open to their suggestions, make thoughtful revisions, and stay true to your vision. Incorporating feedback allows you to see your work from new angles and address issues you might have overlooked, ultimately making your manuscript stronger and more compelling.

7. Ensuring Consistency

Consistency is key to maintaining the credibility and coherence of your manuscript. It's the glue that holds your story together and ensures a seamless reading experience. When details are consistent, readers can fully immerse themselves in your work without being jolted out of the narrative by discrepancies or errors.

Start by checking for consistency in character names, settings, and timelines. It might sound obvious, but it's surprisingly easy to slip up, especially in a longer manuscript. Make sure that a character's name doesn't change halfway through the story unless it's intentional and explained. Double-check that the settings you've described are consistent—if the kitchen is on the left side of the house in one chapter, it shouldn't suddenly be on the right in another.

Timelines are another critical area. Ensure that the sequence of events makes sense and that there are no conflicting details. For instance, if your story spans several years, keep track of your characters' ages and the passage of time. Tools like a timeline chart or even simple notes can help you maintain this consistency.

Factual details also need to be checked. Whether you're writing fiction or non-fiction, getting the facts right is crucial. If your story mentions historical events, scientific principles, or specific cultural practices, make sure your information is accurate and consistent throughout. This attention to detail not only adds credibility but also enhances the reader's trust in you as an author.

Another important aspect of consistency is your writing style and tone. Your narrative voice should remain uniform throughout the manuscript. If you start with a light, humorous tone, shifting abruptly to a dark, serious style can confuse readers and disrupt the flow of your story. Of course, tone can evolve with the plot, but these transitions should be smooth and deliberate.

Consider the following scenario: you're writing a mystery novel with a suspenseful and tense atmosphere. Midway through, if your writing suddenly becomes overly casual or comedic without a clear purpose, it can throw readers off. Maintaining a consistent tone helps keep readers engaged and maintains the story's integrity.

One way to ensure consistency is by creating a style guide for your manuscript. This can include character profiles with detailed descriptions, a map of your fictional world, and notes on the timeline and key events. Refer to this guide as you write and revise to keep all the details aligned.

Reading your manuscript in its entirety is another effective strategy. When you read through your work from start to finish, you're more likely to catch inconsistencies that might have slipped through during the writing process. It's also helpful to get feedback from beta readers who can point out any discrepancies you might have missed.

Consistency in details and presentation helps create a seamless reading experience. It prevents confusion and allows readers to stay fully immersed in your work. When everything fits together logically and smoothly, readers can focus on the story itself rather than being distracted by inconsistencies.

In summary, paying attention to consistency is crucial for maintaining the credibility and coherence of your manuscript. Check for consistent character names, settings, timelines, and factual details. Ensure that your writing style and tone remain uniform throughout the manuscript. By doing so, you'll create a more polished, professional, and engaging story that keeps readers hooked from beginning to end.

8. Fostering Emotional Impact

Editing and revising are your golden opportunities to enhance the emotional impact of your manuscript. This is the time to revisit scenes meant to evoke strong emotions and ensure they are written with the right intensity and sensitivity. By carefully crafting these moments, you can connect with your readers on a deeper level and make your story truly memorable.

Start by identifying the key emotional beats in your story. These are the moments where you want your readers to feel something powerful—whether it's joy, sorrow, fear, or excitement. Once you've pinpointed these scenes, focus on amplifying their impact. Ask yourself if the emotions come through clearly and whether they resonate as strongly as they should.

Descriptive language plays a crucial role in fostering emotional impact. Instead of telling your readers how a character feels, show them through vivid, sensory details. For example, if your character is heartbroken, describe the physical sensations of their pain—the tightness in their chest, the burning in their eyes as they fight back tears, the hollow ache in their stomach. These specific details make the emotion more tangible and relatable.

Pacing is another essential element. The rhythm of your prose can significantly influence how emotions are perceived. Slowing down the narrative during a poignant moment can give readers the space to fully absorb the character's feelings. Conversely, quick, sharp sentences can heighten tension and urgency during a suspenseful scene. Adjust the pacing to match the emotional tone you're aiming for.

Dialogue is a powerful tool for conveying emotion. Natural, authentic dialogue can reveal a lot about a character's inner state. Pay attention to the words your characters choose, their tone, and their speech patterns. Subtext—what's left unsaid—can be just as impactful as spoken words. A character's hesitation, their trailing off, or a sudden change in topic can all suggest deeper emotional undercurrents.

Revisiting the emotional arcs of your characters is also important. Ensure that their emotional journeys are coherent and believable. Characters should grow and change in response to the events of the story, and their emotions should reflect this development. If a character experiences a major loss, show how this affects them over time, not just in the immediate aftermath.

Consider the emotional context of each scene. The setting, the weather, the time of day—all these factors can contribute to the mood and enhance the emotional weight. For instance, a breakup scene might feel more poignant against the backdrop of a rainy evening, with the sound of raindrops echoing the character's tears.

It's also helpful to read emotionally charged scenes aloud. Hearing the words can highlight areas where the emotion might not be coming through as strongly as you'd like. It can also help you catch any awkward phrasings that could disrupt the emotional flow.

Feedback from others can be invaluable here. Beta readers can offer fresh perspectives on whether the emotions in your manuscript are hitting the mark. They can tell you which scenes moved them and which fell flat, giving you clear guidance on where to focus your revisions.

Remember, an emotionally resonant manuscript is more likely to leave a lasting impression on your readers. It's these deep emotional connections that make stories memorable and impactful. By carefully crafting and revising the emotional moments in your manuscript, you can ensure that your story touches your readers' hearts.

So, dive into your manuscript with an eye for emotional depth. Revisit key scenes, use descriptive language, adjust the pacing, and refine your dialogue. Make sure the emotions are authentic and powerful. By fostering emotional impact, you'll create a story that resonates deeply and lingers long after the final page.

9. Refining Your Voice

Your unique voice is what sets your work apart. It's the distinct personality and style that readers come to recognize and love. Through the editing and revising process, you can refine and strengthen this voice, ensuring it comes through clearly and consistently. This is your chance to make your manuscript unmistakably yours, resonating with authenticity and originality.

Start by paying attention to how your personality, perspective, and style are reflected in your writing. Your voice is a blend of these elements, creating a unique tone that's all your own. Think about what makes your writing distinctive. Is it your witty dialogue, your lyrical descriptions, or perhaps your candid and straightforward narrative style?

As you read through your manuscript, listen to how your voice sounds. Does it feel consistent throughout the entire piece? Are there parts where your voice seems to waver or become less distinct? These are the areas where you can focus your revisions.

One way to strengthen your voice is to ensure that your perspective shines through. Your experiences, beliefs, and worldview shape how you tell your story. Don't shy away from letting these aspects influence your writing. Authenticity is compelling. Readers can tell when a writer is being genuine, and it creates a stronger connection.

Consider your word choices and sentence structures. Do they reflect your natural way of speaking or thinking? For instance, if you have a conversational tone, make sure your sentences aren't overly formal or complex. Conversely, if your style is more formal, ensure that your language maintains that level of sophistication throughout.

Dialogue is a great place to infuse your voice. The way your characters speak can reflect your unique style. Maybe you have a knack for witty banter or deep, introspective conversations. Let your strengths in dialogue shine, and ensure that each character's voice is distinct yet complements the overall tone of your manuscript.

Consistency is key. While it's natural for your voice to evolve as you progress through your manuscript, it should remain recognizable. Make sure that the tone you establish at the beginning carries through to the end. If your story starts with a light-hearted, humorous tone, it shouldn't suddenly shift to something completely different without a clear, narrative-driven reason.

Editing is also the time to cut out anything that doesn't feel true to your voice. Sometimes, we write sentences or paragraphs that feel a bit off because we're trying to emulate another writer or fit into a certain style. If it doesn't feel like you, it's okay to let it go. Focus on what feels natural and authentic to you.

Feedback from others can be incredibly helpful in this process. Ask your beta readers or critique partners if they feel your voice is coming through clearly. They can provide insights on which parts feel the most "you" and where you might need to refine further.

Lastly, embrace your uniqueness. Your voice is your biggest asset as a writer. It's what makes your work stand out in a sea of stories. Don't be afraid to take risks and let your personality and perspective color your writing. Authenticity and originality are what readers crave, and your unique voice is what will resonate with them long after they've finished your book.

So, as you refine your manuscript, pay close attention to your voice. Make sure it's consistent, authentic, and unmistakably yours. Let your personality, perspective, and style shine through in every sentence. By doing so, you'll create a manuscript that's not only compelling but also deeply resonant and memorable.

10. Preparing for Publication

Preparing your manuscript for publication is a critical step in your writing journey. A well-edited and thoroughly revised manuscript is crucial for successful publication, whether you're self-publishing or submitting to traditional publishers. Presenting a polished manuscript not only increases your chances of acceptance but also ensures a positive reception from agents, editors, and readers alike. It demonstrates your commitment to quality and professionalism, making a strong impression.

Start by doing a final, thorough read-through of your manuscript. Look for any lingering typos, grammatical errors, or inconsistencies. Even after multiple rounds of editing, small mistakes can slip through, so this final check is essential. Consider reading your manuscript out loud or using a text-to-speech tool to catch errors you might have missed.

Formatting is also an important aspect. Ensure that your manuscript follows the standard formatting guidelines expected by publishers or platforms you're targeting. This typically includes using a readable font like Times New Roman or Arial, setting the font size to 12 points, double-spacing the text, and having one-inch margins on all sides. Proper formatting makes your manuscript look professional and is often a requirement for submission.

If you're aiming for traditional publication, research the submission guidelines of the agents or publishers you're interested in. Each may have specific requirements for how they want manuscripts submitted, including cover letters, synopses, and sample chapters. Adhering to these guidelines shows that you're professional and attentive to detail.

Writing a compelling query letter is another crucial step if you're seeking an agent or traditional publisher. Your query letter should be concise, engaging, and professional, providing a brief overview of your manuscript, your background, and why you believe this agent or publisher would be a good fit. This is your chance to make a great first impression, so take the time to craft a strong, persuasive letter.

For those pursuing self-publishing, there are additional considerations. You'll need to decide on platforms and formats—whether you're publishing as an e-book, a paperback, or both. Each platform, like Amazon Kindle Direct Publishing or IngramSpark, has its own formatting requirements and guidelines. Make sure your manuscript is correctly formatted for each platform to avoid any technical issues.

Investing in a professional cover design is also crucial for self-published authors. Your cover is the first thing potential readers will see, and a professionally designed cover can significantly impact their decision to purchase your book. Consider hiring a professional cover designer who understands the market and can create a cover that captures the essence of your story while appealing to your target audience.

Another important aspect of preparing for publication is creating a strong marketing plan. Think about how you will promote your book and reach your audience. This might include building an author website, engaging with readers on social media, arranging book signings, or setting up promotional giveaways. A well-thought-out marketing strategy can make a big difference in your book's success.

Don't underestimate the value of beta readers and professional editors. Beta readers can provide feedback from a reader's perspective, highlighting any remaining issues with the plot, pacing, or characters. A professional editor can offer a final polish, ensuring your manuscript is the best it can be before it goes out into the world.

Finally, be prepared for the journey ahead. Publishing, whether traditional or self, is a process that requires patience, persistence, and resilience. There will be challenges along the way, but staying committed to your goal and maintaining a professional attitude will serve you well.

In summary, preparing your manuscript for publication is about more than just ensuring it's error-free. It's about presenting a polished, professional work that showcases your commitment to quality and your unique voice. Whether you're submitting to agents, publishers, or self-publishing, taking the time to thoroughly prepare will increase your chances of success and help your book make a strong, lasting impression.

Approaching the Editing and Revising Process

- **Take a Break**: After completing your first draft, take a break before you start editing. This allows you to return to your manuscript with fresh eyes and a more objective perspective.
- **Edit in Stages**: Break the editing process into stages, focusing first on big-picture elements like structure and plot, and then on finer details like grammar and style.
- **Use Tools Wisely**: Utilize grammar-checking tools and style guides, but don't rely solely on them. Manual review is essential for catching subtleties and nuances that automated tools might miss.
- **Read Aloud**: Reading your manuscript aloud can help you catch awkward phrasing, rhythm issues, and errors you might overlook when reading silently.
- **Stay Open to Feedback**: Embrace feedback from others and be willing to make changes. Constructive criticism is invaluable for improving your work.

Editing and revising are not just about correcting mistakes; they are about refining your manuscript to its highest potential. This process is where you polish your prose, sharpen your ideas, and ensure that your work is the best it can be. Embrace this stage with patience and dedication, knowing that each round of editing brings you closer to a manuscript that will resonate with and captivate your readers.

Tools and Resources: Software and other resources to aid in the writing process.

In today's digital age, writers have access to a plethora of tools and resources designed to enhance productivity, streamline the writing process, and improve the quality of their work. These tools can assist you at every stage, from brainstorming and drafting to editing and revising. Here are some of the most useful software and resources that can aid you in your writing journey.

1. Writing Software

Scrivener: Scrivener is a comprehensive writing software that allows you to organize your manuscript, research, and notes in one place. It's particularly useful for large projects, offering features like a corkboard for visualizing your story structure, a binder for easy navigation, and customizable templates. Scrivener's robust organizational tools can help you manage complex narratives and keep track of your progress.

Microsoft Word: A staple in the writing community, Microsoft Word offers powerful word processing capabilities. Its features include track changes for collaborative editing, extensive formatting options, and integration with other Microsoft Office tools. Word is highly versatile and widely used in both professional and academic settings.

Google Docs: Google Docs is a cloud-based word processor that enables real-time collaboration. It's perfect for working with co-authors, editors, or beta readers, as multiple users can comment and edit simultaneously. Google Docs also automatically saves your work, reducing the risk of data loss.

2. Editing Tools

Grammarly: Grammarly is an AI-powered writing assistant that checks for grammar, punctuation, style, and tone. It offers real-time suggestions to improve clarity and correctness, making it a valuable tool for both drafting and editing. Grammarly's browser extension also ensures your writing is polished across various platforms, including emails and social media.

ProWritingAid: ProWritingAid is another robust editing tool that provides detailed reports on grammar, style, readability, and more. It offers in-depth analysis and suggestions for improvement, helping you refine your manuscript. The tool integrates with popular writing software and platforms, making it versatile and user-friendly.

Hemingway Editor: The Hemingway Editor helps you simplify your writing by highlighting complex sentences, passive voice, and adverbs. It's designed to improve readability and make your writing more concise and impactful. The desktop app and online version provide immediate feedback, allowing you to make real-time adjustments.

3. Organization and Planning Tools

Evernote: Evernote is a note-taking app that helps you capture ideas, research, and inspiration on the go. Its organizational features, such as notebooks and tags, make it easy to keep track of your notes and find them when needed. Evernote also allows you to attach files, images, and web clippings, making it a versatile tool for research and planning.

Trello: Trello is a project management tool that uses boards, lists, and cards to help you organize your writing projects. It's great for visual thinkers and can be used to track progress, set deadlines, and collaborate with others. Trello's flexibility makes it suitable for everything from outlining your manuscript to managing your publishing schedule.

MindMeister: MindMeister is a mind mapping tool that helps you brainstorm and organize your ideas visually. It's useful for plotting your story, developing characters, and structuring your manuscript. MindMeister's intuitive interface allows you to create and modify mind maps easily, making the brainstorming process more dynamic and interactive.

4. Research Tools

Zotero: Zotero is a research tool that helps you collect, organize, and cite sources. It's particularly useful for academic writing, allowing you to create a personal library of research materials. Zotero's browser extension makes it easy to save articles, books, and web pages, while its integration with word processors streamlines the citation process.

Evernote: Evernote is a versatile note-taking app that allows you to capture research, ideas, and inspiration in various formats, including text, images, and audio. Its organizational features, such as notebooks and tags, make it easy to categorize and retrieve information. Evernote is especially useful for gathering research materials and keeping them accessible across all your devices.

Scrivener: Beyond its writing capabilities, Scrivener also excels as a research tool. You can import and organize research materials directly within your project, making it easy to reference notes, images, and documents as you write. Scrivener's split-screen feature allows you to view your research alongside your manuscript, enhancing efficiency.

5. Collaboration and Feedback Tools

Google Docs: Google Docs is a powerful tool for collaboration, allowing multiple users to work on a document simultaneously. Its commenting and suggestion features facilitate feedback and revisions, making it ideal for working with co-authors, editors, or beta readers. Google Docs' cloud-based nature ensures that your work is always accessible and up-to-date.

Dropbox: Dropbox is a cloud storage service that enables you to share large files and collaborate with others. It's particularly useful for sharing drafts, research materials, and feedback documents. Dropbox's file synchronization ensures that your files are always backed up and accessible from any device.

Slack: Slack is a communication tool that enhances collaboration through channels, direct messaging, and file sharing. It's useful for coordinating with writing groups, editors, and beta readers. Slack's integration with other tools, like Google Drive and Trello, streamlines project management and communication.

6. Productivity Tools

FocusWriter: FocusWriter is a distraction-free writing environment that helps you concentrate on your writing. It offers a minimalist interface, customizable themes, and goal tracking features. FocusWriter's fullscreen mode eliminates distractions, allowing you to immerse yourself in your writing.

Pomodoro Technique Apps: The Pomodoro Technique is a time management method that involves working in focused intervals (typically 25 minutes) followed by short breaks. Apps like TomatoTimer, Focus Booster, and Be Focused help you implement this technique, improving your productivity and maintaining your focus during writing sessions.

Freedom: Freedom is a website and app blocker that helps you stay focused by limiting access to distracting websites and applications. By setting up scheduled sessions, you can create a distraction-free writing environment, enhancing your productivity and concentration.

7. Writing Communities and Resources

NaNoWriMo: National Novel Writing Month (NaNoWriMo) is an annual event that challenges writers to complete a 50,000-word novel in November. The NaNoWriMo community provides support, motivation, and resources to help you achieve your writing goals. Participating in NaNoWriMo can be a great way to jumpstart your writing project and connect with other writers.

Writer's Digest: Writer's Digest is a comprehensive resource for writers, offering articles, tutorials, webinars, and writing prompts. It covers various aspects of writing, from craft and technique to publishing and marketing. Subscribing to Writer's Digest can provide you with valuable insights and inspiration throughout your writing journey.

Critique Circle: Critique Circle is an online writing community where writers can share their work and receive constructive feedback from peers. Participating in critique groups can help you improve your writing, gain new perspectives, and build connections with other writers. Critique Circle's structured feedback process ensures that you receive detailed and helpful critiques.

By leveraging these tools and resources, you can enhance your writing process, stay organized, and produce high-quality work. Whether you need help with drafting, editing, research, or collaboration, there's a tool out there to support you at every stage of your writing journey. Embrace these resources to streamline your workflow, improve your craft, and bring your writing projects to life.

Chapter 2: Explore Self-Publishing vs. Traditional or Hybrid Publishing

Embarking on the journey to publish your book involves making critical decisions that will shape your career as an author. One of the most significant choices you'll face is deciding which publishing route to take. In this chapter, we will explore the three primary publishing options available to you: self-publishing, traditional publishing, and hybrid publishing. Each of these paths has its unique characteristics, advantages, and challenges. Understanding these differences will empower you to make an informed decision that aligns with your goals and aspirations.

Understanding Your Options: The Differences Between Self-Publishing, Traditional Publishing, and Hybrid Publishing

To navigate the publishing landscape, it's essential to understand what each option entails.

Self-Publishing: This route offers complete control over the publishing process. As a self-published author, you handle everything from writing and editing to cover design and marketing. Platforms like Amazon Kindle Direct Publishing (KDP) and IngramSpark make it relatively straightforward to publish your book. The key benefits include higher royalty rates and full creative control. However, the responsibility for all aspects of the publishing process falls on you, requiring significant time and effort.

Traditional Publishing: In traditional publishing, you submit your manuscript to publishing houses or literary agents. If accepted, the publisher takes on the responsibility of editing, designing, marketing, and distributing your book. This route often involves a rigorous selection process and can be highly competitive. The advantages include professional support and broader distribution channels. However, traditional publishing usually offers lower royalty rates, and authors have less control over the final product.

Hybrid Publishing: Hybrid publishing combines elements of both self-publishing and traditional publishing. Authors often pay for specific services like editing, cover design, and marketing, while retaining more control and higher royalty rates than in traditional publishing. Hybrid publishers can offer valuable resources and support, making it an attractive option for authors who want professional assistance without giving up too much control.

Vanity Press: There is another type of publishing you should be aware of—the vanity press. These entities prey on inexperienced authors, charging exorbitant fees for the "honor" of publishing your work without providing meaningful support or value. Vanity presses often exploit authors' dreams, leaving them with poor-quality books and significant financial losses. We will not spend much time here, but be warned: if you come across this kind of publisher, run.

Pros and Cons: Weighing the Advantages and Disadvantages of Each Publishing Route

Every publishing route comes with its own set of pros and cons. Understanding these will help you weigh your options effectively.

Self-Publishing Pros:

- Complete creative control
- Higher royalty rates
- Speed to market
- Flexibility in marketing and distribution

Write It. Publish It. Sell It.

Self-Publishing Cons:

- Requires significant time and effort
- Upfront costs for professional services
- Limited access to traditional distribution channels
- Responsibility for all aspects of publishing

Traditional Publishing Pros:

- Professional editing, design, and marketing
- Established distribution channels
- Credibility and prestige
- Advance payments (in some cases)

Traditional Publishing Cons:

- Highly competitive and selective
- Lower royalty rates
- Less creative control
- Longer time to market

Hybrid Publishing Pros:

- Professional support and services
- Higher royalty rates than traditional publishing
- More control over the publishing process
- Faster time to market than traditional publishing

Hybrid Publishing Cons:

- Upfront costs for services
- Varying levels of support and quality
- Potential for higher financial risk
- Less credibility than traditional publishing

Case Studies: Real-Life Examples of Authors Who Have Succeeded with Each Method

Examining real-life examples of authors who have succeeded with different publishing methods can provide valuable insights and inspiration. These case studies highlight the diverse paths to success and demonstrate that there is no one-size-fits-all approach. Each author's journey is unique, offering lessons and motivation for your own publishing endeavors.

Self-Publishing Success: Andy Weir and "The Martian"

Consider the remarkable case of Andy Weir, author of "The Martian." Weir's journey began in an unconventional way. He initially self-published his novel on his website, posting chapters for free and receiving feedback from readers. His dedication to accuracy and detail, combined with engaging storytelling, garnered a dedicated following. This grassroots support was pivotal.

As his readership grew, Weir decided to self-publish "The Martian" as an e-book on Amazon Kindle. The book's popularity soared, catching the attention of traditional publishers. Crown Publishing Group eventually picked up the novel, leading to its transformation into a major motion picture. Weir's story illustrates the potential for self-publishing to lead to mainstream success. It underscores the importance of building a strong reader base and leveraging digital platforms to gain visibility.

Traditional Publishing Success: J.K. Rowling and the "Harry Potter" Series

J.K. Rowling's journey with the "Harry Potter" series is a classic example of traditional publishing success. Rowling faced numerous rejections before her manuscript was finally accepted by Bloomsbury Publishing. Her perseverance paid off, and the series went on to achieve unprecedented global acclaim and sales.

Rowling's success story highlights several key aspects of traditional publishing: the importance of perseverance, the role of a supportive and enthusiastic publisher, and the potential for widespread distribution and marketing. Bloomsbury's initial modest print run and strategic marketing efforts, including targeting young readers and leveraging word-of-mouth promotion, were crucial in building the series' momentum. Rowling's experience demonstrates that traditional publishing, despite its challenges, can offer unparalleled opportunities for reach and recognition.

Hybrid Publishing Success: James Altucher and "Choose Yourself!"

The hybrid publishing model has worked well for authors like James Altucher. Altucher utilized the resources of hybrid publisher Choose Yourself Media to publish his book "Choose Yourself!" This approach provided him with professional support while allowing him to maintain control over his work and reap substantial financial benefits.

Altucher's book became a bestseller, in part due to the hybrid model's flexibility and support in areas such as distribution, marketing, and design. Hybrid publishing combines elements of both traditional and self-publishing, offering authors the best of both worlds. For Altucher, this model meant retaining creative control and a larger share of the profits, while still accessing professional services that ensured a high-quality publication.

Lessons Learned

These case studies provide several key takeaways for aspiring authors:

> **Building a Readership**: Andy Weir's success underscores the importance of engaging with readers early on and building a dedicated following, which can be crucial for gaining visibility and attracting publishers.

Perseverance: J.K. Rowling's journey is a testament to the power of perseverance. Facing numerous rejections didn't deter her, and her eventual success highlights the importance of believing in your work and staying persistent.

Choosing the Right Model: James Altucher's experience with hybrid publishing shows that there is no one-size-fits-all approach. Different publishing methods can offer different benefits, and choosing the right one depends on your goals, resources, and preferences.

Leveraging Platforms: Both Weir and Altucher's stories illustrate the power of leveraging digital platforms for distribution and marketing. In today's publishing landscape, having an online presence can significantly boost your chances of success.

Professional Support: Whether through traditional, hybrid, or self-publishing, professional support in editing, design, and marketing is crucial. High-quality production values enhance credibility and reader satisfaction.

Conclusion

By examining the diverse paths to success of authors like Andy Weir, J.K. Rowling, and James Altucher, you can see that success in publishing comes in many forms. Each method—self-publishing, traditional publishing, and hybrid publishing—has its own advantages and challenges. The key is to choose the path that best aligns with your goals, strengths, and circumstances. With dedication, perseverance, and the right strategy, you can find success and connect with readers in meaningful ways.

Write It. Publish It. Sell It.

Making the Decision: How to Choose the Best Publishing Path for Your Book and Career Goals

Choosing the right publishing path involves considering your personal goals, resources, and preferences. Here are some questions to guide your decision:

- **Control vs. Support**: How much control do you want over the publishing process? Are you willing to handle all aspects of publishing, or do you prefer professional support?
- **Financial Investment**: What is your budget for publishing? Are you prepared to invest upfront in professional services, or do you prefer a model where the publisher covers these costs?
- **Timeline**: How quickly do you want to see your book published? Are you willing to go through the potentially lengthy traditional publishing process, or do you need a faster route to market?
- **Distribution and Reach**: How important are wide distribution and prestige to you? Are you aiming for bookstore placement and traditional media coverage, or are you focused on online sales and niche markets?
- **Long-Term Career Goals**: What are your long-term goals as an author? Are you looking to build a career with multiple books, and if so, which publishing path aligns best with your vision?

By carefully considering these factors, you can choose the publishing route that best aligns with your aspirations and resources. Each path has its unique challenges and rewards, and the right choice depends on your individual circumstances and goals.

In the following sections, we will delve deeper into each publishing option, providing detailed insights and guidance to help you make an informed decision. Remember, the journey to publishing your book is a personal and evolving one. Stay open to learning and adapting as you navigate the landscape of self-publishing, traditional publishing, and hybrid publishing.

Understanding Your Options: The differences between self-publishing, traditional publishing, and hybrid publishing.

Deciding how to publish your book is one of the most critical decisions you'll make as an author. Each publishing route—self-publishing, traditional publishing, and hybrid publishing—offers distinct advantages and challenges. Understanding the fundamental differences between these options will empower you to choose the path that best aligns with your goals, resources, and preferences.

Self-Publishing

Self-publishing has revolutionized the literary world, giving authors unprecedented control over their work. Here's what you need to know:

- **Complete Creative Control**: As a self-published author, you retain full control over every aspect of your book, from content and cover design to pricing and marketing. This allows you to maintain your creative vision without external interference.
- **Higher Royalty Rates**: Self-publishing platforms like Amazon Kindle Direct Publishing (KDP) and IngramSpark offer higher royalty rates compared to traditional publishers. You can earn a larger percentage of each sale, which can be financially rewarding if your book sells well.
- **Speed to Market**: Self-publishing enables you to bring your book to market quickly. Once your manuscript is ready, you can publish it within days or weeks, rather than the months or years that traditional publishing often requires.
- **Responsibility for All Aspects**: While self-publishing offers freedom, it also means that you are responsible for all aspects of the publishing process. This includes editing, formatting, cover design, and marketing. You may need to invest in professional services to ensure the quality of your book.

Traditional Publishing

Traditional publishing remains a prestigious and desirable route for many authors. Here are the key features:

- **Professional Support**: Traditional publishers provide a team of professionals to support your book's journey, including editors, designers, marketers, and publicists. This ensures that your book meets high industry standards.
- **Broad Distribution**: Established publishers have extensive distribution networks, allowing your book to reach bookstores, libraries, and international markets. This can significantly increase your book's visibility and sales potential.
- **Credibility and Prestige**: Being published by a reputable traditional publisher can enhance your credibility as an author. It can open doors to media coverage, literary awards, and speaking opportunities.
- **Competitive and Selective**: The traditional publishing process is highly competitive. Securing a publishing deal typically requires finding a literary agent and submitting your manuscript for consideration. The process can be lengthy and uncertain, with no guarantee of acceptance.
- **Lower Royalty Rates**: Traditional publishers usually offer lower royalty rates compared to self-publishing. Additionally, they may retain a significant portion of the revenue to cover the costs of production, distribution, and marketing.

Hybrid Publishing

Hybrid publishing offers a middle ground between self-publishing and traditional publishing. It combines elements of both models:

- **Professional Services with Control**: Hybrid publishers provide professional services such as editing, design, and marketing, while allowing authors to retain more control over their work. You can choose which services you need and pay for them accordingly.
- **Higher Royalties than Traditional Publishing**: While hybrid publishing involves upfront costs, authors typically earn higher royalties compared to traditional publishing. This can make it a financially viable option for many writers.
- **Faster Time to Market**: Hybrid publishing often has a quicker turnaround time than traditional publishing, allowing you to bring your book to

market faster. This is beneficial if you want to capitalize on current trends or time-sensitive topics.
- **Varied Quality and Reputation**: The quality and reputation of hybrid publishers can vary widely. It's essential to research and choose a reputable hybrid publisher to ensure you receive valuable services and support.
- **Financial Investment**: Hybrid publishing usually requires an upfront financial investment from the author. This can range from a few hundred to several thousand dollars, depending on the services provided.

Vanity Press

- While exploring your options, it's crucial to be aware of vanity presses, which present themselves as legitimate publishers but often exploit inexperienced authors:sanificant fees for publishing services, often without providing the professional quality or distribution networks of reputable publishers.
- **Limited Marketing and Support**: Despite high costs, vanity presses typically offer minimal marketing support and limited distribution, leaving authors to struggle with promotion and sales.
- **Predatory Practices**: Vanity presses often use high

-pressure sales tactics to lure authors into costly contracts. They prey on the desire to see one's work in print, without delivering the value that justifies the expense.

- <u>**Warning Signs**: Be cautious of publishers who ask for large upfront payments, promise guaranteed success, or pressure you to sign a contract quickly. Reputable publishers, whether traditional or hybrid, will not charge exorbitant fees for basic services.</u>

Weighing the Options

Understanding the distinctions between self-publishing, traditional publishing, hybrid publishing, and recognizing the risks of vanity presses is crucial in making an informed decision about your publishing journey. Here's a summary to help you weigh your options:

Write It. Publish It. Sell It.

Self-Publishing

- **Pros**: Full creative control, higher royalties, quick time to market.
- **Cons**: Full responsibility for all aspects, upfront costs for quality services, limited access to traditional distribution channels.

Traditional Publishing

- **Pros**: Professional support, broad distribution, enhanced credibility, potential advances.
- **Cons**: Highly competitive, longer time to market, lower royalties, less creative control.

Hybrid Publishing

- **Pros**: Professional services with more control, higher royalties than traditional, quicker time to market.
- **Cons**: Upfront financial investment, varied quality and reputation among hybrid publishers.

Vanity Press

- **Cons**: High upfront costs, limited marketing and support, predatory practices, poor return on investment.

By understanding these options, you can align your choice with your goals, financial situation, and desired level of control over your publishing journey. Each path offers unique opportunities and challenges, and the right choice depends on your personal and professional aspirations.

In the following sections, we will delve deeper into the advantages and disadvantages of each publishing route, explore real-life case studies, and provide practical advice on how to make the best decision for your book and career goals. Equipped with this knowledge, you will be better prepared to navigate the publishing landscape and achieve your dreams of becoming a successful author.

- **Pros and Cons**: Weighing the advantages and disadvantages of each publishing route.

Choosing the right publishing path is a crucial decision that can significantly impact your career as an author. Each route—self-publishing, traditional publishing, and hybrid publishing—has its unique advantages and disadvantages. Understanding these pros and cons will help you make an informed decision that aligns with your goals, resources, and personal preferences.

Making Your Decision

Choosing the best publishing route for your book is a significant decision that depends on various factors. To help you make an informed choice, consider the following questions:

1. What level of control do you want over the publishing process?
2. How much are you willing to invest upfront?
3. What are your financial goals and expectations for royalties?
4. How important is professional support and quality assurance to you?
5. What is your preferred timeline for bringing your book to market?
6. How important is broad distribution and traditional credibility to you?

To help visualize these considerations, here's a graph that outlines the different aspects of self-publishing, hybrid publishing, and traditional publishing. Each publishing route offers unique opportunities and challenges, and the right choice depends on your individual circumstances and goals.

Write It. Publish It. Sell It.

Publishing Decision Comparison

Self-Publishing	Hybrid Publishing	Traditional Publishing
- **Control**: Full control over content, design, and pricing.	- **Control**: Significant control with professional support.	- **Control**: Limited control; publisher handles most aspects.
- **Upfront Investment**: High (editing, cover design, marketing).	- **Upfront Investment**: Moderate (shared costs, some services provided).	- **Upfront Investment**: Low (publisher bears most costs).
- **Financial Goals**: High potential royalties (up to 70%).	- **Financial Goals**: Balanced potential, with professional support boosting quality.	- **Financial Goals**: Lower royalties, but potential for advances.
- **Professional Support and Quality Assurance**: Must outsource or handle yourself.	- **Professional Support and Quality Assurance**: Includes professional editing, design, and marketing services.	- **Professional Support and Quality Assurance**: Comprehensive support from publisher.

• **Time to Market:** Fast (days to weeks).	• **Time to Market:** Moderate (weeks to months).	• **Time to Market:** Slow (months to years).
• **Distribution and Credibility:** Self-driven, often limited to online platforms.	• **Distribution and Credibility:** Wider distribution through partnerships; some traditional credibility.	• **Distribution and Credibility:** Extensive distribution, strong credibility and market presence.

Considerations for Each Publishing Route

Self-Publishing:

1. **Pros**: Full creative control, high potential royalties, fast time to market.
2. **Cons**: High upfront investment, responsibility for all aspects, limited distribution and credibility.
3. **Best For**: Authors who want complete control and are willing to invest time and money upfront.

Hybrid Publishing:

1. **Pros**: Significant control, shared costs, professional support, moderate time to market.
2. **Cons**: Moderate upfront investment, some loss of control, variable distribution.
3. **Best For**: Authors who want a balance of control and support, and are willing to share costs.

Traditional Publishing:

1. **Pros**: Low upfront costs, comprehensive professional support, extensive distribution, high credibility.
2. **Cons**: Limited control, lower royalties, long time to market.
3. **Best For**: Authors who prioritize professional support and broad distribution, and are willing to wait longer for publication.

By carefully weighing the pros and cons of each publishing route, you can align your choice with your personal and professional aspirations. Each path offers unique opportunities and challenges, and the right choice depends on your individual circumstances and goals.

Next Steps

In the next section, we will explore real-life case studies of authors who have succeeded with each method, providing insights and inspiration for your publishing journey. These examples will help you see how different authors navigated their publishing paths and achieved success.

Avoiding Vanity Press Pitfalls: A Cautionary Tale

Not all publishing experiences are positive, as illustrated by the cautionary tale of an author who fell victim to a vanity press. This author, eager to see their work published, signed a contract with a company that promised comprehensive services for a high fee. The result was a poorly edited book with a subpar cover design, minimal marketing support, and limited distribution.

Despite investing thousands of dollars, the author struggled to sell copies and received little return on their investment. This experience underscores the importance of researching publishers thoroughly and avoiding those that charge exorbitant fees without delivering value. The cautionary tale serves as a reminder to be vigilant and seek reputable publishers who offer genuine support and fair terms.

Lessons Learned

Self-Publishing:

- **Leverage Your Audience**: Andy Weir's success was driven by his ability to engage directly with readers. Building a loyal audience before and during the self-publishing process can significantly boost your book's visibility and sales.
- **Quality Matters**: Investing in professional editing, cover design, and formatting can elevate your self-published book to compete with traditionally published works.

Traditional Publishing:

- **Perseverance Pays Off**: J.K. Rowling's journey underscores the importance of persistence. Rejections are part of the process, and success often requires determination and resilience.
- **Trust the Process**: Traditional publishing offers extensive professional support. Trusting your publisher's expertise can help your book reach its full potential.

Hybrid Publishing:

- **Professional Support with Control**: James Altucher's experience highlights the benefits of hybrid publishing, where authors can access professional services while retaining significant control and higher royalties.
- **Choose Reputable Publishers**: Research and select hybrid publishers with a proven track record to ensure you receive quality support and value for your investment.

Avoiding Vanity Presses:

- **Do Your Homework**: Investigate publishers thoroughly, read reviews, and seek recommendations from other authors. Avoid companies that promise guaranteed success for high fees.
- **Know Your Rights**: Understand the terms of your contract and retain rights to your work. Reputable publishers should be transparent and supportive, not exploitative.

By examining these case studies, you can gain a clearer understanding of the potential outcomes of each publishing route. Each path has its unique opportunities and challenges, and learning from the experiences of successful authors can guide you in making the best decision for your book and career goals. In the next section, we will discuss how to choose the right publishing path for you, based on your individual needs and aspirations.

Making the Decision: How to choose the best publishing path for your book and career goals.

Choosing the right publishing path is a pivotal decision that will shape your journey as an author. Each publishing route—self-publishing, traditional publishing, and hybrid publishing—offers unique benefits and challenges. To determine the best option for your book and career goals, consider the following factors and questions.

1. Assess Your Goals and Priorities

Your goals and priorities as an author are fundamental in guiding your decision. Reflect on what you hope to achieve with your book:

- **Creative Control**: How important is it for you to retain full control over your manuscript, cover design, and marketing strategy? If maintaining your creative vision is a top priority, self-publishing or hybrid publishing might be the best fit.
- **Professional Support**: Do you prefer having a team of professionals to handle editing, design, and marketing, allowing you to focus solely on writing? If so, traditional publishing or a reputable hybrid publisher can provide the support you need.
- **Financial Goals**: Consider your financial expectations. Are you willing to invest upfront in professional services with the potential for higher royalties (self-publishing or hybrid publishing)? Or do you prefer the traditional route, which might offer advance payments but lower royalty rates?

- **Speed to Market**: How quickly do you want to see your book published? Self-publishing and hybrid publishing typically offer faster turnaround times compared to traditional publishing.
- **Prestige and Recognition**: Is gaining credibility and recognition through an established publisher important to you? Traditional publishing can enhance your reputation and open doors to media coverage, awards, and speaking opportunities.

2. Evaluate Your Resources

Consider the resources you have at your disposal, including time, money, and expertise:

- **Time Commitment**: Do you have the time to manage all aspects of the publishing process, from editing to marketing? Self-publishing requires significant time and effort, whereas traditional and hybrid publishing can alleviate some of these responsibilities.
- **Financial Investment**: What is your budget for publishing your book? Self-publishing and hybrid publishing often involve upfront costs for professional services. Ensure you have a realistic budget and be prepared for potential financial risks.
- **Skill Set**: Do you have the skills or willingness to learn tasks such as marketing, graphic design, and formatting? Self-publishing demands a diverse skill set or the ability to outsource these tasks effectively.

3. Research the Market

Understanding the market and potential readership for your book can influence your decision:

- **Genre and Audience**: Certain genres perform better in specific publishing routes. For example, niche genres or those with a strong online community may thrive in self-publishing, while genres with broad appeal might benefit from traditional publishing's extensive distribution networks.
- **Market Trends**: Stay informed about trends in the publishing industry. Hybrid publishing is gaining traction as a viable option for many authors. Analyze how similar books in your genre have fared in different publishing models.

4. Consider Long-Term Career Goals

Your long-term aspirations as an author should play a crucial role in your decision:

- **Building a Brand**: If you plan to write multiple books, consider how each publishing route can help you build and sustain your author brand. Consistency in quality and marketing efforts is essential.
- **Career Development**: Think about how each publishing path aligns with your broader career goals. Traditional publishing can enhance your credibility, which might be beneficial for other ventures such as public speaking or consulting. Self-publishing allows for more entrepreneurial opportunities, such as leveraging your books for coaching or online courses.
- **Flexibility**: Evaluate how each option allows for flexibility in your career. Self-publishing offers the most flexibility in terms of creative and business decisions. Traditional publishing can provide stability and support, which might be preferable if you're looking for a more structured approach.

5. Seek Professional Advice and Community Input

Engaging with the writing and publishing community can provide valuable insights and advice:

- **Author Networks**: Connect with other authors who have experience with different publishing routes. Join writing groups, attend conferences, and participate in online forums to gather first-hand accounts and advice.
- **Consult Professionals**: Consider consulting with literary agents, editors, and publishing consultants. They can offer expert guidance based on your manuscript and career goals.
- **Workshops and Webinars**: Participate in workshops and webinars focused on publishing. These can provide in-depth knowledge and answer specific questions you may have about each publishing option.

6. Make an Informed Decision

After evaluating your goals, resources, market insights, and professional advice, you'll be better equipped to make an informed decision. Remember that your choice is not set in stone; many authors switch between different publishing models throughout their careers based on their evolving needs and goals.

Key Questions to Guide Your Decision:

- What are my primary goals for publishing this book (e.g., creative control, professional support, financial gain, speed to market, recognition)?
- How much time and money am I willing to invest in the publishing process?
- What are my strengths and weaknesses in terms of managing the publishing tasks?
- How does my genre and target audience influence my publishing choice?
- What are my long-term career aspirations as an author?
- What insights and advice have I gathered from the writing community and publishing professionals?

By thoroughly considering these questions and the factors outlined, you can choose the publishing path that best aligns with your unique circumstances and aspirations. Whether you opt for self-publishing, traditional publishing, or hybrid publishing, the most important thing is to remain committed to your writing and passionate about sharing your work with the world.

In the next section, we will delve into practical steps and actionable advice for navigating your chosen publishing route, ensuring you are well-prepared for the journey ahead.

Chapter 3: Understanding Marketing vs. Promoting Your Book

Congratulations! Your manuscript is polished, and your book is on the brink of publication. However, the journey doesn't end with seeing your book in print or available online. One of the most critical aspects of a book's success is how well it is marketed and promoted. In this chapter, we will explore the fundamental differences between marketing and promoting your book, providing you with the tools and strategies to ensure your work reaches its intended audience and achieves the recognition it deserves.

Marketing Fundamentals: The Basics of Book Marketing and Why It Matters

Book marketing is a comprehensive, long-term strategy that encompasses all activities related to identifying, reaching, and engaging your target audience. It involves understanding who your readers are, what they want, and how to connect with them effectively. Marketing is about creating a sustained presence and building relationships that encourage readers to not only buy your book but also recommend it to others.

Effective marketing is crucial because it lays the foundation for your book's success. It helps you:

- Establish your author brand and build credibility.
- Generate awareness and interest in your book.
- Drive sales and create a loyal reader base.
- Position your book within the competitive literary market.

Promotion Strategies: How to Effectively Promote Your Book Through Various Channels

Promotion, on the other hand, refers to the specific, time-bound activities designed to boost your book's visibility and sales at particular moments—such as during your book launch or around significant events and holidays. Promotion strategies can include:

- Book tours (virtual or in-person).
- Launch parties.
- Giveaways and contests.
- Speaking engagements and signings.
- Special discount campaigns.

We'll explore how to create and implement these promotional tactics to maximize their impact and reach.

Building a Brand: Creating an Author Brand That Resonates with Your Target Audience

Your author brand is more than just your name or the titles of your books. It's the promise you make to your readers about what they can expect from your work. A strong author brand communicates your unique voice, style, and values, helping you connect with your target audience on a deeper level.

Building a compelling author brand involves:

- Defining your unique selling points (USPs).
- Crafting a consistent and authentic message.
- Developing a visual identity, including your website, social media profiles, and book covers.
- Engaging with your audience in a way that reflects your brand's personality.

We'll guide you through the steps to create an author brand that stands out and resonates with readers.

Write It. Publish It. Sell It.

Social Media and Digital Marketing: Leveraging Online Platforms to Reach More Readers

In today's digital age, social media and online platforms are indispensable tools for reaching and engaging with your audience. Effective digital marketing strategies can help you expand your reach and build a community around your book.

Key aspects of social media and digital marketing include:

- Choosing the right platforms (e.g., Facebook, Twitter, Instagram, TikTok) based on your target audience.
- Creating and sharing engaging content that promotes your book and reflects your author brand.
- Using paid advertising to boost visibility and drive traffic to your book's sales pages.
- Building an email list to maintain direct communication with your readers.

We'll delve into practical tips and techniques for leveraging digital marketing to enhance your book's presence online.

Public Relations: Using Media and Public Appearances to Boost Your Book's Visibility

Public relations (PR) involves managing your reputation and relationship with the public, media, and other key stakeholders. Effective PR can significantly enhance your book's visibility and credibility.

PR strategies include:

- Writing and distributing press releases.
- Securing media coverage through interviews, reviews, and features.
- Participating in book fairs, literary festivals, and other public events.
- Networking with influencers, bloggers, and other authors to gain endorsements and recommendations.

We'll explore how to use PR to create buzz around your book and establish a positive public image.

By understanding the distinction between marketing and promoting your book, and mastering the fundamentals of each, you can develop a comprehensive strategy that ensures your book reaches its full potential. In the following sections, we will provide detailed guidance and actionable steps to help you navigate the complexities of book marketing and promotion, ultimately achieving success in the literary marketplace.

Marketing Fundamentals: The basics of book marketing and why it matters.

Book marketing is the cornerstone of a successful author's career. It involves a comprehensive strategy designed to identify, reach, and engage your target audience, ensuring that your book gains the visibility and traction it needs in a crowded market. Understanding the basics of book marketing and its importance can set the stage for your book's success and establish a foundation for your long-term career as an author.

1. Identifying Your Target Audience

The first step in any marketing strategy is to identify your target audience. Knowing who your readers are is crucial because it influences every aspect of your marketing plan. Consider factors such as age, gender, interests, reading preferences, and buying behaviors. Create a detailed profile of your ideal reader to guide your marketing efforts.

- **Research**: Conduct market research to understand your potential readers. Use tools like surveys, social media analytics, and online forums to gather insights.
- **Reader Personas**: Develop reader personas—fictional representations of your ideal readers. These personas help you tailor your marketing messages and strategies to better resonate with your audience.

Write It. Publish It. Sell It.

The first step in any marketing strategy is to identify your target audience. Knowing who your readers are is crucial because it influences every aspect of your marketing plan. Think about it: trying to sell a young adult fantasy novel to a group of retirees who primarily read historical fiction probably isn't going to work very well, right? That's why understanding your audience is so important. It helps ensure that your book reaches the right people—those who are most likely to be interested in what you've written.

So, how do you get to know your readers? Start by considering some basic factors such as age, gender, interests, reading preferences, and buying behaviors. Are your readers teenagers who love fast-paced, adventurous stories, or are they middle-aged professionals who prefer thoughtful, character-driven narratives? The more specific you can be, the better.

One effective way to gather this information is through market research. Tools like surveys, social media analytics, and online forums can provide valuable insights into your potential readers. For instance, you could create a survey asking about reading habits and preferences and share it on your social media channels or through your email newsletter. The responses can give you a clearer idea of who your readers are and what they're looking for in a book.

Social media platforms like Facebook, Instagram, and Twitter have analytics tools that can help you understand the demographics of your followers. These insights can reveal trends in age, location, interests, and engagement levels. Online forums and reader communities, such as Goodreads, are also fantastic places to see what people are saying about books similar to yours. Pay attention to the discussions and reviews to identify common likes, dislikes, and unmet needs.

Once you have gathered enough information, it's time to develop reader personas. These are fictional representations of your ideal readers, created based on the data you've collected. Give them names, backgrounds, and specific interests. For example, you might have a persona named "Jane," a 35-year-old graphic designer who loves reading mystery novels in her free time and prefers e-books over paperbacks because of her on-the-go lifestyle.

Creating these personas helps you to humanize your target audience and tailor your marketing messages accordingly. When you write a blog post, craft a social media update, or design an ad campaign, you can think about how it would resonate with "Jane" or any other persona you've developed. This approach makes your marketing efforts feel more personal and targeted, which can significantly improve their effectiveness.

With your reader personas in hand, you can now tailor your marketing strategy to better resonate with your audience. If "Jane" is one of your personas, you might focus on promoting your e-book version and highlighting the elements of your mystery novel that align with her interests, such as plot twists and strong female protagonists. You could also consider which platforms "Jane" frequents and direct your efforts there—perhaps running ads on Instagram or joining mystery book groups on Goodreads.

Remember, identifying your target audience is not a one-time task. As your career evolves and you publish more books, your audience might change too. Keep revisiting and updating your reader personas to ensure they remain accurate and useful. Regularly engage with your readers to stay in tune with their evolving preferences and needs.

Understanding your audience deeply can lead to more effective and engaging marketing campaigns, higher reader satisfaction, and ultimately, better sales. When readers feel that a book is written for them, they are more likely to become loyal fans and recommend your work to others. So, take the time to identify and understand your target audience. Conduct thorough market research, develop detailed reader personas, and let these insights guide your marketing strategies. By doing so, you'll be well-equipped to connect with your readers on a meaningful level, making your book marketing efforts more impactful and successful.

2. Creating a Marketing Plan

A well-thought-out marketing plan serves as a roadmap for your marketing activities. It outlines your goals, strategies, tactics, and the metrics you'll use to measure success. Key components of a marketing plan include:

- **Goals**: Define clear, measurable goals for your marketing efforts. These could include increasing book sales, growing your email list, or enhancing your social media presence.
- **Strategies**: Outline the broad approaches you'll take to achieve your goals. For example, if your goal is to increase book sales, your strategies might include online advertising, content marketing, and book tours.
- **Tactics**: Break down your strategies into specific, actionable tactics. If your strategy is online advertising, your tactics could include Facebook ads, Google Ads, and Instagram promotions.
- **Metrics**: Identify the key performance indicators (KPIs) you'll track to measure your success. Common KPIs in book marketing include sales numbers, website traffic, email open rates, and social media engagement.

Creating a marketing plan might seem daunting, but think of it as your roadmap to success. It outlines where you want to go and how you're going to get there. Let's chat about how to put together a solid marketing plan that will help you achieve your goals.

First, think about what you want to achieve. Setting clear, measurable goals is essential. Maybe you want to increase book sales, grow your email list, or boost your social media presence. Whatever your aim, having specific goals will give you something concrete to work towards.

For example, you might decide you want to sell 1,000 copies of your book within the first three months. Or perhaps you aim to add 500 new email subscribers in the next quarter. Clear goals give you direction and make it easier to track your progress.

Next, let's talk about strategies. These are the broad approaches you'll use to achieve your goals. Think of strategies as the big-picture ideas that will guide your efforts. For instance, if your goal is to increase book sales, your strategies might include online advertising, content marketing, and organizing book tours. These strategies provide a framework for your marketing activities and ensure that everything you do is aligned with your overall goals.

Now, let's get into the nitty-gritty details with tactics. These are the specific actions you'll take to implement your strategies. Tactics are where your plan gets practical and actionable. If online advertising is one of your strategies, your tactics might include running Facebook ads, creating Google Ads campaigns, and promoting your book on Instagram. Each tactic should be a clear step that supports your strategy and helps you move closer to your goal.

Finally, let's talk about metrics. How will you know if your efforts are paying off? Identifying the key performance indicators (KPIs) you'll track is crucial for measuring success. Common KPIs in book marketing include sales numbers, website traffic, email open rates, and social media engagement. For example, if you're running a social media campaign, you might track the number of likes, shares, comments, and click-through rates on your posts. Monitoring these metrics will show you what's working and where you might need to make adjustments.

So, let's put this all together with an example. Suppose your goal is to increase book sales by 1,000 copies in the next three months. Here's how your plan might look: Your strategies could include online advertising, content marketing, and book tours. To implement these strategies, you might run Facebook ads targeting readers interested in your genre, write and publish blog posts related to your book's themes, and schedule virtual book tours and live readings on social media platforms. You would then track the number of books sold each month, monitor website traffic and blog engagement, and measure the reach and engagement of your social media posts and ads.

Having a clear marketing plan helps you stay organized and focused. It ensures that every action you take is purposeful and contributes to your overall objectives. This roadmap will guide you through the complexities of book marketing, helping you reach your goals more effectively. Think of your marketing plan as a living document that includes your goals, strategies, actionable tactics, and the metrics to measure success. By following this roadmap, you'll navigate the marketing landscape with confidence and drive your book's success.

So, take some time to sit down and map out your plan. It's a worthwhile investment that will pay off in helping you achieve your publishing dreams. Happy planning!

3. Building an Author Platform

An author platform is your online presence and the means by which you connect with readers. A strong platform can significantly enhance your marketing efforts. Essential elements of an author platform include:

- **Website**: Your website serves as your digital home base. It should include an author bio, book information, a blog, and a way for readers to contact you. Make sure it's professional, user-friendly, and regularly updated.
- **Email List**: Building an email list allows you to maintain direct communication with your readers. Offer incentives like free chapters, exclusive content, or discounts to encourage sign-ups. Regularly send newsletters to keep your audience engaged.
- **Social Media**: Choose social media platforms that align with your target audience. Share engaging content, interact with your followers, and use these platforms to promote your book and build your author brand.

Think of your author platform as your online presence and the primary way you connect with your readers. A strong platform can significantly enhance your marketing efforts, making it easier to reach and engage with your audience. Let's dive into the essential elements of a solid author platform.

First, your website serves as your digital home base. It's the place where readers can learn more about you and your work. Your website should include an engaging author bio, detailed information about your books, a blog where you can share insights and updates, and a way for readers to contact you. Make sure it's professional, user-friendly, and regularly updated. A well-maintained website helps establish your credibility and keeps readers coming back for more.

Next, let's talk about building an email list. This is one of the most powerful tools in your marketing arsenal because it allows you to maintain direct communication with your readers. To encourage sign-ups, offer incentives like free chapters, exclusive content, or special discounts. Once people join your list, regularly send newsletters to keep them engaged. Share updates about your writing process, upcoming releases, and any events or promotions. Your email list is a direct line to your most dedicated fans, so nurture it carefully.

Now, social media. Social media platforms are fantastic for connecting with readers and building your author brand. Choose platforms that align with your target audience—whether it's Facebook, Instagram, Twitter, or another platform. Share engaging content that reflects your personality and interests. This could be behind-the-scenes looks at your writing process, book recommendations, personal anecdotes, or discussions about topics related to your books. Interact with your followers by responding to comments, joining conversations, and showing appreciation for their support. Social media is not just about promoting your book; it's about building relationships and creating a community around your work.

By focusing on these key elements—your website, email list, and social media presence—you can create a robust author platform that supports your marketing efforts. Your website acts as a central hub of information, your email list provides a direct communication channel, and your social media presence helps you engage with a wider audience.

Building a strong author platform takes time and effort, but it's worth it. It enhances your visibility, strengthens your connection with readers, and ultimately helps you sell more books. So, invest in your online presence, engage with your audience, and watch your author platform grow.

By maintaining a professional, user-friendly website, nurturing an active and engaged email list, and leveraging social media to connect with readers, you'll create a dynamic author platform that can significantly boost your marketing efforts and help you achieve your publishing goals.

4. Content Marketing

Content marketing involves creating and sharing valuable content to attract and engage your target audience. It's a long-term strategy that builds trust and establishes your authority as an author. Effective content marketing tactics include:

- **Blogging**: Write blog posts related to your book's themes, writing tips, or industry insights. Consistent, high-quality blogging can drive traffic to your website and boost your search engine rankings.
- **Guest Blogging**: Contribute articles to other websites and blogs in your niche. This expands your reach and introduces you to new audiences.
- **Podcasts and Videos**: Create podcasts or video content to reach readers who prefer these formats. Discuss your book, share behind-the-scenes insights, or offer writing advice.

Content marketing is all about creating and sharing valuable content to attract and engage your target audience. It's a long-term strategy that builds trust and establishes your authority as an author. Let's explore some effective content marketing tactics you can use to connect with your readers.

First, let's talk about blogging. Blogging is a fantastic way to share your thoughts and expertise while driving traffic to your website. Write blog posts related to your book's themes, offer writing tips, or provide industry insights. Consistent, high-quality blogging can boost your search engine rankings and help more people discover your work. Think of your blog as a place where readers can get to know you better and learn more about the subjects you're passionate about.

Another powerful tactic is guest blogging. By contributing articles to other websites and blogs in your niche, you can expand your reach and introduce yourself to new audiences. Look for blogs that cater to your target readers and pitch them article ideas that provide value and showcase your knowledge. Guest blogging not only helps you reach more people but also enhances your credibility as an expert in your field.

Don't forget about podcasts and videos. Creating podcasts or video content is a great way to connect with readers who prefer these formats. You could start a podcast where you discuss your book, share behind-the-scenes insights, or offer writing advice. Or, create video content that gives readers a glimpse into your writing process, offers tips, or talks about the themes and characters in your book. Podcasts and videos are engaging and personal, helping you build a deeper connection with your audience.

Content marketing is not just about promoting your book; it's about providing value to your readers and building relationships. By sharing your knowledge and insights, you can establish yourself as an authority and gain the trust of your audience. This trust is crucial because readers are more likely to buy books from authors they respect and admire.

So, let's put this all together. Start with blogging on your website, sharing posts that are relevant and interesting to your readers. Then, look for opportunities to guest blog on other sites to reach new audiences. Finally, consider creating podcasts or videos to diversify your content and engage with readers in different ways.

Content marketing takes time and effort, but it's a powerful way to build your brand, connect with your audience, and ultimately sell more books. By consistently providing valuable content, you'll create a loyal following of readers who are excited about your work and eager to support you.

Remember, the goal of content marketing is to build trust and establish your authority. So, focus on creating content that is informative, engaging, and relevant to your readers. Over time, this will help you grow your audience and achieve your publishing goals.

5. Leveraging Book Reviews and Testimonials

Positive reviews and testimonials can greatly influence potential readers. They provide social proof that your book is worth reading. Strategies to gather and leverage reviews include:

- **Advance Review Copies (ARCs)**: Send ARCs to book bloggers, influencers, and loyal readers before your launch. Encourage them to leave reviews on platforms like Amazon, Goodreads, and social media.
- **Review Campaigns**: Run campaigns to solicit reviews, such as offering free copies in exchange for honest reviews. Make it easy for readers to leave reviews by providing direct links.
- **Showcasing Testimonials**: Highlight positive reviews and testimonials on your website, social media, and marketing materials. Use quotes from reputable sources to build credibility.

Positive reviews and testimonials can significantly influence potential readers. They provide social proof that your book is worth reading, which can be a powerful motivator for new readers to give your book a chance. Let's explore some strategies to gather and leverage reviews effectively.

One of the best ways to start collecting reviews is by sending out Advance Review Copies (ARCs). Reach out to book bloggers, influencers, and loyal readers before your book's official launch and offer them an ARC. These early readers can help create buzz around your book by leaving reviews on platforms like Amazon, Goodreads, and social media. Make sure to politely encourage them to share their honest thoughts, as genuine reviews are most impactful.

Next, consider running review campaigns. These campaigns can be as simple as offering free copies of your book in exchange for honest reviews. You can promote these campaigns through your email list, social media, and book-related forums. To make it as easy as possible for readers to leave reviews, provide them with direct links to the review pages on

Amazon, Goodreads, or other relevant sites. This removes any barriers and increases the likelihood that they'll follow through.

Once you start receiving positive reviews and testimonials, don't let them go unnoticed. Highlight these reviews on your website, social media, and any marketing materials you produce. A dedicated section on your website for testimonials can showcase the positive feedback in an organized way. Quotes from reputable sources or well-known reviewers can be particularly effective in building credibility. Use these quotes in your promotional graphics, email newsletters, and even in your book's cover design if possible.

For example, you might include a testimonial from a respected book blogger on your website's homepage. Or, you could create a social media graphic featuring a glowing review from a satisfied reader. These positive endorsements act as powerful marketing tools, convincing potential readers that your book is worth their time.

Gathering and leveraging reviews and testimonials isn't just about getting praise; it's about building trust with your potential readers. When they see that others have enjoyed and valued your book, they're more likely to take the plunge and purchase it themselves.

So, start by sending out ARCs to build early momentum, run targeted review campaigns to gather more feedback, and then showcase these testimonials across all your marketing channels. By effectively leveraging positive reviews, you can enhance your book's reputation and attract more readers.

Remember, the key to leveraging reviews and testimonials is to be proactive and strategic. Make it easy for readers to leave reviews, actively seek out feedback, and prominently display positive testimonials to build credibility and trust. This approach will help you maximize the impact of your reviews and boost your book's success.

6. Paid Advertising

Paid advertising can amplify your marketing efforts by reaching a larger audience. Effective channels for book advertising include:

- **Social Media Ads**: Platforms like Facebook, Instagram, and Twitter offer targeted advertising options that can help you reach specific demographics.
- **Search Engine Ads**: Google Ads can drive traffic to your book's sales page by targeting keywords related to your book.
- **Book Promotion Sites**: Use book promotion services like BookBub, which has a large audience of avid readers. These services can generate significant visibility and sales.

Paid advertising can be a powerful way to amplify your marketing efforts and reach a larger audience. Let's dive into some effective channels for book advertising and how you can use them to your advantage.

First up, social media ads. Platforms like Facebook, Instagram, and Twitter offer targeted advertising options that allow you to reach specific demographics. Think about who your ideal readers are—what are their interests, age range, and online behaviors? Social media ads let you tailor your campaigns to these precise groups, making your marketing efforts more efficient and effective. For instance, you can create eye-catching ads that target fantasy lovers aged 18-35 on Instagram, or promote your latest thriller to mystery enthusiasts on Facebook. The key is to use compelling visuals and engaging copy that grabs attention and entices users to click through to learn more about your book.

Next, consider search engine ads. Google Ads can drive traffic to your book's sales page by targeting keywords related to your book. When someone searches for terms like "best new romance novels" or "thrilling mystery books," your ad can appear at the top of the search results. This type of advertising is particularly effective because it reaches people who are actively looking for new books to read. Crafting a compelling ad that highlights the unique selling points of your book and includes a strong call-to-action can help convert these searchers into buyers.

Another powerful tool in your advertising arsenal is book promotion sites like BookBub. These services have large audiences of avid readers who are always on the lookout for new books. BookBub, in particular, is known for its ability to generate significant visibility and sales. While getting a featured deal on BookBub can be competitive, it's worth the effort due to the potential payoff. Even if you don't land a featured deal, BookBub's pay-per-click ads and other promotional options can still provide a substantial boost to your book's visibility.

To make the most of your paid advertising efforts, here are a few tips:

- **Set a Budget**: Determine how much you're willing to spend on advertising each month. Start with a small budget and scale up as you see positive results.
- **Track Performance**: Use the analytics tools provided by each platform to monitor the performance of your ads. Pay attention to metrics like click-through rates, conversion rates, and return on investment (ROI).
- **Test and Optimize**: Don't be afraid to experiment with different ad creatives, targeting options, and ad placements. A/B testing can help you identify what works best and refine your strategy over time.
- **Stay Consistent**: Consistency is key in advertising. Regularly update your ads and keep your campaigns running to maintain visibility and momentum.

By leveraging social media ads, search engine ads, and book promotion sites, you can reach a wider audience and boost your book's visibility. Paid advertising, when done correctly, can complement your organic marketing efforts and drive significant results. So, consider incorporating these channels into your marketing strategy and watch your book reach new heights.

7. Measuring and Adjusting Your Strategy

Continuous measurement and adjustment are vital to the success of your marketing efforts. Regularly review your KPIs and assess which strategies are working and which need refinement. Be prepared to pivot and try new tactics based on your findings.

- **Analytics Tools**: Use tools like Google Analytics, social media insights, and email marketing analytics to track your performance.
- **Feedback**: Solicit feedback from your readers to understand their preferences and improve your marketing approach.

Continuous measurement and adjustment are vital to the success of your marketing efforts. Regularly reviewing your key performance indicators (KPIs) and assessing which strategies are working and which need refinement is essential for staying on track. Be prepared to pivot and try new tactics based on your findings. Let's talk about how you can effectively measure and adjust your strategy.

First, make use of analytics tools. Tools like Google Analytics, social media insights, and email marketing analytics are invaluable for tracking your performance. Google Analytics can show you how many people are visiting your website, where they're coming from, and what they're doing once they get there. Social media platforms like Facebook, Instagram, and Twitter offer insights into how your posts are performing, who's engaging with them, and what content resonates most with your audience. Email marketing platforms like Mailchimp or ConvertKit provide analytics on open rates, click-through rates, and subscriber growth.

By regularly reviewing these analytics, you can see patterns and trends that inform your marketing decisions. For example, if you notice that your blog posts about writing tips are getting a lot of traffic and engagement, you might decide to create more content on that topic. Or, if you see that a particular social media ad is performing well, you might allocate more budget to that ad and create similar ones.

In addition to using analytics tools, it's crucial to solicit feedback from your readers. This feedback can give you insights that numbers alone can't provide. Consider sending out surveys or simply asking for feedback via email or social media. Ask your readers what they like about your content, what they'd like to see more of, and how they found out about your book. This direct input can help you understand your audience's preferences and tailor your marketing approach accordingly.

For instance, if readers mention that they love your behind-the-scenes videos but would like to see more live Q&A sessions, you can incorporate that feedback into your content strategy. Or, if they found your book through a guest blog post you wrote, you might focus more on guest blogging as a promotional tactic.

Remember, the goal is to be flexible and willing to adjust your strategy based on what you learn. Marketing is not a one-size-fits-all approach, and what works for one author might not work for another. By continuously measuring your performance and being open to change, you can refine your tactics and improve your results over time.

So, here's your action plan: Regularly check your analytics to see how your efforts are paying off. Use tools like Google Analytics, social media insights, and email marketing analytics to gather data. Combine this with direct feedback from your readers to get a comprehensive understanding of what's working and what's not. And don't be afraid to pivot. If something isn't working, try a new approach. Marketing is an ongoing process of learning, adapting, and improving.

By staying on top of your analytics and actively seeking feedback, you'll be well-equipped to adjust your strategy and continue moving toward your goals. Keep measuring, keep adjusting, and keep pushing forward. You've got this!

Why Book Marketing Matters

Book marketing is essential because it bridges the gap between you and your readers. Without effective marketing, even the best-written book may struggle to find its audience. Marketing creates awareness, builds relationships, and drives sales. It's the engine that powers your book's success and fuels your growth as an author.

By mastering the fundamentals of book marketing, you lay the groundwork for a successful and sustainable author career. In the following sections, we will delve deeper into specific promotion strategies, building your author brand, leveraging social media, and using public relations to enhance your book's visibility. With these tools and knowledge, you will be well-equipped to navigate the complex landscape of book marketing and achieve your literary goals.

Promotion Strategies: How to effectively promote your book through various channels.

Once you have a solid marketing foundation, it's time to dive into specific promotion strategies that can effectively boost your book's visibility and drive sales. Promotion involves targeted, time-bound activities designed to generate immediate interest and engagement. Here, we'll explore various channels and tactics you can use to promote your book successfully.

1. Book Tours (Virtual and In-Person)

Book tours are a traditional yet powerful way to promote your book. They can be conducted virtually or in-person, each with its own set of advantages.

> **Virtual Book Tours**: These tours involve visiting various blogs, websites, and online platforms to promote your book. They are cost-effective and have the potential to reach a global audience.
>
> - **Blog Stops**: Partner with book bloggers to feature your book on their blogs. This can include interviews, guest posts, reviews, and giveaways.
> - **Webinars and Live Streams**: Host live webinars or participate in virtual author events on platforms like Zoom, Facebook Live, or YouTube. Engage with your audience in real-time through Q&A sessions and discussions about your book.
> - **Podcasts**: Appear on podcasts that cater to your target audience. Share insights about your writing process, the story behind your book, and more.

In-Person Book Tours: These tours involve visiting bookstores, libraries, and literary festivals. They allow for personal interaction with readers, which can be highly impactful.

- **Book Signings**: Arrange book signings at local bookstores and libraries. Promote these events through social media, email newsletters, and local media.
- **Literary Festivals**: Participate in literary festivals and book fairs. These events provide excellent opportunities to network with other authors and industry professionals while promoting your book to an engaged audience.

Book tours are a traditional yet powerful way to promote your book, and they can be conducted either virtually or in-person, each with its own set of advantages. Let's explore both options and see how they can help you connect with your audience and boost your book's visibility.

Virtual Book Tours

Virtual book tours involve visiting various blogs, websites, and online platforms to promote your book. They are cost-effective and have the potential to reach a global audience, making them an excellent choice if you're looking to maximize your reach without the logistical challenges of travel.

Imagine partnering with book bloggers to feature your book on their blogs. These blog stops can include interviews, guest posts, reviews, and giveaways. By engaging with established book bloggers, you can tap into their readership and introduce your book to new fans.

Hosting live webinars or participating in virtual author events on platforms like Zoom, Facebook Live, or YouTube is another fantastic way to promote your book. These events allow you to engage with your audience in real-time through Q&A sessions and discussions about your book. Think about the excitement of discussing your story, answering readers' questions, and sharing behind-the-scenes insights about your writing process—all from the comfort of your home.

Podcasts are also a great avenue for virtual book tours. By appearing on podcasts that cater to your target audience, you can share insights about your writing process, the story behind your book, and much more. Podcasts have loyal listeners who trust the hosts' recommendations, making them a valuable platform for book promotion.

In-Person Book Tours

In-person book tours involve visiting bookstores, libraries, and literary festivals. These tours allow for personal interaction with readers, which can be highly impactful and create lasting connections.

Think about arranging book signings at local bookstores and libraries. These events give you the opportunity to meet readers face-to-face, sign copies of your book, and have meaningful conversations. Promote these events through social media, email newsletters, and local media to draw in a crowd.

Participating in literary festivals and book fairs is another fantastic way to promote your book in person. These events provide excellent opportunities to network with other authors and industry professionals while promoting your book to an engaged audience. Imagine the buzz of a literary festival, with readers eager to discover new authors and books—your presence there can make a significant impact.

Combining Virtual and In-Person Strategies

You don't have to choose between virtual and in-person book tours; in fact, combining both strategies can be highly effective. Start with a virtual tour to build momentum and reach a wide audience, then follow up with in-person events to deepen those connections.

For example, you might kick off your book launch with a series of blog stops and podcast appearances, followed by a webinar or live stream event. Once your virtual tour has generated buzz, you can plan a series of in-person book signings and appearances at local literary festivals.

Conclusion

Book tours, whether virtual or in-person, are a powerful way to promote your book. Virtual tours offer cost-effective, global reach through blog stops, webinars, live streams, and podcasts. In-person tours provide the personal touch of meeting readers face-to-face at book signings, libraries, and literary festivals. By leveraging both virtual and in-person strategies, you can maximize your book's visibility and create meaningful connections with your readers. So, start planning your book tour today and get ready to share your story with the world.

2. Launch Parties

A book launch party is a celebratory event that marks the release of your book. It can generate excitement and buzz, both online and offline.

- **Physical Launch Parties**: Host a launch event at a local venue such as a bookstore, café, or community center. Invite friends, family, readers, and media. Include activities like readings, Q&A sessions, and book signings.
- **Virtual Launch Parties**: Host a live virtual event where you can engage with a broader audience. Use platforms like Zoom, Facebook Live, or Instagram Live to interact with attendees. Incorporate interactive elements like live readings, contests, and giveaways to keep the audience engaged.

A book launch party is a celebratory event that marks the release of your book. It's an excellent way to generate excitement and buzz, both online and offline. Let's explore how you can organize both physical and virtual launch parties to create a memorable and impactful event.

Physical Launch Parties

Hosting a physical launch party is a fantastic way to celebrate your book's release with friends, family, readers, and media. Choose a local venue that suits the vibe of your book and your audience. This could be a bookstore, a cozy café, or a community center.

Write It. Publish It. Sell It.

Imagine the atmosphere at a local bookstore, where the shelves are lined with your book, and the space is filled with people excited to celebrate your achievement. At the event, you can include activities like readings, where you share an excerpt from your book to give attendees a taste of your writing. A Q&A session can follow, allowing readers to ask questions about your book, your writing process, or your inspiration. Book signings are another highlight, giving you the chance to connect personally with your readers as you autograph their copies.

To make your launch party even more engaging, consider adding some interactive elements. Perhaps a small trivia contest about your book or its themes, with signed copies as prizes. You could also have a photo booth with props related to your book, where attendees can take pictures to remember the event.

Virtual Launch Parties

If you want to reach a broader audience, hosting a virtual launch party is an excellent option. Platforms like Zoom, Facebook Live, or Instagram Live allow you to interact with attendees from around the world, making your launch accessible to all your fans, no matter where they are.

Picture hosting a live virtual event where you can engage directly with your audience. You can start with a live reading from your book, followed by a discussion or Q&A session where attendees can ask questions in real-time. This interaction can be incredibly rewarding, as it allows you to connect with your readers on a personal level.

To keep the virtual audience engaged, incorporate interactive elements like contests and giveaways. For example, you could hold a live contest where participants answer questions related to your book, with winners receiving signed copies or exclusive content. Giveaways are also a great way to maintain excitement and encourage participation.

Consider using a virtual backdrop related to your book's theme to create a visually appealing setting. Encourage attendees to share their experiences on social media using a specific hashtag, which helps spread the word about your book even further.

Combining Both Approaches

Combining physical and virtual launch parties can maximize your reach and impact. You could host a small, intimate physical launch event and live-stream it to your virtual audience. This way, you get the personal touch of an in-person event while also engaging with a global audience.

Conclusion

A book launch party, whether physical or virtual, is a powerful way to celebrate the release of your book and generate excitement. Physical launch parties allow for personal interactions with readings, Q&A sessions, and book signings at local venues. Virtual launch parties offer a broader reach, engaging with readers worldwide through live readings, contests, and giveaways on platforms like Zoom, Facebook Live, or Instagram Live. By combining both approaches, you can create a memorable and impactful launch event that reaches and engages a wide audience. So, start planning your book launch party today and celebrate your achievement with your readers!

3. Giveaways and Contests

Giveaways and contests are effective ways to generate interest and increase your book's visibility. They can attract new readers and encourage word-of-mouth promotion.

- **Social Media Giveaways**: Run giveaways on platforms like Instagram, Twitter, and Facebook. Ask participants to like, share, and comment on your posts for a chance to win a free copy of your book. This increases engagement and expands your reach.
- **Goodreads Giveaways**: Use Goodreads' giveaway feature to reach its vast community of readers. This can generate reviews and visibility among avid readers.

- **Contests**: Host contests related to your book's themes or characters. For example, ask readers to submit fan art, short stories, or personal anecdotes. Offer book-related prizes to the winners.

Giveaways and contests are highly effective strategies to generate interest and increase your book's visibility. They not only attract new readers but also encourage word-of-mouth promotion. Let's dive into how you can leverage these tactics to boost your book's presence.

Social Media Giveaways

Social media giveaways are a fantastic way to engage with your audience and expand your reach. Platforms like Instagram, Twitter, and Facebook are ideal for running these promotions. Imagine creating a buzz around your book by asking participants to like, share, and comment on your posts for a chance to win a free copy. This not only increases engagement on your posts but also helps spread the word to a broader audience as participants share your content with their followers.

For example, you could post an eye-catching image of your book on Instagram, and in the caption, ask your followers to tag three friends and comment on why they're excited to read your book. In return, they get entered into a draw to win a signed copy. This simple yet effective tactic can significantly boost your book's visibility and attract new readers.

Goodreads Giveaways

Goodreads is a goldmine for reaching avid readers, and its giveaway feature is a powerful tool to get your book noticed. By offering a few copies of your book through a Goodreads giveaway, you can generate a lot of interest and attract a dedicated audience who loves to read and review books. This can lead to valuable reviews and increased visibility among a community that trusts Goodreads for book recommendations.

Setting up a Goodreads giveaway is straightforward. You create an entry for your book, specify the number of copies you're giving away, and set the duration of the giveaway. Readers can enter the giveaway with a single click, making it easy for them to participate. Once the giveaway ends, Goodreads randomly selects the winners, and you send them their copies. The added bonus is that many participants often add your book to their "Want to Read" lists, keeping your book on their radar even if they don't win.

Contests

Contests are a creative and interactive way to engage your audience. Hosting contests related to your book's themes or characters can inspire readers to connect more deeply with your work. For example, you could ask readers to submit fan art, short stories, or personal anecdotes inspired by your book. Offering book-related prizes to the winners adds an exciting incentive for participation.

Imagine hosting a contest where readers create fan art of their favorite scene or character from your book. You could then showcase the entries on your social media channels, giving participants exposure and encouraging others to join in. Alternatively, you might run a short story contest where readers write a brief tale set in the world of your book. The winning stories could be featured on your blog or in your newsletter, providing a platform for your readers while also enriching your content.

These contests not only generate buzz but also build a sense of community among your readers. They feel more connected to your book and are more likely to share their experiences with others, further promoting your work through word-of-mouth.

Conclusion

Giveaways and contests are powerful tools in your marketing arsenal. Social media giveaways can significantly boost engagement and expand your reach, while Goodreads giveaways tap into a vast community of avid readers. Contests, on the other hand, foster creativity and deeper engagement with your book's themes and characters. By incorporating these strategies into your marketing plan, you can generate excitement, attract new readers, and encourage word-of-mouth promotion. So, get creative, plan your giveaways and contests, and watch your book's visibility soar!

4. Speaking Engagements and Signings

Public speaking engagements and book signings provide opportunities to connect with readers and promote your book in person.

- **Library Talks**: Offer to speak at local libraries about your book, writing process, or related topics. Libraries often welcome author events and can help promote them to their patrons.
- **Book Clubs**: Reach out to book clubs and offer to attend their meetings (virtually or in-person) to discuss your book. This can lead to meaningful discussions and new fans.
- **Schools and Universities**: If your book is relevant to academic subjects, offer to speak at schools or universities. This can also lead to bulk purchases of your book for classes or libraries.

Public speaking engagements and book signings are incredible opportunities to connect with readers and promote your book in person. Trust me, I've found the stage to be an incredibly effective way to sell books. This strategy isn't just for non-fiction authors like me—it works wonders for fiction writers too, especially if you can secure speaking opportunities at fantasy events.

Imagine giving a talk at your local library. Libraries are fantastic venues because they love hosting author events and can help promote them to their patrons. Picture yourself discussing your book, sharing your writing process, and talking about topics that fascinate your audience. If you've written a fantasy novel, you could dive into your world-building process or explain the inspiration behind your characters. These events are a perfect way to interact directly with readers and build a loyal following.

Book clubs are another great option. Reach out to local book clubs and offer to join their meetings, either virtually or in-person. These gatherings provide an intimate setting where readers can discuss your book and ask you questions. It's a wonderful opportunity for meaningful interactions and can turn club members into passionate advocates for your work.

Schools and universities also offer unique opportunities. If your book ties into academic subjects, why not offer to speak at educational institutions? Imagine talking to students about your book and its themes, and how it connects to what they're studying. This can even lead to bulk purchases for classes or libraries. It's a win-win—you get to share your knowledge, and students get to dive deeper into their studies through your book.

Now, if you're a fiction author, especially writing in the fantasy genre, speaking at fantasy events can be a game-changer. Picture yourself at a fantasy convention, sharing the stage with other authors, and talking about your world-building process, character development, or the mythology in your book. These events attract fans who are eager to discover new stories and authors, making them the perfect audience for your book.

Let me share a bit about my own experience. As a public speaker who has written several non-fiction books, I've seen firsthand how effective these engagements can be. Speaking directly to an audience allows me to share my passion and connect with people on a personal level. This connection often translates into increased interest and book sales. And this approach works just as well for fiction authors. By engaging with readers at events, you create memorable experiences that resonate long after the event ends, turning attendees into enthusiastic supporters of your work.

So, why not embrace the stage? Public speaking engagements and book signings offer you a chance to connect with readers, share your story, and promote your book in a powerful way. Whether you're speaking at libraries, book clubs, schools, universities, or fantasy events, these opportunities allow you to engage directly with your audience, boost your visibility, and increase your book sales. It's all about creating those personal connections that make readers excited to support you and your work. So go ahead, share your story, and watch your readership grow.

5. Special Discount Campaigns

Discount campaigns can attract new readers and boost sales, especially when timed strategically.

- **Ebook Discounts**: Use platforms like Amazon KDP Select to run limited-time promotions and discounts on your ebook. Lowering the price or offering the book for free for a short period can increase downloads and reviews.
- **Bundling**: Bundle your book with other authors' works or offer it as part of a series at a discounted rate. This can attract readers who are looking for a good deal and introduce them to your other works.
- **Holiday Promotions**: Take advantage of holidays and special occasions to run themed promotions. For example, offer discounts during the holiday season, on your book's anniversary, or on significant dates related to your book's content.

Discount campaigns are a fantastic way to attract new readers and boost sales, especially when you time them strategically. Let's talk about how you can leverage these campaigns to get your book in front of more readers.

First, let's discuss ebook discounts. Platforms like Amazon KDP Select offer excellent opportunities to run limited-time promotions and discounts on your ebook. Imagine lowering the price or even offering your book for free for a short period. This can significantly increase downloads and reviews, giving your book a surge of visibility. People love a good deal, and a temporary discount can make your book irresistible. Plus, once readers get a taste of your writing, they might be more inclined to buy your other books at full price.

Another effective strategy is bundling. Think about partnering with other authors or offering your book as part of a series at a discounted rate. Bundles can be particularly appealing to readers looking for a great deal. For example, if you've written a fantasy series, offering the first three books at a lower price can entice readers to commit to the whole series. Similarly, teaming up with authors in the same genre to create a bundle can introduce your work to a broader audience. It's a win-win—you share your readership, and they share theirs, expanding your reach.

Holiday promotions are another golden opportunity. Holidays and special occasions are perfect times to run themed promotions. Picture this: during the holiday season, you offer a special discount on your book, making it an ideal gift option. Or, celebrate your book's anniversary with a price drop to attract new readers. You can even tie promotions to significant dates related to your book's content. For instance, if your novel revolves around a historical event, offer a discount on the anniversary of that event. These timely promotions create a sense of urgency and relevance, encouraging readers to take advantage of the deal.

The key to successful discount campaigns is timing and visibility. Plan your promotions around times when readers are most likely to be looking for new books, such as holidays or during other promotional events. Promote your discounts through your email list, social media channels, and even through paid advertising if your budget allows. The more people who know about the discount, the more effective it will be.

So, to sum up: use ebook discounts to boost visibility and gather reviews, bundle your books to offer great deals and expand your audience, and take advantage of holidays and special occasions for timely promotions. By strategically planning and promoting these discount campaigns, you can attract new readers and significantly increase your book sales.

Remember, the goal is to get your book into as many hands as possible, and a well-timed discount can be just the push readers need to give your book a chance. So go ahead, plan your next discount campaign, and watch the magic happen. Happy promoting!

6. Utilizing Email Marketing

Email marketing is a direct way to communicate with your readers and keep them informed about your book's promotions and events.

- **Newsletters**: Send regular newsletters to your email list with updates, exclusive content, and promotions. Engage your subscribers with interesting stories, behind-the-scenes looks, and personal insights.
- **Exclusive Offers**: Reward your email subscribers with exclusive offers, such as early access to new releases, special discounts, or bonus content. This fosters loyalty and encourages readers to stay connected.

Email marketing is a direct and effective way to communicate with your readers and keep them informed about your book's promotions and events. Let's dive into how you can make the most of this powerful tool to engage your audience and drive book sales.

First, think about the value of regular newsletters. These are your golden opportunity to connect with your readers on a consistent basis. By sending out newsletters, you can keep your audience updated with the latest news about your books, share exclusive content, and promote upcoming events or promotions. Imagine your subscribers eagerly opening your emails to read interesting stories, get behind-the-scenes looks at your writing process, or gain personal insights about your journey as an author. These newsletters should be engaging and valuable, making readers look forward to each one.

Creating engaging newsletters is about more than just promoting your book. Share anecdotes from your writing life, sneak peeks of new projects, or even personal updates that let your readers get to know you better. For example, if you've just finished a draft, share your excitement and perhaps a little teaser from the manuscript. Or, if you're attending a literary festival, let your subscribers know where they can find you. The goal is to build a relationship with your readers, making them feel like they're part of your journey.

Next, let's talk about exclusive offers. Rewarding your email subscribers with exclusive offers is a fantastic way to foster loyalty and keep them engaged. Think about offering early access to your new releases. Imagine the thrill your readers will feel knowing they get to read your latest book before anyone else. Special discounts or bonus content can also make your subscribers feel valued. For instance, you could offer a discount code for your book's anniversary or provide exclusive short stories or deleted scenes that aren't available anywhere else.

These exclusive offers not only make your subscribers feel special but also encourage them to stay connected and open your emails regularly. The more value you provide, the more likely they are to remain engaged and loyal.

Email marketing also allows you to segment your audience and tailor your messages. For example, you can create different segments for new subscribers, long-time fans, or those who have purchased your books before. This way, you can send targeted emails that speak directly to each group's interests and needs, making your communication more effective.

To get started with email marketing, you'll need a platform that helps you manage your email list and send out your newsletters. Services like Mailchimp, ConvertKit, or Substack are user-friendly and offer various features to help you create and automate your email campaigns. Make sure to include sign-up forms on your website and promote your newsletter on social media to grow your list.

In summary, email marketing is an essential tool for building and maintaining a strong connection with your readers. Regular newsletters filled with engaging content and personal insights keep your audience informed and interested. Exclusive offers reward your subscribers and foster loyalty. By utilizing email marketing effectively, you can enhance your book's promotion, engage with your readers on a deeper level, and drive book sales. So, start crafting those emails and watch your relationship with your readers flourish. Happy emailing!

7. Engaging with Influencers and Bloggers

Collaborating with influencers and bloggers can amplify your promotional efforts and reach a wider audience.

- **Book Reviews and Features**: Reach out to book bloggers and influencers who review books in your genre. Offer them a free copy of your book in exchange for an honest review or feature on their platform.
- **Social Media Takeovers**: Arrange social media takeovers with influencers or bloggers. During the takeover, you can interact with their followers, share content, and promote your book.
- **Author Interviews**: Participate in interviews on popular blogs, podcasts, or YouTube channels. Share your experiences and insights, and mention your book to attract new readers.

Collaborating with influencers and bloggers can significantly amplify your promotional efforts and help you reach a wider audience. These partnerships can be powerful tools in getting your book noticed by potential readers who trust and follow these voices.

Book Reviews and Features

One effective way to engage with influencers and bloggers is by reaching out to those who review books in your genre. Offering them a free copy of your book in exchange for an honest review or feature on their platform can be incredibly beneficial. Think about it: when a respected book blogger or influencer shares their thoughts about your book, their followers are likely to take notice. These reviews and features provide social proof that can drive new readers to check out your work.

For example, if you've written a mystery novel, look for bloggers who specialize in crime and thriller genres. Send them a personalized email introducing yourself and your book, and explain why you think their audience would enjoy it. By making a genuine connection and showing that you've done your research, you're more likely to get a positive response.

Social Media Takeovers

Another engaging strategy is arranging social media takeovers with influencers or bloggers. During a takeover, you temporarily manage their social media account, interacting with their followers, sharing content, and promoting your book. This gives you direct access to a new and potentially large audience.

Imagine taking over a popular bookstagram account for a day. You could share behind-the-scenes glimpses of your writing process, post about your inspirations, and host a live Q&A session where followers can ask you questions about your book. This kind of direct engagement can create a buzz around your book and attract new readers who are already interested in your genre.

Author Interviews

Participating in interviews on popular blogs, podcasts, or YouTube channels is another excellent way to reach new readers. These platforms often have dedicated followings, and an interview allows you to share your experiences and insights while mentioning your book.

Picture yourself on a well-known podcast that discusses books and writing. You get to share your journey as an author, discuss the themes and characters in your book, and offer advice to aspiring writers. Not only does this position you as an expert in your field, but it also introduces your book to listeners who trust the podcast host's recommendations

Putting It All Together

To effectively engage with influencers and bloggers, start by researching those who align with your genre and audience. Reach out with personalized messages that show you're familiar with their work and explain why you think their followers would enjoy your book. Be genuine and respectful in your communications.

When arranging social media takeovers, plan your content in advance to ensure it's engaging and relevant. Use a mix of posts, stories, and live interactions to keep followers interested. And for author interviews, prepare thoughtful responses and share insights that will resonate with the audience.

Engaging with influencers and bloggers is about building relationships and expanding your reach. By leveraging their platforms, you can amplify your promotional efforts and connect with a broader audience. So, start reaching out, making connections, and watch your book's visibility grow.

8. Leveraging Paid Advertising

Paid advertising can effectively boost your book's visibility and attract potential readers.

- **Social Media Ads**: Use platforms like Facebook, Instagram, and Twitter to run targeted ad campaigns. Define your audience based on demographics, interests, and behaviors to ensure your ads reach the right people.
- **Google Ads**: Run search and display ads on Google to drive traffic to your book's sales page. Target specific keywords related to your book to attract interested readers.
- **Book Promotion Services**: Use book promotion sites like BookBub, which have a large audience of dedicated readers. These services can significantly increase your book's visibility and sales during promotional campaigns.

Hey there! Let's talk about a really powerful tool to boost your book's visibility and attract potential readers: paid advertising. It might sound a bit daunting, but with the right approach, it can be a game-changer for your book's success. Let's dive into some strategies together.

Social Media Ads

Have you thought about using social media ads? Platforms like Facebook, Instagram, and Twitter offer amazing opportunities to run targeted ad campaigns. Picture this: you can define your audience based on demographics, interests, and behaviors. This means your ads will reach the people most likely to be interested in your book. Imagine running a Facebook ad that targets users who love your genre, follow similar authors, or are members of book-related groups. On Instagram, you can create visually stunning ads that grab attention and drive engagement. And on Twitter, quick, catchy ads can spread like wildfire through retweets and shares. The key here is to create ads that speak directly to your ideal readers, making them curious enough to check out your book.

Google Ads

Now, let's talk about Google Ads. These can be incredibly effective in driving traffic to your book's sales page. By running search and display ads, you can target specific keywords related to your book. For example, if you've written a historical fiction novel, you might target keywords like "best historical fiction books" or "new historical novels." When people search for these terms, your ad appears at the top of their search results—how cool is that? Display ads can also place your book's ad on websites your target audience visits, keeping your book top of mind as they browse the internet.

Book Promotion Services

And then there are book promotion services like BookBub. These services have huge audiences of dedicated readers who are actively looking for new books to read. Imagine your book being featured in a BookBub email, reaching thousands of subscribers who love your genre. The visibility and potential for increased sales and reviews are tremendous. It's a great way to get your book in front of a lot of eyes quickly.

Making It Work

To get started, set a clear budget and define your objectives. How much are you willing to spend, and what do you hope to achieve? Whether it's driving more traffic to your sales page, increasing book sales, or boosting your overall visibility, having a clear goal will guide your strategy.

For social media ads, create engaging visuals and copy that resonate with your audience. Use the targeting options to narrow down your audience and keep track of your ad performance. See what works best and tweak your approach as needed.

With Google Ads, choose the right keywords and write compelling ad copy that makes people want to click. Monitor your campaigns and adjust your keywords and bids to get the best results.

And when you're using book promotion services, make sure you understand their audience and how to best present your book. A well-timed promotion can lead to significant spikes in sales and visibility.

Conclusion

Paid advertising might seem a bit overwhelming at first, but it's an incredible way to give your book the spotlight it deserves. By leveraging social media ads, Google Ads, and book promotion services, you can reach a targeted audience and spark interest in your book. Set clear goals, create compelling ads, and keep an eye on your campaigns to ensure you're hitting the mark.

So, take a deep breath and dive into the world of paid advertising. Experiment with different platforms, see what works best for you, and watch as your book reaches new heights. You've got this, and your book deserves all the attention it can get. Happy promoting!

By implementing a combination of these promotion strategies, you can create a comprehensive plan that maximizes your book's exposure and drives sales. Remember to track the effectiveness of each tactic and adjust your approach based on what works best for your audience. In the next sections, we will explore how to build a strong author brand, leverage social media and digital marketing, and use public relations to further enhance your book's visibility and success.

Building a Brand: Creating an author brand that resonates with your target audience.

Your author brand is your unique identity in the literary world. It's the combination of your voice, style, personality, and the themes you explore in your work. A strong author brand helps you stand out, build credibility, and create a loyal reader base. Here's how to create a compelling author brand that resonates with your target audience.

1. Define Your Unique Selling Points (USPs)

Your USPs are the qualities that make you and your work unique. They distinguish you from other authors and attract readers who resonate with your style and themes.

- **Identify Your Strengths**: Reflect on what sets your writing apart. Is it your distinctive voice, your expertise in a particular genre, your innovative storytelling techniques, or your engaging characters?
- **Highlight Your Themes**: Consider the recurring themes and messages in your books. Are you known for uplifting stories of resilience, thought-provoking explorations of social issues, or thrilling adventures?
- **Understand Your Audience**: Think about the types of readers who are drawn to your work. What are their interests, values, and preferences? Tailor your USPs to align with their expectations.

Hey there! Let's chat about something super important: your Unique Selling Points, or USPs. These are the qualities that make you and your work stand out in the crowd. Think of them as the special ingredients that distinguish you from other authors and attract readers who resonate with your style and themes. Let's explore how you can identify and highlight your USPs.

Write It. Publish It. Sell It.

Identify Your Strengths

First, take a moment to reflect on what sets your writing apart. What are the strengths that make your work unique? Maybe it's your distinctive voice—do you have a way with words that captures emotions perfectly or paints vivid pictures in readers' minds? Or perhaps it's your expertise in a particular genre. Are you the go-to author for gripping mysteries, heartfelt romances, or epic fantasies? Think about your storytelling techniques. Do you weave intricate plots that keep readers guessing or create characters that feel like real people with whom readers can't help but fall in love? Identifying these strengths is the first step in defining your USPs.

Highlight Your Themes

Next, consider the recurring themes and messages in your books. What are the common threads that run through your stories? Are you known for uplifting tales of resilience and hope that inspire readers to persevere? Maybe your books delve into thought-provoking explorations of social issues, challenging readers to think deeply about the world around them. Or perhaps your stories are thrilling adventures that take readers on a rollercoaster ride of excitement and suspense. Whatever your themes, make sure they shine through as key elements of your USPs.

Understand Your Audience

Finally, think about the types of readers who are drawn to your work. Who are they? What are their interests, values, and preferences? Understanding your audience helps you tailor your USPs to align with their expectations. For example, if your readers love emotionally rich stories with complex characters, emphasize your knack for creating deep, relatable protagonists. If they're fans of fast-paced action and suspense, highlight your ability to craft edge-of-your-seat plot twists.

By understanding what your readers love about your books, you can better communicate the unique qualities that make your work special. This not only attracts new readers but also strengthens the bond with your existing audience.

Conclusion

Defining your Unique Selling Points is all about celebrating what makes you and your work unique. Reflect on your strengths, highlight the themes that resonate in your stories, and understand what your audience loves about your books. These USPs are your secret sauce—they set you apart from other authors and draw readers to your work. So, take some time to think about what makes your writing special and shout it from the rooftops. Your readers will love you for it, and you'll stand out in the crowded world of books. Happy writing!

2. Craft a Consistent and Authentic Message

Consistency and authenticity are key to building a trustworthy and relatable brand. Your message should reflect who you are as an author and what readers can expect from your books.

- **Develop Your Voice**: Your authorial voice is a crucial part of your brand. It should be consistent across all your communications, from your books to your blog posts, social media updates, and newsletters. Whether your tone is witty, serious, inspirational, or quirky, make sure it reflects your personality and writing style.
- **Create a Tagline**: A concise tagline can effectively communicate your brand's essence. It should capture the core of what you offer as an author. For example, if you write cozy mysteries, a tagline like "Unraveling Whodunits with Charm and Wit" can be memorable and informative.
- **Share Your Story**: Your personal journey as an author can be a powerful part of your brand. Share your experiences, challenges, and successes with your audience. This not only humanizes you but also fosters a deeper connection with your readers.

Let's talk about something really important for building a strong connection with your readers: crafting a consistent and authentic message. Consistency and authenticity are key to building a trustworthy and relatable brand. Your message should reflect who you are as an author and what readers can expect from your books.

First, think about developing your voice. Your authorial voice is a crucial part of your brand. It should be consistent across all your communications, from your books to your blog posts, social media updates, and newsletters. Whether your tone is witty, serious, inspirational, or quirky, make sure it reflects your personality and writing style. This consistency helps readers know what to expect from you and creates a sense of familiarity and trust.

Next, consider creating a tagline. A concise tagline can effectively communicate your brand's essence. It should capture the core of what you offer as an author. For example, if you write cozy mysteries, a tagline like "Unraveling Whodunits with Charm and Wit" can be memorable and informative. This simple phrase can instantly give readers a sense of your style and what they can look forward to in your books.

Sharing your story is another powerful way to connect with your readers. Your personal journey as an author can be a compelling part of your brand. Share your experiences, challenges, and successes with your audience. This not only humanizes you but also fosters a deeper connection with your readers. When they see the real person behind the words, they're more likely to feel a bond and become loyal fans.

So, let's put it all together: develop a voice that consistently reflects your personality and writing style, create a memorable tagline that captures the essence of your work, and share your personal journey to foster a deeper connection with your readers. This combination of consistency and authenticity will help you build a strong, trustworthy brand that resonates with your audience. Keep being true to yourself and your readers will appreciate and support you. Happy writing!

3. Develop a Visual Identity

Your visual identity includes the design elements that represent your brand. It should be cohesive and easily recognizable, reinforcing your brand's message.

- **Logo and Color Scheme**: Design a logo that reflects your brand's personality. Choose a color scheme that complements your genre and style. For example, a romance author might use soft, warm colors, while a thriller author might opt for darker, more intense hues.
- **Book Covers**: Your book covers are a crucial part of your visual identity. They should be professionally designed and aligned with your brand's aesthetics. Consistent cover styles across your books can create a strong visual identity that readers recognize.
- **Website Design**: Your website should be a central hub for your brand. Ensure it is visually appealing, easy to navigate, and reflective of your brand's style. Use your logo, color scheme, and consistent design elements throughout your site.

Hey there! Let's chat about developing a visual identity for your brand. Your visual identity includes all the design elements that represent you and your work. It's about creating a cohesive and recognizable look that reinforces your brand's message and makes you stand out. Let's dive into some key components of building a strong visual identity.

First up, think about your logo and color scheme. Your logo is a visual symbol of your brand's personality. It should be unique and memorable, giving readers an instant connection to your work. Along with your logo, choose a color scheme that complements your genre and style. For instance, if you're a romance author, you might go for soft, warm colors like pinks and pastels. If you write thrillers, darker, more intense hues like black, red, and grey might be more fitting. These colors will set the tone and mood of your brand, making it easier for readers to recognize and connect with you.

Next, let's talk about book covers. Your book covers are one of the most crucial parts of your visual identity. They should be professionally designed and aligned with your brand's aesthetics. Consistency is key here—having a consistent cover style across your books can create a strong visual identity that readers recognize. Think about your favorite series and how their covers instantly remind you of the books. That's the kind of impact you want your covers to have. Invest in good design and make sure your covers reflect the essence of your stories.

Your website design is another essential element. Your website should be the central hub for your brand, a place where readers can learn about you, explore your books, and stay updated on your latest news. Make sure it's visually appealing and easy to navigate. Use your logo, color scheme, and consistent design elements throughout your site. This creates a seamless experience for visitors, reinforcing your brand every step of the way. Imagine your readers feeling at home every time they visit your site, recognizing the familiar colors and style that they've come to associate with your books.

In summary, developing a visual identity is all about creating a cohesive and recognizable look that represents your brand. Design a logo that reflects your personality, choose a color scheme that complements your genre, ensure your book covers are professionally designed and consistent, and create a visually appealing website that ties everything together. By paying attention to these details, you'll build a strong visual identity that helps you stand out and connect with your readers. So, go ahead and start crafting your visual identity—your readers will love it!

4. Engage with Your Audience

Building a brand is not just about presenting an image; it's about building relationships with your readers. Engage with your audience in meaningful ways to create a loyal community.

- **Social Media Interaction**: Choose social media platforms where your target audience is most active. Post regularly, share interesting content, and interact with your followers. Respond to comments, participate in discussions, and show appreciation for your readers' support.
- **Email Newsletters**: Regular newsletters are an excellent way to keep your audience informed and engaged. Share updates about your writing progress,

upcoming releases, events, and exclusive content. Personalize your emails to make your readers feel valued.
- **Reader Feedback**: Encourage feedback from your readers and show that you value their opinions. Use surveys, polls, and direct questions to engage your audience and learn more about their preferences. Incorporate their feedback to improve your work and strengthen your connection with them.

Building a brand isn't just about presenting an image—it's about building relationships with your readers. Engaging with your audience in meaningful ways helps create a loyal community that supports you and your work. Here are some strategies to help you connect with your readers and foster those valuable relationships.

Social Media Interaction

Social media is a fantastic tool for connecting with your readers. Choose platforms where your target audience is most active. Whether it's Facebook, Instagram, Twitter, or TikTok, find out where your readers hang out and join the conversation. Post regularly and share interesting content that resonates with your audience. This could be behind-the-scenes looks at your writing process, book recommendations, or personal updates.

But it's not just about posting content—interaction is key. Respond to comments on your posts, participate in discussions, and show appreciation for your readers' support. For example, if a reader shares a photo of your book or posts a review, take a moment to thank them or start a conversation. This kind of personal interaction makes your readers feel valued and more connected to you.

Email Newsletters

Regular newsletters are another excellent way to keep your audience informed and engaged. Use your newsletters to share updates about your writing progress, upcoming releases, events, and exclusive content. Think of it as a way to bring your readers into your world.

Personalize your emails to make your readers feel special. Address them by name and share personal anecdotes or stories that make your newsletters feel like a conversation. For instance, you might share a funny story about a writing mishap or a personal milestone. By making your readers feel like they're part of your journey, you'll build a stronger connection with them.

Reader Feedback

Encouraging feedback from your readers is crucial. Show them that you value their opinions by asking for their thoughts and suggestions. Use surveys, polls, and direct questions to engage your audience and learn more about their preferences.

For example, you could run a poll to ask readers which character they'd like to see more of in your next book, or what kind of content they enjoy most in your newsletters. Incorporating their feedback not only improves your work but also strengthens your connection with them. When readers see that you're listening and responding to their input, they'll feel more invested in your success.

Conclusion

Engaging with your audience is all about building meaningful relationships. Use social media to interact with your readers, post interesting content, and participate in conversations. Keep your audience informed and engaged with regular, personalized email newsletters. And always encourage feedback to show that you value your readers' opinions. By connecting with your audience in these ways, you'll create a loyal community that supports and champions your work. So, go ahead and start building those relationships—your readers will thank you for it!

5. Maintain Consistency Across All Platforms

Consistency builds trust and reinforces your brand identity. Ensure that your message, voice, and visuals are uniform across all platforms where you have a presence.

- **Website and Blog**: Your website and blog should consistently reflect your brand's voice and style. Regularly update them with fresh content that aligns with your brand's themes and interests.
- **Social Media Profiles**: Use the same profile picture, cover photo, and bio across all social media platforms. This consistency makes it easier for readers to recognize and connect with you.
- **Marketing Materials**: Ensure that your marketing materials—such as bookmarks, flyers, and press kits—are branded consistently. Use the same colors, fonts, and logos to create a cohesive look.

Let's talk about something super important for building trust and reinforcing your brand identity: maintaining consistency across all your platforms. Consistency helps readers easily recognize and connect with you, no matter where they find you. Here's how you can ensure your message, voice, and visuals are uniform across all your platforms.

Website and Blog

Your website and blog are your digital homes, and they should consistently reflect your brand's voice and style. Imagine a reader visiting your website and instantly feeling that it matches the vibe of your books. Regularly update your site with fresh content that aligns with your brand's themes and interests. Whether you're sharing new blog posts, updating your bio, or adding book-related news, keep everything in sync with your brand's identity. This way, your readers will always feel connected and engaged with your world.

Social Media Profiles

Consistency on social media is key. Use the same profile picture, cover photo, and bio across all your social media platforms. This makes it easier for readers to recognize you and ensures a seamless experience when they follow you from one platform to another. Think about your favorite brands—you can probably recognize them instantly on any platform because they maintain a consistent look and feel. Aim for the same with your author brand. It might be a great headshot, a logo, or a distinctive cover image that ties everything together.

Marketing Materials

Your marketing materials—like bookmarks, flyers, and press kits—should all be branded consistently. Use the same colors, fonts, and logos to create a cohesive look. Imagine handing out a beautifully designed bookmark at a book signing that perfectly matches your website and social media profiles. This kind of consistency not only looks professional but also reinforces your brand in the minds of your readers. When everything from your online presence to your physical marketing materials is aligned, it creates a strong, recognizable brand identity.

Putting It All Together

So, let's put this into action. Start by auditing your current platforms and materials to ensure everything aligns with your brand's voice, style, and visuals. Update your website and blog regularly with content that reflects your themes and interests. Make sure your social media profiles have the same profile picture, cover photo, and bio. And check that all your marketing materials are using consistent colors, fonts, and logos.

Maintaining this level of consistency builds trust with your readers. They know what to expect from you and feel a stronger connection because everything is familiar and cohesive. It's like having a signature style that people instantly recognize and love.

By keeping your message, voice, and visuals uniform across all platforms, you're creating a seamless, professional, and engaging experience for your readers. So, go ahead and make sure your brand shines consistently everywhere. Your readers will appreciate the effort and feel even more connected to your world. Happy branding!

6. Showcase Your Expertise and Passion

Your brand should highlight your expertise and passion for your subject matter. This not only establishes you as an authority but also attracts readers who share your interests.

- **Content Creation**: Create content that showcases your knowledge and passion. Write articles, blog posts, or social media updates that delve into topics related to your books. This can include behind-the-scenes looks at your writing process, insights into your research, or discussions about themes in your work.
- **Speaking Engagements and Workshops**: Participate in speaking engagements, workshops, and panels to share your expertise. This not only builds your credibility but also increases your visibility and expands your reach.

Highlighting these aspects of your brand not only establishes you as an authority but also attracts readers who share your interests. Here are some ways to make your knowledge and enthusiasm shine.

Content Creation

Creating content that showcases your knowledge and passion is a great way to connect with your audience. Think about writing articles, blog posts, or social media updates that delve into topics related to your books. For example, you could share behind-the-scenes looks at your writing process—maybe a sneak peek at your daily routine, your favorite writing tools, or how you overcome writer's block. Insights into your research are also fascinating; if your book involves historical elements, explain how you dig up those details or the interesting facts you discovered along the way.

Discussions about the themes in your work can also engage your readers deeply. For instance, if your book explores themes of resilience or social justice, write about why these topics matter to you and how they shape your storytelling. This not only shows your expertise but also your genuine passion for the subjects you write about, creating a strong connection with readers who care about the same things.

Speaking Engagements and Workshops

Participating in speaking engagements, workshops, and panels is another excellent way to share your expertise. Imagine giving a talk at a literary festival or hosting a workshop on writing techniques. These opportunities allow you to directly interact with your audience, share your knowledge, and showcase your passion in real-time.

When you speak at events, you not only build your credibility as an expert but also increase your visibility and expand your reach. People who attend these events are likely interested in your subject matter, making them potential readers. Plus, these engagements can lead to networking opportunities with other professionals, further boosting your profile.

For example, if you're a historical fiction author, you might participate in a panel discussing the importance of historical accuracy in storytelling. Or, if you write science fiction, you could lead a workshop on world-building. These activities demonstrate your expertise and passion, making you more relatable and authoritative in your field.

Conclusion

Showcasing your expertise and passion is all about creating content that reflects your knowledge and enthusiasm. Write articles, blog posts, and social media updates that offer insights into your writing process, research, and themes. Engage in speaking engagements and workshops to share your knowledge directly with your audience. By doing these things, you'll establish yourself as an authority and attract readers who share your interests.

Remember, it's not just about telling people what you know—it's about showing them why you care. Your passion is contagious, and when readers see how deeply you care about your subject, they're more likely to connect with you and your work. So, go ahead and let your expertise and enthusiasm shine.

7. Foster a Community

Building a community around your brand can create a loyal and engaged readership. Foster a sense of belonging and connection among your readers.

- **Online Groups**: Create and manage online groups or forums where readers can discuss your books, share their thoughts, and interact with you. Platforms like Facebook Groups or Discord can be excellent for this purpose.
- **Exclusive Content**: Offer exclusive content to your community members, such as sneak peeks, bonus chapters, or early access to new releases. This rewards their loyalty and keeps them engaged.
- **Reader Events**: Host reader events, both online and offline. These can include book clubs, Q&A sessions, and live readings. Engaging directly with your readers helps build a strong and supportive community.

Creating a community around your brand is a powerful way to build a loyal and engaged readership. It's about fostering a sense of belonging and connection among your readers. Let's explore how you can cultivate this community and make your readers feel like they're part of something special.

Online Groups

One of the best ways to build a community is by creating and managing online groups or forums. Platforms like Facebook Groups or Discord are excellent for this purpose. Imagine having a dedicated space where readers can discuss your books, share their thoughts, and interact with you directly. These groups allow readers to connect with each other over their shared love of your work, creating a supportive and enthusiastic community.

For instance, you could start a Facebook Group where members can post their favorite quotes from your books, discuss plot theories, or share fan art. Regularly participate in these discussions to show your readers that you value their input and enjoy engaging with them. This kind of interaction can deepen their connection to you and your work.

Exclusive Content

Offering exclusive content to your community members is another great way to keep them engaged and reward their loyalty. Think about what special content you can share that they won't find anywhere else. This could be sneak peeks of your upcoming books, bonus chapters, or even early access to new releases.

For example, you might share a behind-the-scenes look at your writing process, or a bonus scene that didn't make it into your latest book. These exclusive glimpses make your readers feel special and appreciated, reinforcing their commitment to your community.

Reader Events

Hosting reader events, both online and offline, is a fantastic way to engage directly with your audience. These events can include book clubs, Q&A sessions, and live readings. By interacting with your readers in real time, you can build a strong and supportive community around your brand.

Imagine hosting a live Q&A session on Instagram or Facebook, where readers can ask you questions about your books, characters, or writing process. Or consider organizing a virtual book club where you can discuss your book with a small group of readers. These events create personal connections and show your readers that you value their support and enjoy spending time with them.

For offline events, consider book signings, readings at local libraries, or even meet-and-greets at literary festivals. These face-to-face interactions can be incredibly impactful, leaving lasting impressions on your readers.

Conclusion

Fostering a community around your brand is all about creating a sense of belonging and connection among your readers. Use online groups to facilitate discussions, offer exclusive content to reward loyalty, and host reader events to engage directly with your audience. By building this community, you'll create a loyal and supportive readership that feels personally connected to you and your work.

Remember, it's not just about promoting your books—it's about nurturing relationships with your readers and making them feel valued. So, go ahead and start fostering that community. Your readers will love being a part of it, and you'll enjoy the deeper connections that come from building a strong, engaged audience.

8. Evolve with Your Audience

As your career progresses, be open to evolving your brand in response to your audience's preferences and feedback. Staying attuned to their needs ensures your brand remains relevant and appealing.

- **Monitor Trends**: Keep an eye on trends within your genre and the broader literary community. Adapt your brand and marketing strategies to stay current and resonate with your audience.
- **Feedback Loop**: Maintain a continuous feedback loop with your readers. Use their input to refine your brand and improve your offerings.

By defining your unique selling points, crafting a consistent and authentic message, developing a visual identity, engaging with your audience, maintaining consistency, showcasing your expertise, fostering a community, and evolving with your audience, you can build a strong and resonant author brand. A compelling brand not only attracts readers but also creates lasting connections, turning casual readers into dedicated fans.

In the next sections, we will explore leveraging social media and digital marketing, and using public relations to further enhance your book's visibility and success.

Social Media and Digital Marketing: Leveraging online platforms to reach more readers.

In today's digital age, social media and online platforms are indispensable tools for authors looking to expand their reach and connect with readers. Effective use of these channels can significantly enhance your book's visibility and foster a loyal community around your work. Here's how to leverage social media and digital marketing to promote your book and engage with your audience.

1. Choosing the Right Platforms

Not all social media platforms are created equal, and it's essential to choose the ones that best align with your target audience and content.

- **Facebook**: With its broad user base and versatile features, Facebook is ideal for building a community, hosting events, and sharing a variety of content types. Facebook Groups can foster deeper engagement by creating a space for fans to interact directly with you and each other.
- **Twitter**: Twitter's fast-paced environment is perfect for real-time updates, engaging in industry conversations, and networking with other authors and readers. Use hashtags effectively to reach a wider audience and join relevant discussions.
- **Instagram**: Instagram's visual nature makes it excellent for sharing book covers, quotes, behind-the-scenes looks, and more. Features like Stories, IGTV, and Reels allow for creative content that can attract and engage followers.
- **YouTube**: If you're comfortable with video content, YouTube is a powerful platform for book trailers, author interviews, writing tips, and more. Video content can create a personal connection with your audience.

- **TikTok**: Known for its short-form video content, TikTok is increasingly popular among younger readers. Use trends, challenges, and creative videos to showcase your book and connect with a new audience.
- **LinkedIn**: For non-fiction authors, LinkedIn is a valuable platform for establishing professional credibility, sharing expertise, and networking with industry professionals.

Choosing the right social media platforms is essential to connect effectively with your readers, as not all platforms are created equal. Facebook's broad user base and versatile features make it ideal for building a community, hosting events, and sharing various content types. Imagine using Facebook Groups to foster deeper engagement, allowing fans to interact directly with you and each other, creating a loyal readership. Twitter's fast-paced environment is perfect for real-time updates and engaging in industry conversations. By using hashtags effectively, you can reach a wider audience and join relevant discussions, sharing quick thoughts and linking to your latest blog posts or articles.

Instagram's visual nature is excellent for sharing book covers, quotes, and behind-the-scenes looks. Features like Stories, IGTV, and Reels allow for creative content that can captivate your audience, like posting a beautiful image of your writing setup or a teaser quote from your next book. YouTube, if you're comfortable with video content, is a powerful platform for book trailers, author interviews, and writing tips, creating a personal connection with your audience through visual and auditory engagement. TikTok's short-form video content is increasingly popular among younger readers. Using trends, challenges, and creative videos, you can showcase your book and connect with a new audience in a fun and dynamic way.

LinkedIn, for non-fiction authors, is invaluable for establishing professional credibility, sharing expertise, and networking with industry professionals. Posting articles, sharing insights from your book, and connecting with others in your field can position you as an expert and lead to speaking engagements and collaborations. By selecting the platforms that best fit your content and audience, you can create meaningful connections and effectively promote your work. So, explore these platforms and find the ones that align with your goals—your readers are out there waiting to connect with you!

2. Creating Engaging Content

Engaging content is key to building a strong online presence. Here are some ideas for content that resonates with readers:

- **Behind-the-Scenes**: Share glimpses into your writing process, research, and daily life as an author. This content humanizes you and builds a personal connection with your readers.
- **Teasers and Excerpts**: Post short excerpts or teasers from your book to intrigue potential readers and generate excitement.
- **Visuals**: High-quality images, infographics, and videos can capture attention and convey your message more effectively. Use tools like Canva to create visually appealing graphics.
- **Interactive Content**: Engage your audience with polls, quizzes, and questions. Encourage them to share their thoughts and participate in discussions.
- **Live Sessions**: Host live Q&A sessions, readings, and virtual book launches. Live content allows for real-time interaction and builds a sense of community.
- **User-Generated Content**: Encourage readers to share their own photos, reviews, and experiences related to your book. Reposting this content not only boosts engagement but also fosters a sense of belonging among your audience.

Creating engaging content is key to building a strong online presence. Sharing behind-the-scenes glimpses into your writing process, research, and daily life as an author humanizes you and builds a personal connection with your readers. Imagine posting about the quirky habits you have while writing or the unique research adventures you've embarked on for your book. This type of content makes you relatable and gives readers a peek into the life of an author. Posting short excerpts or teasers from your book can intrigue potential readers and generate excitement. A well-chosen passage can hook a reader, making them eager to read more.

High-quality visuals, like images, infographics, and videos, can capture attention and convey your message more effectively. Tools like Canva can help you create visually appealing graphics that stand out on social media. Think about designing a beautiful quote image from your book or an infographic that highlights interesting facts related to your story. Interactive content, such as polls, quizzes, and questions, engages your audience by encouraging them to share their thoughts and participate in discussions. Asking your followers to vote on a character's fate or complete a fun quiz about your book's world can drive engagement and make them feel involved.

Hosting live sessions, such as Q&A sessions, readings, and virtual book launches, allows for real-time interaction and builds a sense of community. Picture yourself hosting a live reading of a favorite chapter, followed by a Q&A where readers can ask you anything. This direct interaction can deepen your connection with your audience and create memorable experiences. Encouraging user-generated content by asking readers to share their own photos, reviews, and experiences related to your book can boost engagement and foster a sense of belonging. Reposting this content shows that you value your readers' contributions and helps build a community around your work.

By incorporating behind-the-scenes looks, teasers, high-quality visuals, interactive elements, live sessions, and user-generated content, you can create a diverse and engaging content strategy that resonates with your audience and strengthens your online presence. Your readers will appreciate the variety and the effort you put into connecting with them, making them more likely to stay engaged and loyal to your brand.

3. Building a Content Calendar

A content calendar helps you plan and organize your social media posts, ensuring consistency and variety. Here's how to create one:

- **Set Goals**: Define what you want to achieve with your social media efforts, whether it's increasing followers, driving book sales, or boosting engagement.
- **Plan Content Themes**: Outline the types of content you'll post each day or week, such as writing tips on Mondays, book excerpts on Wednesdays, and live Q&As on Fridays.

Write It. Publish It. Sell It.

- **Schedule Posts**: Use scheduling tools like Hootsuite, Buffer, or Later to plan and automate your posts. This saves time and ensures that your content goes live at optimal times.
- **Monitor and Adjust**: Track the performance of your posts using analytics tools. Adjust your content strategy based on what resonates most with your audience.

Building a content calendar is a fantastic way to plan and organize your social media posts, ensuring consistency and variety. Start by setting clear goals for what you want to achieve with your social media efforts, whether it's increasing followers, driving book sales, or boosting engagement. Having a clear vision helps guide your content creation and measure success.

Next, plan your content themes. Outline the types of content you'll post each day or week. For instance, you could share writing tips on Mondays to help aspiring writers, post book excerpts on Wednesdays to intrigue potential readers, and host live Q&As on Fridays to directly engage with your audience. This variety keeps your feed interesting and ensures you're covering all aspects of your brand.

Scheduling your posts is the next step. Use tools like Hootsuite, Buffer, or Later to plan and automate your posts. This not only saves you time but also ensures your content goes live at optimal times when your audience is most active. Imagine setting up a week's worth of posts in one sitting, freeing up more time for you to focus on writing and engaging with your readers.

Finally, it's crucial to monitor and adjust your strategy. Track the performance of your posts using analytics tools provided by social media platforms. Pay attention to which types of content resonate most with your audience. If you notice that your followers engage more with behind-the-scenes content or interactive posts, adjust your strategy to include more of those. This continuous monitoring and tweaking help you stay relevant and responsive to your audience's preferences.

By setting goals, planning content themes, scheduling posts, and monitoring performance, you create a structured yet flexible approach to your social media strategy. This ensures you're consistently providing valuable and engaging content, helping to grow your online presence and connect with your readers more effectively. So, start building your content calendar today and watch how it transforms your social media game!

4. Engaging with Your Audience

Engagement is about building relationships and fostering a sense of community. Here are some tips for effective engagement:

- **Respond Promptly**: Reply to comments, messages, and mentions in a timely manner. Show appreciation for your readers' support and participation.
- **Be Authentic**: Authenticity builds trust. Share your genuine thoughts, experiences, and emotions. Your audience will appreciate your transparency and honesty.
- **Create Conversations**: Ask questions, start discussions, and encourage your followers to share their opinions. This not only increases engagement but also provides valuable insights into your readers' preferences.
- **Showcase Readers**: Highlight your readers by sharing their reviews, fan art, and other user-generated content. Recognizing your audience's contributions fosters loyalty and encourages others to engage.

Engaging with your audience is all about building relationships and fostering a sense of community. Here are some tips to help you connect more effectively with your readers:

Start by responding promptly to comments, messages, and mentions. When you reply quickly, you show appreciation for your readers' support and participation, making them feel valued. Imagine the positive impression you create by promptly thanking someone for a kind comment or answering a question about your book.

Being authentic is another key aspect. Authenticity builds trust, so share your genuine thoughts, experiences, and emotions. Your audience will appreciate your transparency and honesty. For example, if you're struggling with a tough part of your writing process, share that experience. It makes you relatable and shows your readers the real person behind the books they love.

Creating conversations is a great way to engage your audience. Ask questions, start discussions, and encourage your followers to share their opinions. This not only boosts engagement but also provides valuable insights into your readers' preferences. For instance, you could ask what type of characters they enjoy most or which book genres they're currently reading. These interactions make your followers feel involved and valued.

Showcasing your readers is another effective engagement strategy. Highlight their reviews, fan art, and other user-generated content. When you recognize your audience's contributions, it fosters loyalty and encourages others to engage. Imagine sharing a beautifully drawn piece of fan art or a heartfelt review from a reader. It not only makes the creator feel special but also shows that you appreciate and value your readers' input.

By responding promptly, being authentic, creating conversations, and showcasing your readers, you can build strong, meaningful relationships with your audience. These efforts will help you foster a supportive and engaged community around your work, making your readers feel more connected to you and your stories. So, go ahead and start engaging—your readers are waiting to connect with you!

5. Leveraging Paid Advertising

Paid advertising can amplify your reach and attract new readers. Here's how to make the most of paid ads:

- **Targeted Ads**: Use social media platforms' targeting features to reach specific demographics, interests, and behaviors. This ensures that your ads are seen by the most relevant audience.
- **Ad Formats**: Experiment with different ad formats, such as image ads, video ads, carousel ads, and sponsored posts. Each format has its strengths and can cater to different marketing goals.

- **A/B Testing**: Run A/B tests to compare different ad creatives, headlines, and targeting options. This helps you identify what works best and optimize your campaigns for better results.
- **Budgeting**: Set a clear budget for your ad campaigns and monitor your spending. Start with a modest budget and scale up based on the performance and ROI of your ads.

Leveraging paid advertising can significantly amplify your reach and attract new readers. Here's how to make the most of paid ads and ensure your investment pays off:

First, take advantage of targeted ads. Social media platforms offer sophisticated targeting features that allow you to reach specific demographics, interests, and behaviors. By honing in on the most relevant audience, you ensure that your ads are seen by people who are most likely to be interested in your book. For example, if you've written a young adult fantasy novel, you can target users who follow popular YA fantasy authors, participate in related groups, or show interest in fantasy movies and series.

Experimenting with different ad formats is also crucial. Platforms like Facebook, Instagram, and Twitter offer a variety of formats, including image ads, video ads, carousel ads, and sponsored posts. Each format has its strengths and can cater to different marketing goals. For instance, video ads might be great for creating engaging book trailers, while carousel ads can showcase multiple aspects of your book, such as different covers, key quotes, or reader reviews.

A/B testing is a powerful tool to optimize your ad campaigns. By running A/B tests, you can compare different ad creatives, headlines, and targeting options to see what resonates most with your audience. For example, you might test two different headlines—one highlighting a gripping plot point and another featuring a compelling character quote. Analyzing the performance of each variant helps you identify what works best, allowing you to refine your strategy for better results.

Budgeting is another critical aspect of paid advertising. Set a clear budget for your ad campaigns and keep a close eye on your spending. It's wise to start with a modest budget to test the waters and scale up based on the performance and ROI of your ads. Monitoring your ad spend and adjusting your budget as needed ensures that you're investing wisely and maximizing your returns.

By leveraging targeted ads, experimenting with different ad formats, running A/B tests, and carefully budgeting your campaigns, you can make the most of paid advertising. These strategies will help you reach a wider audience, attract new readers, and ultimately drive more sales for your book. So, dive into the world of paid ads with confidence and watch your readership grow!

6. Building and Nurturing an Email List

Email marketing is a powerful tool for maintaining direct communication with your readers. Here's how to build and nurture your email list:

- **Lead Magnets**: Offer valuable incentives, such as free chapters, exclusive content, or discounts, to encourage sign-ups. Promote these lead magnets on your website and social media.
- **Segmentation**: Segment your email list based on readers' preferences, behaviors, and demographics. This allows you to send more personalized and relevant content.
- **Regular Newsletters**: Send regular newsletters with updates, behind-the-scenes content, and special offers. Keep your emails engaging and varied to maintain reader interest.
- **Automated Campaigns**: Use email marketing tools like Mailchimp, ConvertKit, or AWeber to set up automated campaigns. Welcome new subscribers, follow up with readers who've purchased your book, and re-engage inactive subscribers.

Building and nurturing an email list is a powerful way to maintain direct communication with your readers and keep them engaged. Here's how to effectively build and nurture your email list:

Start by offering lead magnets. These are valuable incentives that encourage people to sign up for your email list. Think about offering free chapters of your book, exclusive content that can't be found elsewhere, or special discounts. Promote these lead magnets on your website and social media to attract new subscribers. For instance, you could have a sign-up form on your website that offers a free eBook or a sneak peek at your upcoming novel in exchange for an email address.

Segmentation is crucial for making your emails more personalized and relevant. Segment your email list based on readers' preferences, behaviors, and demographics. This allows you to tailor your content to different groups of subscribers. For example, you might have one segment for readers who enjoy your mystery novels and another for those who prefer your romance books. By sending targeted content, you increase the likelihood that your readers will find your emails interesting and engaging.

Regular newsletters are a great way to keep your audience updated and engaged. Send out newsletters with updates on your writing progress, behind-the-scenes content, and special offers. Make sure your emails are engaging and varied to maintain reader interest. Share stories about your writing journey, give sneak peeks of upcoming projects, or offer exclusive discounts on your books. The goal is to make your readers look forward to your emails.

Automated campaigns can help you stay in touch with your subscribers without overwhelming yourself. Use email marketing tools like Mailchimp, ConvertKit, or AWeber to set up automated campaigns. For instance, you can create a welcome series for new subscribers, follow up with readers who've purchased your book to ask for reviews, and re-engage subscribers who haven't opened your emails in a while. Automation ensures that your readers receive timely and relevant communications, helping to nurture your relationship with them.

By offering lead magnets, segmenting your email list, sending regular newsletters, and setting up automated campaigns, you can build and nurture a strong email list. This direct communication channel allows you to keep your readers informed, engaged, and excited about your work.

Start implementing these strategies today and watch your email list—and your reader engagement—grow!

7. Collaborating with Influencers and Bloggers

Collaborating with influencers and bloggers can expand your reach and lend credibility to your book. Here's how to approach collaborations:

- **Identify Influencers**: Look for influencers and bloggers who cater to your target audience. Consider their follower count, engagement rates, and relevance to your book's genre.
- **Build Relationships**: Engage with influencers by commenting on their posts, sharing their content, and sending personalized messages. Building a genuine relationship increases the likelihood of collaboration.
- **Offer Value**: When reaching out to influencers, highlight how a collaboration can benefit them. Offer free copies of your book, propose co-hosting a giveaway, or suggest creating exclusive content together.
- **Track Results**: Monitor the impact of influencer collaborations on your book's visibility and sales. Use unique discount codes or trackable links to measure their effectiveness.

Collaborating with influencers and bloggers can significantly expand your reach and lend credibility to your book. Here's how to effectively approach these collaborations:

First, identify influencers and bloggers who cater to your target audience. Look for those whose followers match the demographics and interests of your ideal readers. Consider their follower count, engagement rates, and relevance to your book's genre. For example, if you've written a fantasy novel, seek out influencers who regularly review and discuss fantasy books and have a dedicated following of fantasy enthusiasts.

Building genuine relationships with influencers is crucial. Start by engaging with their content—comment on their posts, share their articles or videos, and send personalized messages expressing your appreciation for their work. This kind of authentic interaction shows that you value their content and are genuinely interested in what they do, increasing the likelihood that they'll be open to collaborating with you.

When reaching out to influencers, focus on offering value and highlighting how a collaboration can benefit them. For instance, you might offer free copies of your book for them to review or propose co-hosting a giveaway to attract more followers to both of your platforms. You could also suggest creating exclusive content together, such as an interview or a behind-the-scenes look at your writing process. This mutual benefit approach makes the collaboration appealing and worthwhile for influencers.

Tracking the results of your influencer collaborations is essential to understand their impact on your book's visibility and sales. Use unique discount codes or trackable links to measure the effectiveness of each collaboration. This data will help you determine which influencers are driving the most engagement and sales, allowing you to refine your strategy and focus on the most successful partnerships.

By identifying relevant influencers, building genuine relationships, offering mutual value, and tracking the results, you can effectively collaborate with influencers and bloggers to expand your reach and enhance your book's credibility. These partnerships can introduce your work to new audiences, create buzz, and ultimately drive more readers to your book. So, start reaching out and building those valuable connections today!

8. Utilizing Analytics and Adjusting Strategies

Continuous improvement is key to successful digital marketing. Regularly analyze your performance and adjust your strategies accordingly:

- **Analytics Tools**: Use tools like Google Analytics, Facebook Insights, Twitter Analytics, and Instagram Insights to track your performance. Pay attention to metrics such as engagement, reach, click-through rates, and conversions.

- **Evaluate Content**: Identify which types of content perform best and resonate most with your audience. Focus on creating more of what works and refining or eliminating what doesn't.
- **Adjust Campaigns**: Based on your analysis, adjust your social media and digital marketing campaigns. Experiment with new strategies, platforms, and content formats to keep your marketing efforts fresh and effective.

Continuous improvement is the key to successful digital marketing. Regularly analyzing your performance and adjusting your strategies accordingly ensures that you stay on the right track and keep growing. Let's dive into how you can make the most of analytics and refine your marketing efforts.

First, make use of analytics tools. Platforms like Google Analytics, Facebook Insights, Twitter Analytics, and Instagram Insights provide valuable data about your performance. Pay attention to metrics such as engagement, reach, click-through rates, and conversions. These metrics help you understand how your audience is interacting with your content and where you're seeing the most success.

Evaluating your content is the next step. Identify which types of content perform best and resonate most with your audience. Maybe your behind-the-scenes posts get the most engagement, or perhaps your video content drives the highest click-through rates. Focus on creating more of what works and refining or eliminating what doesn't. This ensures you're always providing value to your audience and keeping them engaged.

Based on your analysis, adjust your social media and digital marketing campaigns. If you notice that a particular type of post isn't performing well, try something new. Experiment with different strategies, platforms, and content formats to keep your marketing efforts fresh and effective. For instance, if you've been focusing mainly on Facebook and not seeing the desired results, maybe it's time to give Instagram or TikTok a try. Or, if static images aren't driving engagement, consider creating more video content or interactive posts.

By strategically leveraging social media and digital marketing, you can reach more readers, build a strong online presence, and create a community around your book. Continuous improvement through regular analysis and strategic adjustments keeps your marketing dynamic and effective.

In the next section, we will explore how to use public relations to further enhance your book's visibility and establish your reputation as an author. Public relations efforts can complement your digital marketing strategy, providing additional avenues for reaching potential readers and building your brand. Stay tuned to learn more about leveraging PR for your book's success!

Public Relations: Using media and public appearances to boost your book's visibility.

Public relations (PR) plays a crucial role in boosting your book's visibility and establishing your reputation as an author. Effective PR strategies can generate media coverage, create buzz, and build credibility, ultimately helping you reach a broader audience. Here's how to leverage media and public appearances to promote your book successfully.

1. Crafting a Compelling Press Kit

A well-prepared press kit is essential for capturing the attention of journalists, bloggers, and media outlets. Your press kit should include:

- **Author Bio**: A concise and engaging biography that highlights your background, achievements, and expertise. Tailor it to reflect your personality and the themes of your book.
- **Book Synopsis**: A brief, captivating summary of your book that piques interest. Highlight the main plot points, unique aspects, and why readers will find it compelling.
- **Press Release**: A professional press release announcing your book's launch. Include key details such as the release date, a brief overview, and any relevant accolades or endorsements.

- **High-Quality Images**: Provide high-resolution images of your book cover, author photo, and any other relevant visuals. These images should be suitable for both print and online media.
- **Contact Information**: Make it easy for media representatives to reach you or your publicist. Include an email address, phone number, and links to your social media profiles.

Crafting a Compelling Press Kit

A well-prepared press kit is essential for capturing the attention of journalists, bloggers, and media outlets. Your press kit should include key elements that present you and your book in the best light possible. Here's a template to help you get started:

1. Author Bio

Example:

Jane Doe: Captivating Storyteller and Mystery Enthusiast

Jane Doe is a seasoned writer with a passion for unraveling intricate tales of mystery and suspense. With a background in criminal psychology, she brings a unique perspective to her storytelling, weaving together complex characters and thrilling plotlines that keep readers on the edge of their seats. Jane's debut novel, "Whispering Shadows," quickly climbed the bestseller lists, earning praise for its gripping narrative and deep psychological insight. When she's not writing, Jane enjoys exploring abandoned places, which often serve as inspiration for her next mystery.

Tailor your bio to reflect your personality and the themes of your book. Highlight your background, achievements, and expertise in a concise and engaging way.

2. Book Synopsis

Example:

Whispering Shadows: A Novel by Jane Doe

In "Whispering Shadows," readers are introduced to Detective Emily Hart, a seasoned investigator haunted by her past. When a series of bizarre murders rocks the quiet town of Ravenswood, Emily must confront her deepest fears to uncover the truth. As she delves deeper into the mystery, she discovers secrets that challenge her perception of reality. With its intricate plot, rich character development, and unexpected twists, "Whispering Shadows" is a must-read for fans of psychological thrillers.

Provide a brief, captivating summary of your book. Highlight the main plot points, unique aspects, and why readers will find it compelling.

---

3. Press Release

Example:

FOR IMMEDIATE RELEASE

Jane Doe Unveils Her Gripping Debut Novel, "Whispering Shadows"

[City, State, Date] – Jane Doe, a new voice in the mystery genre, is thrilled to announce the release of her debut novel, "Whispering Shadows." Scheduled for release on [Release Date], this psychological thriller promises to captivate readers with its intricate plot and compelling characters.

"Whispering Shadows" has already received acclaim from early reviewers, including praise from renowned author John Smith, who calls it "a masterful blend of suspense and psychological depth."

Write It. Publish It. Sell It.

For more information, review copies, or to schedule an interview, please contact Jane Doe at [Email Address] or [Phone Number].

Include key details such as the release date, a brief overview, and any relevant accolades or endorsements.

---

4. High-Quality Images

Example:

Ensure you include:

- **Book Cover Image:** High-resolution image suitable for print and online media.
- **Author Photo:** Professional, high-resolution photo.
- **Additional Visuals:** Any other relevant images, such as event photos or illustrations related to your book.

Provide high-resolution images that are suitable for both print and online media. These visuals help media outlets present your story professionally.

5. Contact Information

Example:

For media inquiries, please contact:

Jane Doe
Email: janedoe@example.com
Phone: (123) 456-7890
Website: www.janedoeauthor.com
Social Media: Twitter | Facebook | Instagram

Make it easy for media representatives to reach you or your publicist. Include an email address, phone number, and links to your social media profiles.

By including these elements in your press kit, you'll present a professional and engaging package that captures the attention of journalists, bloggers, and media outlets, making it easier for them to feature your book and your story.

2. Writing and Distributing Press Releases

A well-crafted press release can generate media coverage and create buzz around your book. Here's how to write and distribute an effective press release:

- **Headline**: Craft a compelling headline that grabs attention and clearly conveys the main news of your release.
- **Opening Paragraph**: Start with a strong opening that summarizes the key points. Answer the who, what, when, where, and why questions.
- **Body**: Provide more detailed information about your book, including unique selling points, background information, and any relevant quotes or testimonials.
- **Call to Action**: Conclude with a clear call to action, such as visiting your website, purchasing your book, or attending an event.

Write It. Publish It. Sell It.

- **Distribution**: Use PR distribution services like PR Newswire, Business Wire, or a specialized book publicity service. Additionally, send your press release directly to journalists, bloggers, and media outlets that cover your genre or industry.

A well-crafted press release can generate media coverage and create buzz around your book. Here's how to write and distribute an effective press release:

1. Headline

Example:

Mystery Author Jane Doe Unveils Thrilling Debut Novel, "Whispering Shadows"

Craft a compelling headline that grabs attention and clearly conveys the main news of your release.

2. Opening Paragraph

Example:

[City, State, Date] – Jane Doe, a captivating new voice in the mystery genre, is excited to announce the release of her debut novel, "Whispering Shadows," on [Release Date]. This psychological thriller promises to grip readers with its intricate plot and unforgettable characters.

Start with a strong opening that summarizes the key points. Answer the who, what, when, where, and why questions.

3. Body

Example:

"Whispering Shadows" follows Detective Emily Hart as she navigates a series of bizarre murders in the quiet town of Ravenswood. Haunted by her past and driven by an unrelenting quest for justice, Emily uncovers secrets that challenge her perception of reality. The novel has already garnered praise from early reviewers, including bestselling author John Smith, who describes it as "a masterful blend of suspense and psychological depth."

Jane Doe's background in criminal psychology adds an authentic layer of intrigue to her storytelling, making "Whispering Shadows" a must-read for fans of the genre. The book delves into themes of redemption, the complexity of human nature, and the blurred lines between reality and illusion.

Provide more detailed information about your book, including unique selling points, background information, and any relevant quotes or testimonials.

---

4. Call to Action

Example:

Readers can purchase "Whispering Shadows" starting [Release Date] at major retailers and online bookstores. For more information about the book and upcoming events, visit www.janedoeauthor.com.

Conclude with a clear call to action, such as visiting your website, purchasing your book, or attending an event.

5. Contact Information

Example:

For media inquiries, please contact:

Jane Doe
Email: janedoe@example.com
Phone: (123) 456-7890
Website: www.janedoeauthor.com
Social Media: Twitter | Facebook | Instagram

Distribution

Once your press release is polished and ready to go, it's time to distribute it. Here's how to get it into the right hands:

> **PR Distribution Services**: Use services like PR Newswire, Business Wire, or a specialized book publicity service to reach a wide audience. These platforms can help your release get noticed by journalists and media outlets.
>
> **Direct Outreach**: Send your press release directly to journalists, bloggers, and media outlets that cover your genre or industry. Personalize your email to show that you've done your homework and explain why your book would be of interest to their readers.
>
> **Social Media**: Share your press release on your social media channels. Tag relevant influencers, book bloggers, and media outlets to increase visibility.
>
> **Author Website**: Post your press release on your author website. This not only makes it easily accessible for anyone interested but also boosts your site's content and SEO.

Follow Up: Don't hesitate to follow up with the contacts you've sent your press release to. A polite follow-up can keep your book top of mind and increase your chances of coverage.

By following this template and distribution strategy, you can craft a compelling press release that effectively generates media coverage and builds excitement around your book.

3. Securing Media Coverage

Media coverage can significantly boost your book's visibility and credibility. Here's how to secure media coverage effectively:

- **Identify Relevant Media Outlets**: Research media outlets, blogs, podcasts, and influencers that cover your genre or topics related to your book. Create a list of potential contacts.
- **Personalize Your Pitch**: Craft personalized pitches for each media outlet or journalist. Highlight why your book is relevant to their audience and offer unique angles or story ideas.
- **Follow Up**: After sending your initial pitch, follow up with a polite reminder if you haven't received a response. Be persistent but respectful.
- **Provide Review Copies**: Offer free review copies of your book to journalists and bloggers. Encourage them to write reviews, conduct interviews, or feature your book in their coverage.

Securing Media Coverage

Media coverage can significantly boost your book's visibility and credibility. Here's how to secure media coverage effectively:

Write It. Publish It. Sell It.

1. Identify Relevant Media Outlets

Example:

Research and List Creation

Start by researching media outlets, blogs, podcasts, and influencers that cover your genre or topics related to your book. Look for those with audiences that align with your target readers. Create a detailed list of potential contacts, including journalists, bloggers, and podcast hosts.

Example List:

- **Mystery Writers Weekly** (Magazine)
- **Book Lovers Blog** (Blog)
- **The Reader's Nook** (Podcast)
- **Jane Smith** (Influencer on Instagram)

Research media outlets, blogs, podcasts, and influencers that cover your genre or topics related to your book. Create a list of potential contacts.

---

2. Personalize Your Pitch

Example:

Crafting Personalized Pitches

Subject: Exclusive Sneak Peek of "Whispering Shadows" for Mystery Writers Weekly

Dear [Recipient's Name],

I'm Jane Doe, the author of the upcoming psychological thriller "Whispering Shadows." Given your audience's love for gripping mysteries, I believe my book would be a perfect fit for Mystery Writers Weekly.

"Whispering Shadows" follows Detective Emily Hart as she unravels a series of bizarre murders in the quiet town of Ravenswood. With its intricate plot and deep psychological insights, the book has already garnered praise from early reviewers, including bestselling author John Smith.

I'd love to discuss the possibility of featuring "Whispering Shadows" in your publication. I can provide a review copy and am available for interviews or guest articles.

Thank you for considering my book for Mystery Writers Weekly. I look forward to hearing from you.

Best regards,
Jane Doe
Email: janedoe@example.com
Phone: (123) 456-7890
Website: www.janedoeauthor.com

Craft personalized pitches for each media outlet or journalist. Highlight why your book is relevant to their audience and offer unique angles or story ideas.

---

3. Follow Up

Example:

Polite Follow-Up Email

Subject: Follow-Up: Feature Opportunity for "Whispering Shadows"

Dear [Recipient's Name],

I hope this email finds you well. I'm following up on my previous email regarding the opportunity to feature my book, "Whispering Shadows," in Mystery Writers Weekly.

I understand you're busy, but I wanted to check in and see if there might be any interest. I'm happy to provide more information or answer any questions you might have.

Thank you again for considering my book. I look forward to the possibility of working together.

Best regards,
Jane Doe
Email: janedoe@example.com
Phone: (123) 456-7890
Website: www.janedoeauthor.com

After sending your initial pitch, follow up with a polite reminder if you haven't received a response. Be persistent but respectful.

---

4. Provide Review Copies

Example:

Offering Free Review Copies

Hi [Recipient's Name],

I'm thrilled to offer you a free review copy of my upcoming psychological thriller, "Whispering Shadows." Given your interest in mystery novels, I believe you'll find it intriguing.

Please let me know if you'd like a digital or physical copy, and I'll send it your way immediately. I'm also available for interviews or any other feature you might consider.

Thank you for your time and interest. I look forward to your thoughts on the book.

Best regards,
Jane Doe
Email: janedoe@example.com
Phone: (123) 456-7890
Website: www.janedoeauthor.com

Offer free review copies of your book to journalists and bloggers. Encourage them to write reviews, conduct interviews, or feature your book in their coverage.

Conclusion

By identifying relevant media outlets, personalizing your pitches, following up respectfully, and providing review copies, you can effectively secure media coverage for your book. This strategy will help increase your book's visibility and establish credibility, making it more likely to reach a wider audience.

4. Participating in Interviews and Features

Interviews and features are excellent opportunities to share your story and promote your book. Here's how to make the most of these opportunities:

- **Prepare Your Key Messages**: Identify the key messages you want to convey during your interviews. Focus on the unique aspects of your book, your writing process, and your personal journey.
- **Practice Your Delivery**: Practice answering common interview questions and delivering your key messages concisely and confidently. Rehearse with a friend or in front of a mirror.
- **Be Engaging and Authentic**: During interviews, be genuine and enthusiastic. Share personal anecdotes and insights to connect with your audience on a deeper level.
- **Promote Your Interviews**: Once your interviews or features are published, share them across your social media channels, website, and email newsletters to maximize their reach.

Participating in interviews and features is a fantastic way to share your story and promote your book. When it comes to choosing between pay-to-play interviews and free interviews, there's a strong case for leaning towards the pay-to-play opportunities, especially if you're looking for greater reach and a more targeted audience.

First, think about the key messages you want to convey. Identify the unique aspects of your book, your writing process, and your personal journey. These are the points that will resonate most with your audience and make your interview memorable. Having these messages clear in your mind will help you stay focused and ensure you communicate effectively.

Next, practice your delivery. It's important to answer common interview questions confidently and concisely. Try rehearsing with a friend or in front of a mirror to get comfortable with your responses. This preparation will help you speak more naturally and handle any unexpected questions with ease.

During the interview, be engaging and authentic. Show your genuine enthusiasm for your book and share personal anecdotes that connect with your audience on a deeper level. Authenticity builds trust and makes your story more relatable, which is crucial for creating a lasting impression.

Promoting your interviews once they're published is key to maximizing their reach. Share them across your social media channels, your website, and in your email newsletters. Encourage your followers to check out the interview and share it with others. This helps you leverage the exposure and bring more attention to your book.

Now, let's talk about the value of pay-to-play interviews. These opportunities often offer significant exposure because they're featured on platforms with large, engaged audiences. While they do require an investment, they can be worth it because they guarantee coverage and often come with additional promotional support. Pay-to-play interviews also demand a high level of professionalism and preparation, ensuring that you know your book inside and out and can speak about it confidently.

On the other hand, free interviews can also be valuable, but they might require more effort to secure and may not always reach as large an audience. They're typically earned through networking and pitching and can build credibility since they're seen as genuine endorsements by the media outlet.

In summary, participating in interviews and features, especially pay-to-play ones, can significantly boost your book's visibility. By preparing your key messages, practicing your delivery, being engaging and authentic, and promoting your interviews, you can make the most of these opportunities. Pay-to-play interviews, in particular, offer great reach and require you to be at the top of your game, making them a worthwhile investment for serious authors looking to expand their audience. So, dive into these opportunities with confidence and watch your readership grow!

5. Leveraging Book Reviews and Endorsements

Positive book reviews and endorsements can greatly enhance your book's credibility and appeal. Here's how to leverage them:

- **Request Reviews**: Reach out to book reviewers, bloggers, and influencers who specialize in your genre. Offer them free copies of your book in exchange for honest reviews.
- **Highlight Endorsements**: If you receive endorsements from well-known authors, industry experts, or celebrities, prominently feature them on your book cover, website, and marketing materials.
- **Create a Review Campaign**: Run a campaign encouraging readers to leave reviews on platforms like Amazon, Goodreads, and Barnes & Noble. Positive reviews can influence potential readers and boost your book's visibility.

Leveraging book reviews and endorsements can significantly enhance your book's credibility and appeal. Positive feedback from readers and respected figures can make a big difference in attracting new readers. Here's how you can effectively leverage these powerful tools:

First, actively request reviews. Reach out to book reviewers, bloggers, and influencers who specialize in your genre. Offering them free copies of your book in exchange for honest reviews is a great way to get your book into the hands of people who can spread the word. Personalized pitches showing you've done your homework about their work can increase your chances of a positive response. Honest and thoughtful reviews from reputable sources can lend significant credibility to your book.

Next, highlight endorsements prominently. If you receive endorsements from well-known authors, industry experts, or celebrities, make sure to feature them on your book cover, website, and all your marketing materials. These endorsements act as powerful testimonials that can sway potential readers. Imagine the impact of a glowing review from a well-known author on your book's cover—it immediately signals quality and trustworthiness to potential readers.

Running a review campaign is another effective strategy. Encourage your readers to leave reviews on major platforms like Amazon, Goodreads, and Barnes & Noble. These platforms are where potential readers often look first for recommendations and insights into a book. Consider setting up a campaign with incentives, like a small giveaway for those who leave a review, or simply remind your readers through your newsletter and social media channels about how much their reviews help. Positive reviews not only influence potential readers but also boost your book's visibility in search results and recommendations on these platforms.

By actively requesting reviews, prominently featuring endorsements, and running a dedicated review campaign, you can leverage book reviews and endorsements to build your book's credibility and attract new readers. These efforts create a positive buzz around your book, helping it stand out in a crowded market. So, start reaching out, highlighting those endorsements, and encouraging reviews to give your book the best chance of success!

6. Organizing Public Appearances and Events

Public appearances and events provide valuable opportunities to connect with readers and promote your book in person. Here's how to organize successful events:

- **Book Signings**: Arrange book signings at local bookstores, libraries, and literary festivals. Promote these events through your social media channels, email newsletters, and local media.
- **Speaking Engagements**: Offer to speak at conferences, workshops, schools, and community organizations. Tailor your presentations to align with the interests of your audience and the themes of your book.
- **Virtual Events**: Host virtual events such as webinars, live readings, and Q&A sessions. Use platforms like Zoom, Facebook Live, or Instagram Live to reach a broader audience.

Organizing public appearances and events provides invaluable opportunities to connect with readers and promote your book in person. Let's explore how to make these events successful and engaging for your audience.

First, consider arranging book signings. Book signings at local bookstores, libraries, and literary festivals are fantastic ways to meet your readers face-to-face. These events offer a personal touch, allowing you to interact directly with your audience. Promote your book signings through your social media channels, email newsletters, and local media to ensure a good turnout. Imagine the excitement of readers who get to meet you in person and have their copies signed, creating memorable experiences that they'll share with others.

Next, think about speaking engagements. Offer to speak at conferences, workshops, schools, and community organizations. Tailor your presentations to align with the interests of your audience and the themes of your book. For example, if your book covers historical events, you could present a talk on the historical accuracy and research involved in your writing. Speaking engagements not only help you promote your book but also establish you as an authority in your field, enhancing your credibility and reach.

Don't forget the power of virtual events. Hosting virtual events such as webinars, live readings, and Q&A sessions can help you reach a broader audience who might not be able to attend in person. Use platforms like Zoom, Facebook Live, or Instagram Live to make these events accessible. Virtual events are convenient and can attract a diverse group of readers from different locations. Engage your audience with interactive elements, like taking questions in real-time or hosting a live discussion about your book's themes and characters.

By organizing book signings, speaking engagements, and virtual events, you can effectively connect with readers and promote your book. These events provide a platform to showcase your personality and passion, making your book promotion more dynamic and engaging. So, start planning your public appearances and events, and get ready to build meaningful connections with your readers!

7. Networking with Industry Professionals

Building relationships with industry professionals can open doors to new opportunities and enhance your PR efforts. Here's how to network effectively:

- **Attend Industry Events**: Participate in book fairs, literary festivals, writing conferences, and networking events. Engage with other authors, publishers, agents, and media representatives.
- **Join Professional Organizations**: Become a member of professional organizations such as the Authors Guild, Society of Children's Book Writers and Illustrators (SCBWI), or Romance Writers of America (RWA). These organizations offer valuable networking opportunities and resources.
- **Collaborate with Peers**: Collaborate with fellow authors on joint promotions, panel discussions, or anthology projects. Cross-promoting each other's work can expand your reach and introduce you to new audiences.

Networking with industry professionals is a powerful way to open doors to new opportunities and enhance your PR efforts. Building these relationships can significantly boost your visibility and credibility as an author. Here's how to network effectively:

First, make it a point to attend industry events. Participating in book fairs, literary festivals, writing conferences, and networking events can put you in direct contact with other authors, publishers, agents, and media representatives. Engage actively in these settings—introduce yourself, participate in discussions, and exchange contact information. Imagine the connections you can make at a literary festival, where you might meet a publisher interested in your next project or an agent who loves your writing style.

Joining professional organizations is another excellent strategy. Become a member of groups like the Authors Guild, Society of Children's Book Writers and Illustrators (SCBWI), or Romance Writers of America

(RWA). These organizations offer valuable networking opportunities and resources, such as workshops, webinars, and conferences. Being part of these groups not only provides you with industry insights but also allows you to connect with like-minded professionals who can offer support and guidance.

Collaborating with peers can also enhance your network. Team up with fellow authors on joint promotions, panel discussions, or anthology projects. Cross-promoting each other's work can expand your reach and introduce you to new audiences. For instance, co-hosting a webinar with another author can attract their followers to your work and vice versa. Working together on an anthology project can also bring diverse audiences together, boosting visibility for all involved.

By attending industry events, joining professional organizations, and collaborating with peers, you can build a robust network of industry professionals. These relationships can lead to new opportunities, from publishing deals to promotional partnerships. Networking effectively not only enhances your PR efforts but also enriches your professional journey, providing support, inspiration, and valuable connections. So, start engaging with the industry today and watch how these relationships can propel your career forward!

8. Utilizing Social Media for PR

Social media is a powerful tool for amplifying your PR efforts and engaging with your audience. Here's how to use social media effectively:

- **Share Media Coverage**: Promote any media coverage, interviews, and reviews you receive on your social media channels. Tag the media outlets and journalists to increase visibility.
- **Engage with Followers**: Regularly interact with your followers by responding to comments, participating in discussions, and sharing behind-the-scenes content.
- **Use Hashtags**: Utilize relevant hashtags to increase the discoverability of your posts. Create a unique hashtag for your book to encourage user-generated content.

Write It. Publish It. Sell It.

- **Run Contests and Giveaways**: Host contests and giveaways to generate excitement and engagement. Encourage participants to share your book on social media for additional entries.

Utilizing social media for PR is a powerful way to amplify your efforts and engage with your audience. Let's dive into how you can make the most of social media to boost your book's visibility and connect with readers.

First, share any media coverage you receive on your social media channels. Whenever you get interviews, reviews, or features, promote them widely. Tag the media outlets and journalists involved to increase visibility and show appreciation. This not only broadens your reach but also builds relationships with media professionals who might continue to support your work. Imagine sharing a glowing review from a popular book blog on your Instagram or Twitter, tagging the reviewer to acknowledge their work, and watching as your followers engage with the content.

Engaging with your followers is crucial. Regularly interact with them by responding to comments, participating in discussions, and sharing behind-the-scenes content. Show your readers that you're approachable and interested in what they have to say. For example, if someone comments on your post about loving a particular character, reply with a thank you and maybe a fun fact about that character. This kind of engagement builds a loyal community around your work.

Using hashtags effectively can significantly increase the discoverability of your posts. Utilize relevant hashtags related to your book's genre, themes, and audience interests. Additionally, create a unique hashtag for your book to encourage user-generated content. For instance, if your book is titled "Mystery at Maplewood," you might use #MaplewoodMystery. Encourage your readers to use this hashtag when they post about your book, making it easier for others to find related content and join the conversation.

Running contests and giveaways is another excellent way to generate excitement and engagement. Host contests where participants can win a copy of your book or related merchandise. Encourage them to share your book on their social media for additional entries. This not only boosts visibility but also creates a buzz around your book. For example, you could run a giveaway asking readers to post a picture of themselves with your book and tag you in the post for a chance to win a signed copy or special edition.

By effectively utilizing social media, you can amplify your PR efforts, build credibility, and connect with a broader audience. Share your media coverage, engage with your followers, use hashtags strategically, and run exciting contests and giveaways to keep your audience engaged and your book in the spotlight.

In the next section, we will explore additional advanced strategies for maintaining momentum and sustaining your book's success over the long term. Stay tuned to learn more about how to keep your book thriving in the competitive market.

Chapter 4: Learn What You Should Spend Money On

Navigating the financial aspects of publishing your book can be daunting, but making wise investments can significantly enhance your book's quality and reach. Understanding where to allocate your budget and where to find cost-effective solutions is crucial for a successful publishing journey. In this chapter, we will guide you through creating a budget, identifying essential investments, finding affordable alternatives, and avoiding common financial pitfalls.

Budgeting for Success: Creating a Budget for Your Book Publishing Journey

Creating a detailed budget is the first step to financial success in your publishing journey. A well-planned budget helps you manage your expenses, prioritize your spending, and ensure you have the resources necessary to bring your book to life. Here's how to get started:

- **Estimate Your Costs**: Begin by listing all potential expenses associated with publishing your book. This includes writing-related costs, production expenses, marketing, and distribution fees.
- **Set Financial Goals**: Determine your financial goals, such as how much you're willing to spend, your expected return on investment, and your sales targets.
- **Allocate Funds Wisely**: Prioritize your spending based on the areas that will have the most significant impact on your book's success. Allocate more funds to essential aspects such as editing and cover design.
- **Track Your Spending**: Use budgeting tools or spreadsheets to track your expenses and stay within your budget. Regularly review your budget and adjust as needed to avoid overspending.

Essential Investments: Identifying Key Areas Where Spending Money Can Enhance Your Book's Quality and Reach

Investing in certain key areas can greatly improve the quality of your book and its chances of success. Here are the essential investments you should consider:

- **Professional Editing**: A well-edited book is crucial for maintaining credibility and ensuring a positive reader experience. Invest in professional editing services, including developmental editing, copyediting, and proofreading.
- **Cover Design**: Your book cover is the first impression potential readers will have. A professionally designed cover can attract attention and convey the essence of your book. Hire a skilled cover designer to create a visually appealing and marketable cover.
- **Formatting and Typesetting**: Proper formatting and typesetting enhance readability and professionalism. Invest in services to ensure your book is formatted correctly for both print and digital editions.
- **Marketing and Promotion**: Allocate a portion of your budget to marketing and promotional activities. This includes paid advertising, book trailers, PR campaigns, and promotional events.
- **ISBN and Distribution**: Purchase ISBNs (International Standard Book Numbers) and distribution packages to ensure your book is properly cataloged and available through various retail channels.

Cost-Effective Solutions: Finding Affordable Alternatives for Various Publishing Expenses

While it's important to invest in key areas, there are also ways to save money without compromising quality. Here are some cost-effective solutions:

- **Freelance Services**: Hire freelance editors, designers, and formatters from reputable platforms like Upwork, Fiverr, or Reedsy. Freelancers often offer competitive rates and flexible services.
- **DIY Options**: If you have the skills, consider doing some tasks yourself, such as formatting your book using tools like Scrivener or Vellum. DIY solutions can save money but require time and effort.

- **Barter and Trade**: Collaborate with other authors or creatives and offer your skills in exchange for their services. This can be a mutually beneficial arrangement that saves both parties money.
- **Pre-made Covers**: Purchase pre-made book covers from online marketplaces. These covers are often more affordable than custom designs and can still look professional and attractive.
- **Print-on-Demand Services**: Use print-on-demand services like Amazon KDP or IngramSpark to avoid large upfront printing costs. This allows you to print copies as they are sold, reducing financial risk.

Financial Pitfalls: Common Money Mistakes and How to Avoid Them

Avoiding financial pitfalls is crucial to staying on budget and maximizing your return on investment. Here are some common money mistakes and tips on how to avoid them:

- **Overestimating Sales**: Be realistic about your sales projections. Overestimating sales can lead to overspending on inventory and marketing. Start with conservative estimates and adjust based on actual performance.
- **Skipping Professional Services**: Cutting corners on essential services like editing and cover design can hurt your book's quality and reputation. Always prioritize these investments, even if it means allocating less to other areas.
- **Ignoring Marketing**: Failing to invest in marketing can result in poor book sales. Even the best-written book needs effective marketing to reach its audience. Allocate a reasonable portion of your budget to marketing efforts.
- **Not Tracking Expenses**: Failing to track your expenses can lead to overspending and financial stress. Use budgeting tools and regularly review your finances to stay on top of your spending.
- **Underpricing Your Book**: Setting your book's price too low can undermine its perceived value and limit your profit margins. Research similar books in your genre to determine a competitive and profitable price point.

By creating a detailed budget, identifying essential investments, finding cost-effective solutions, and avoiding common financial pitfalls, you can navigate the financial aspects of publishing with confidence and success. In the following sections, we will delve deeper into each of these areas, providing practical advice and actionable tips to help you make the most of your publishing budget.

Budgeting for Success: Creating a budget for your book publishing journey.

Creating a detailed budget is a crucial step in ensuring the success of your book publishing journey. A well-planned budget helps you manage your expenses, prioritize your spending, and allocate resources effectively. Here's how to create a comprehensive budget that sets you up for success.

1. Estimate Your Costs

The first step in creating a budget is to estimate all potential costs associated with publishing your book. These costs can be categorized into four main areas: writing-related expenses, production costs, marketing expenses, and distribution fees.

Writing-Related Expenses:

- **Research**: Costs related to research materials, access to libraries, or subscriptions to databases.
- **Writing Tools**: Software like Scrivener, Grammarly, or other writing aids.

Production Costs:

- **Editing**: Fees for developmental editing, copyediting, and proofreading.
- **Cover Design**: Costs for hiring a professional cover designer.
- **Interior Formatting**: Fees for formatting the book for print and digital editions.
- **Illustrations**: If your book requires illustrations, factor in the cost of hiring an illustrator.
- **ISBNs**: Purchase of International Standard Book Numbers for print and digital versions.

Marketing Expenses:

- **Book Launch**: Costs for organizing a book launch event, whether virtual or in-person.
- **Advertising**: Budget for paid ads on platforms like Facebook, Amazon, and Google.
- **PR and Promotions**: Fees for hiring a publicist or running promotional campaigns.
- **Review Copies**: Costs of sending out review copies to bloggers, reviewers, and influencers.
- **Marketing Materials**: Flyers, bookmarks, posters, and other promotional materials.

Distribution Fees:

- **Print-On-Demand**: Fees associated with print-on-demand services like Amazon KDP and IngramSpark.
- **Ebook Distribution**: Costs for distributing your ebook through platforms like Amazon, Apple Books, and Kobo.
- **Shipping**: Costs of shipping physical copies to bookstores, libraries, and readers.

Writing-Related Expenses

First, let's discuss research and writing tools. Investing in research materials and writing aids like Scrivener or Grammarly is essential. Quality research ensures your book is accurate and well-informed, which can make a huge difference in its credibility and depth. Writing tools can enhance your writing process, helping you stay organized and produce polished, professional-quality work. Relying on free resources might limit your access to valuable information and reduce the efficiency of your writing process.

Production Costs

Editing is perhaps one of the most critical investments. Professional editors provide a fresh perspective, catching errors and improving the structure, flow, and readability of your manuscript. Developmental editing helps shape the story, copyediting ensures grammatical precision, and proofreading catches those last pesky typos. Skimping on editing can result in a manuscript full of errors, which can turn off readers and hurt your reputation as an author.

Cover design is another area where you shouldn't cut corners. A professional cover designer knows how to create a visually appealing and market-appropriate cover that grabs attention and entices potential readers. A poorly designed cover can make your book look unprofessional, no matter how good the content is inside.

Interior formatting ensures that your book looks good and reads well in both print and digital formats. Professional formatting can prevent issues like awkward page breaks, inconsistent fonts, or formatting errors that distract from the reading experience. Free or DIY formatting options might not meet industry standards, leading to a subpar presentation.

If your book requires illustrations, hiring a professional illustrator is vital. Quality illustrations can significantly enhance your book, especially for genres like children's books or graphic novels. Amateur illustrations can detract from the overall quality and appeal of your book.

Purchasing ISBNs for both print and digital versions of your book is also important. An ISBN helps catalog your book properly, making it easier for readers to find and purchase. Free options often don't provide the same level of professionalism and might limit your distribution options.

Marketing Expenses

When it comes to marketing, investing in a well-organized book launch, advertising, PR, and promotions is essential for gaining visibility and attracting readers. A book launch event, whether virtual or in-person, creates buzz and excitement. Paid advertising on platforms like Facebook, Amazon, and Google targets specific demographics, increasing your book's reach.

Hiring a publicist or running promotional campaigns can significantly boost your book's exposure. A publicist can secure media coverage and interviews that you might not be able to obtain on your own. Free promotional efforts often lack the same reach and effectiveness.

Sending out review copies to bloggers, reviewers, and influencers can generate valuable reviews and word-of-mouth promotion. Investing in physical copies and shipping shows that you value their time and opinions, encouraging them to share their thoughts with their audience.

Marketing materials like flyers, bookmarks, and posters can enhance your promotional efforts at events and in bookstores. These tangible items help keep your book in the minds of potential readers and give you a professional edge.

Distribution Fees

Lastly, consider the importance of print-on-demand and ebook distribution services. Print-on-demand options like Amazon KDP and IngramSpark allow you to print books as they are ordered, reducing the need for large print runs and inventory costs. These services take care of the printing and shipping logistics, letting you focus on marketing and sales. Free distribution options might not offer the same quality or reach, limiting your book's availability.

Ebook distribution through platforms like Amazon, Apple Books, and Kobo is also crucial. These platforms often charge a fee or take a percentage of your sales, but they provide access to a vast audience of readers. Skimping on these services can drastically reduce your book's visibility and sales potential.

Shipping costs for physical copies are another necessary expense. Ensuring your books reach bookstores, libraries, and readers in good condition is crucial for maintaining a professional image. Free shipping options might not offer the same reliability and quality, potentially harming your reputation.

Conclusion

In conclusion, investing in the various aspects of book production, marketing, and distribution is crucial for your book's success. While free options might seem appealing to save costs, they often come with limitations that can hurt your book's quality, visibility, and credibility. By allocating resources effectively and investing in professional services, you ensure that your book stands out in the market, attracts readers, and builds your reputation as a serious author. So, don't cut corners—invest in your book's future and watch it thrive!

2. Set Financial Goals

Define clear financial goals for your book publishing journey. These goals will help you stay focused and measure your success.

- **Revenue Targets**: Determine how much you aim to earn from book sales in the first year.
- **Break-Even Point**: Calculate the point at which your book's revenue will cover all your expenses.
- **Profit Margin**: Set a target for your profit margin after reaching the break-even point.

Setting clear financial goals is essential for your book publishing journey. These goals will help you stay focused, make informed decisions, and measure your success. Let's dive into the key financial goals you should consider:

Revenue Targets

Start by determining your revenue targets. How much do you aim to earn from book sales in the first year? Setting a specific revenue goal gives you a clear target to work towards and helps you gauge the effectiveness of your marketing and sales strategies. For instance, if you aim to sell 1,000 copies of your book at $15 each, your revenue target would be $15,000. Break this down further into monthly or quarterly targets to keep track of your progress and make necessary adjustments along the way.

Break-Even Point

Next, calculate your break-even point. This is the point at which your book's revenue will cover all your expenses. Understanding your break-even point is crucial as it helps you determine how many copies you need to sell to start making a profit. To calculate this, sum up all your production costs (editing, cover design, formatting, ISBNs), marketing expenses (book launch, advertising, PR), and distribution fees (print-on-demand, ebook distribution, shipping). Divide this total by the selling price of your book to find out how many copies you need to sell to break even. For example, if your total expenses are $5,000 and your book sells for $15, you need to sell approximately 334 copies to break even.

Profit Margin

Once you've reached the break-even point, set a target for your profit margin. This is the percentage of revenue that remains after all expenses have been paid. Establishing a profit margin goal helps you focus on maximizing your earnings and ensuring the long-term sustainability of your writing career. For instance, you might aim for a 20% profit margin, meaning that after covering all your costs, you want 20% of your revenue to be profit. To achieve this, you may need to explore strategies like increasing your book's price, reducing costs, or finding new revenue streams such as speaking engagements, workshops, or merchandise related to your book.

Conclusion

Setting financial goals for your book publishing journey is not just about aiming high but also about being realistic and strategic. By determining clear revenue targets, calculating your break-even point, and setting a profit margin goal, you can create a roadmap for financial success. These goals will keep you focused, help you measure your progress, and guide your decision-making process. Remember, achieving financial success with your book takes time, effort, and a well-thought-out plan. So, set your goals, track your progress, and adjust your strategies as needed to ensure a successful publishing journey.

3. Allocate Funds Wisely

Prioritize your spending based on the areas that will have the most significant impact on your book's success. Allocate more funds to essential aspects such as editing and cover design, while looking for cost-effective solutions in other areas.

High Priority:

- **Editing**: Investing in professional editing ensures your book is polished and well-written.
- **Cover Design**: A compelling cover design can attract readers and boost sales.

Medium Priority:

- **Marketing**: Effective marketing is crucial for reaching your audience, but you can find cost-effective ways to promote your book.
- **Formatting**: Ensure your book is properly formatted for readability and professionalism.

Low Priority:

- **Additional Features**: Consider luxury items like custom illustrations or high-end marketing materials only if your budget allows.

Allocating your funds wisely is crucial to ensure your book's success while staying within budget. It's all about prioritizing spending on the areas that will have the most significant impact and finding cost-effective solutions for others. Let's break this down together.

Write It. Publish It. Sell It.

First off, editing should be at the top of your list. Investing in professional editing is non-negotiable. A well-edited book is polished, free of errors, and enjoyable to read. Professional editors can enhance your book's structure, clarity, and overall quality, making it more appealing to readers and increasing its chances of success. Trust me, nothing turns off a reader faster than typos and poor grammar.

Next, cover design is equally important. A compelling cover design is crucial for attracting readers and boosting sales. Your book cover is the first thing potential readers see, and a professionally designed cover can make your book stand out in a crowded market. It's worth every penny because a high-quality cover significantly impacts your book's visibility and appeal.

When it comes to marketing, it's definitely vital for reaching your audience and driving book sales, but you don't have to spend a fortune. There are many cost-effective ways to promote your book. Utilize social media, engage with book bloggers, and collaborate with influencers to spread the word. Leverage free or low-cost tools and platforms to maximize your marketing efforts without breaking the bank.

Proper formatting ensures your book is readable and professional-looking in both print and digital formats. While it's important, you can find reasonably priced formatting services or even learn to format your book yourself using software tools. The key is to meet industry standards and provide a pleasant reading experience without overspending.

Lastly, think about additional features like custom illustrations or high-end marketing materials only if your budget allows. These extras can enhance your book, but they're not essential to its initial success. Focus on the core elements first, and if you have extra funds, you can invest in these additional features later.

By prioritizing your spending on professional editing and cover design, and finding cost-effective solutions for marketing and formatting, you ensure your book is well-prepared for success while staying within your financial limits. Additional features can wait until you have the budget for them. This strategic allocation of funds can make a significant difference in your book's journey from manuscript to bestseller. So, let's get smart about where we spend, ensuring every dollar works hard to make your book shine.

4. Track Your Spending

Use budgeting tools or spreadsheets to track your expenses and stay within your budget. Regularly review your budget to ensure you are on track and adjust as needed to avoid overspending.

- **Budgeting Tools**: Utilize tools like Excel, Google Sheets, or budgeting apps to monitor your spending.
- **Expense Tracking**: Record every expense related to your book, no matter how small, to get a clear picture of your total costs.
- **Regular Reviews**: Set aside time each month to review your budget and make any necessary adjustments.

Tracking your spending is a crucial part of managing your book's budget effectively. By using budgeting tools or spreadsheets, you can ensure you stay within your financial limits and make informed decisions about where to allocate your resources. Let's talk about how to do this in a way that's practical and easy to manage.

First, utilize budgeting tools like Excel, Google Sheets, or budgeting apps. These tools can help you monitor your spending with ease. Setting up a spreadsheet in Excel or Google Sheets allows you to list all your expected expenses and track actual costs as they occur. Budgeting apps can also be helpful, providing pre-built templates and automated features to simplify the process.

Next, make sure you're diligent about expense tracking. Record every expense related to your book, no matter how small, to get a clear picture of your total costs. This includes everything from major expenses like editing and cover design to smaller costs like shipping review copies or purchasing marketing materials. Keeping detailed records helps you see where your money is going and prevents any surprise costs from slipping through the cracks.

Regularly reviewing your budget is another essential step. Set aside time each month to go over your expenses and see how they align with your budget. This monthly review allows you to make any necessary adjustments before you overspend. If you notice that you're spending more on marketing than anticipated, for example, you can reallocate funds from other areas or find more cost-effective marketing strategies.

By using budgeting tools, meticulously tracking every expense, and conducting regular reviews, you can manage your book's budget effectively. This approach ensures you stay on track financially and can make adjustments as needed to avoid overspending. It's all about being proactive and organized, allowing you to focus more on the creative aspects of your book while keeping your finances in check. So, get those tools ready, start tracking your expenses, and regularly review your budget to keep everything on course. This way, you can enjoy the journey of publishing your book without the stress of financial surprises.

5. Plan for Contingencies

Unexpected expenses can arise during the publishing process. Allocate a portion of your budget for contingencies to cover unforeseen costs.

- **Emergency Fund**: Set aside 10-15% of your total budget as an emergency fund to cover unexpected expenses.
- **Flexible Spending**: Be prepared to reallocate funds from less critical areas if necessary.

Planning for contingencies is a smart strategy to ensure you're prepared for any unexpected expenses that may arise during the publishing process. Here's how you can effectively allocate a portion of your budget to handle unforeseen costs and keep your project on track.

First, establish an emergency fund. Allocate 10-15% of your total budget as a cushion to cover any unexpected expenses. This fund acts as a financial safety net, allowing you to handle surprises without derailing your entire budget. For example, if your total budget is $10,000, set aside $1,000 to $1,500 specifically for emergencies. This way, if you encounter unexpected costs—like additional editing rounds, last-minute marketing opportunities, or unexpected distribution fees—you have the resources to cover them without stress.

Next, maintain flexible spending within your budget. Be prepared to reallocate funds from less critical areas if necessary. This flexibility means that if you need more money for an essential aspect of your project, you can adjust your spending accordingly. For instance, if your initial cover design requires more work than anticipated, you might shift funds from your marketing or additional features budget to cover the extra costs.

To manage this effectively, keep a close eye on your budget and regularly review your expenses. By monitoring your spending and maintaining a flexible approach, you can make informed decisions about reallocating funds as needed. This proactive management helps ensure that you can handle any financial surprises that come your way.

Planning for contingencies is all about being prepared and adaptable. Setting aside an emergency fund and maintaining flexible spending options within your budget can save you from financial headaches and allow you to focus on successfully bringing your book to market. So, make sure to allocate that 10-15% for unexpected expenses and stay flexible with your spending. This approach will give you peace of mind and ensure you're ready to tackle any challenges that arise during your publishing journey.

6. Analyze and Adjust

After your book is published, analyze your financial performance and adjust your budget for future projects. Learn from your experience to improve your budgeting process.

- **Financial Analysis**: Compare your actual expenses and revenue against your budget and financial goals.
- **Identify Trends**: Look for patterns in your spending and revenue to identify areas for improvement.
- **Adjust Future Budgets**: Use the insights gained from your analysis to create more accurate budgets for future projects.

Once your book is published, it's essential to analyze your financial performance and adjust your budget for future projects. Learning from your experience will help you improve your budgeting process and ensure greater success with your next book. Here's how to go about it:

Financial Analysis

Start by comparing your actual expenses and revenue against your initial budget and financial goals. Did you spend more or less than you planned? How did your revenue stack up against your expectations? This comparison will give you a clear picture of your financial performance and highlight areas where you may need to make adjustments. For instance, if you allocated a large portion of your budget to marketing but didn't see the expected return, it might be worth re-evaluating your marketing strategies.

Identify Trends

Look for patterns in your spending and revenue to identify areas for improvement. Did certain expenses consistently exceed your budget? Were there revenue streams that performed better than others? Identifying these trends can help you understand where your money was well spent and where it might have been wasted. For example, if you notice that investing in professional editing significantly improved your book's reception and sales, you might decide to allocate more funds to editing in future projects.

Adjust Future Budgets

Use the insights gained from your analysis to create more accurate budgets for future projects. Adjust your spending in areas that underperformed and consider increasing your budget in areas that yielded positive results. This continuous improvement approach ensures that each new project benefits from the lessons learned during previous ones. For instance, if you found that attending book fairs provided excellent networking opportunities and boosted your sales, you might allocate more funds to travel and event participation in your next budget.

Conclusion

By estimating your costs, setting financial goals, allocating funds wisely, tracking your spending, planning for contingencies, and analyzing and adjusting your budget, you can navigate the financial aspects of publishing with confidence and success. This comprehensive approach ensures that you're prepared for any challenges and can make informed decisions to enhance your book's quality and reach.

In the next section, we will delve into essential investments, identifying key areas where spending money can significantly enhance your book's quality and reach. By focusing on these critical investments, you can maximize your book's potential and achieve greater success in the competitive publishing market. So, let's take the lessons learned from your financial analysis and use them to build a stronger, more effective strategy for your future projects.

Write It. Publish It. Sell It.

Essential Investments: Identifying key areas where spending money can enhance your book's quality and reach.

Essential Investments: Identifying Key Areas Where Spending Money Can Enhance Your Book's Quality and Reach

Investing wisely in key areas can significantly enhance your book's quality, appeal, and reach. By allocating your budget to these essential elements, you can ensure that your book stands out in a competitive market and resonates with readers. Here are the critical areas where spending money can have the most impact:

1. Professional Editing

Editing is perhaps the most critical investment you can make in your book. A well-edited manuscript is essential for readability, credibility, and overall quality.

- **Developmental Editing**: This type of editing focuses on the structure, content, and overall narrative of your book. A developmental editor will help you refine your plot, improve pacing, develop characters, and enhance the thematic depth of your story.
    - **Cost**: Developmental editing can range from $0.03 to $0.07 per word.
- **Copyediting**: Copyediting involves correcting grammar, punctuation, syntax, and consistency. A copyeditor ensures that your manuscript is polished and free of errors.

    - **Cost**: Copyediting typically costs between $0.02 and $0.04 per word.

- **Proofreading**: The final stage of editing, proofreading, involves catching any remaining typos, spelling mistakes, and minor errors.

    - **Cost**: Proofreading usually costs around $0.01 to $0.03 per word.

Hey there, new authors! Let's have a candid conversation about one of the most critical aspects of your book's success: professional editing. Trust me, I've learned this lesson the hard way, and I don't want you to make the same mistakes I did. You might think you can skip this step or find free alternatives, but let me tell you why investing in professional editing is absolutely essential.

First off, editing is not just about fixing typos—it's about transforming your manuscript into a polished, compelling, and high-quality book. Let's break down the types of editing you need and why each is crucial.

Developmental Editing

Think of developmental editing as the foundation of your book. This type of editing focuses on the structure, content, and overall narrative. A developmental editor helps you refine your plot, improve pacing, develop characters, and enhance the thematic depth of your story. They're like a personal trainer for your manuscript, pushing it to be the best it can be. You might balk at the cost, which can range from $0.03 to $0.07 per word, but the investment is worth it. Without this foundational work, your story might lack coherence and fail to engage readers.

Copyediting

Next up is copyediting, which involves correcting grammar, punctuation, syntax, and consistency. A copyeditor ensures that your manuscript is polished and free of errors. Imagine reading a book filled with grammatical mistakes and awkward sentences—it's distracting and unprofessional. Copyediting typically costs between $0.02 and $0.04 per word, and it's a step you can't afford to skip if you want your book to be taken seriously.

Proofreading

Finally, there's proofreading, the last line of defense against typos, spelling mistakes, and minor errors. Proofreading usually costs around $0.01 to $0.03 per word. It might seem like a small detail, but a few overlooked errors can make a big difference in how readers perceive your book. A clean, error-free manuscript shows that you care about quality and respect your readers.

The Wake-Up Call

Here's the wake-up call: you cannot do this for free. Sure, you might have a friend who's good at spotting typos or a family member who loves to read, but professional editing is a skill honed over years of experience. Free alternatives simply don't compare. Skimping on editing might save you money upfront, but it can cost you dearly in the long run—poor reviews, lost credibility, and a book that doesn't sell.

Investing in professional editing is an investment in your book's success. It's about presenting your best work to the world and respecting your readers' time and money. So, take it from someone who learned the hard way: don't cut corners on editing. Spend the money, get it done right, and set your book up for success. You, your book, and your readers deserve nothing less.

2. Cover Design

Your book cover is the first thing potential readers will see, making it a crucial element in attracting attention and conveying the essence of your book.

- **Professional Cover Designer**: Hire an experienced cover designer who understands the market and genre conventions. A professional cover can significantly increase your book's appeal and sales.

- **Cost**: Professional cover design can range from $300 to $1,000 or more, depending on the designer's experience and the complexity of the design.

This is the very first thing potential readers will see, and trust me, it's crucial for attracting attention and conveying the essence of your book. I learned this the hard way, and I want you to avoid the mistakes I made. Here's why investing in a professional cover designer is non-negotiable.

The Importance of a Professional Cover Designer

Your book cover is like the packaging of a product—if it doesn't look appealing, people won't pick it up, no matter how amazing the content inside might be. A professional cover designer understands the market and genre conventions. They know what elements attract readers in your specific genre and how to make your book stand out on a crowded shelf or a busy webpage.

Hiring an experienced cover designer can significantly increase your book's appeal and sales. Think about it: a stunning, genre-appropriate cover grabs attention, creates intrigue, and can be the deciding factor for a potential reader choosing your book over another. It's not just about looking good; it's about signaling to readers that your book is worth their time and money.

The Investment

Yes, professional cover design comes with a cost. You can expect to pay anywhere from $300 to $1,000 or more, depending on the designer's experience and the complexity of the design. But here's the thing—this is not an area where you want to cut corners. A poorly designed cover can make your book look amateurish and turn off potential readers before they even read the first page.

The Wake-Up Call

Here's your wake-up call: DIY covers or cheap alternatives simply won't cut it in today's competitive market. Sure, you can try to design your cover yourself or hire a bargain-basement designer, but these options often lack the professional touch that makes a book stand out. A professional designer brings expertise, creativity, and an understanding of what sells.

Investing in a professional cover designer is about giving your book the best possible chance to succeed. It's about respecting your readers and showing them that you've put in the effort to create something truly special. So, don't skimp on this crucial element. Spend the money, hire a pro, and watch your book shine. Remember, your cover is the first impression readers will have of your book—make it a great one!

3. Interior Formatting

Proper interior formatting ensures that your book is readable and professionally presented, whether in print or digital format.

- **Print Formatting**: Professional formatting for print editions ensures that your book meets industry standards and is visually appealing. This includes proper margins, fonts, spacing, and chapter headings.
  - **Cost**: Print formatting services typically range from $200 to $500.

- **Ebook Formatting**: Formatting for digital editions involves creating files that are compatible with various e-readers and platforms. This includes ensuring proper text flow, clickable links, and navigation.
  - **Cost**: Ebook formatting services generally cost between $100 and $300.

Hello, future bestsellers! Let's chat about a crucial yet often overlooked aspect of book publishing: interior formatting. Proper interior formatting ensures that your book is readable and professionally presented, whether in print or digital format. Trust me, I learned the importance of this the hard way, and I want to help you avoid the same pitfalls. Here's why investing in professional formatting is essential for your book's success.

Print Formatting

When it comes to print editions, professional formatting ensures that your book meets industry standards and is visually appealing. This includes proper margins, fonts, spacing, and chapter headings. Imagine picking up a book where the text is too close to the edge, the font changes randomly, or the spacing is inconsistent—it's distracting and can make the reading experience unpleasant.

A professionally formatted book, on the other hand, is a joy to read. Everything is where it should be, and it looks polished and inviting. This kind of attention to detail shows your readers that you care about their reading experience. The cost for print formatting services typically ranges from $200 to $500, and it's worth every penny to ensure your book looks its best.

Ebook Formatting

Formatting for digital editions is just as important as print. Ebooks need to be compatible with various e-readers and platforms, and this requires a different set of skills. Proper ebook formatting includes ensuring that the text flows correctly, links are clickable, and navigation is smooth. Think about how frustrating it is to read an ebook with broken links or text that doesn't resize properly on your device.

Professional ebook formatting makes sure your digital book looks great and functions well across all devices. This not only enhances the reader's experience but also reduces the likelihood of negative reviews based on technical issues. Ebook formatting services generally cost between $100 and $300, a small investment for the potential return in reader satisfaction and sales.

The Wake-Up Call

Here's the wake-up call: you cannot afford to overlook interior formatting. DIY options or cheap services often result in subpar formatting that can distract and frustrate readers. This can lead to poor reviews and a damaged reputation, both of which are hard to recover from. Professional formatting is a small price to pay for ensuring that your book is presented in the best possible light.

By investing in professional print and ebook formatting, you're not just making your book look good—you're showing your readers that you respect their time and attention. Proper formatting enhances readability, making your book more enjoyable and accessible. So, don't skimp on this vital step. Allocate the necessary funds, hire a professional, and ensure your book meets the highest standards. Your readers—and your future self—will thank you.

4. Illustrations and Graphics

If your book requires illustrations or graphics, investing in high-quality artwork can greatly enhance its appeal and value.

- **Illustrations**: Whether you need cover art, interior illustrations, or diagrams, hire a professional illustrator to create visually compelling images that complement your text.
  - **Cost**: The cost of illustrations can vary widely depending on the complexity and number of illustrations needed, typically ranging from $50 to $500 per illustration.

Hey there, creative minds! Let's dive into another critical aspect of your book's presentation: illustrations and graphics. If your book requires visual elements, investing in high-quality artwork can significantly enhance its appeal and value. Trust me, I've seen firsthand how powerful great illustrations can be, and I want to share why this investment is worth every penny.

The Power of Professional Illustrations

Whether you need cover art, interior illustrations, or diagrams, hiring a professional illustrator is essential. A talented illustrator can create visually compelling images that complement your text and bring your story to life. Imagine a children's book without vibrant, engaging illustrations or a technical book without clear, helpful diagrams—it just wouldn't have the same impact.

Professional illustrations do more than just make your book look good; they enhance the reader's experience and help convey your message more effectively. High-quality artwork can captivate readers, draw them into your world, and make your book memorable. This is especially crucial for genres like children's books, graphic novels, and instructional manuals where visuals play a central role.

The Investment

Now, let's talk about costs. The price of illustrations can vary widely depending on the complexity and number of illustrations needed. You might pay anywhere from $50 to $500 per illustration. While this might seem steep, think of it as an investment in your book's overall quality and marketability. High-quality illustrations can make your book stand out, attract more readers, and even justify a higher price point.

The Wake-Up Call

Here's your wake-up call: don't try to cut corners with illustrations and graphics. Free or low-cost alternatives often lack the professionalism and creativity that a skilled illustrator brings to the table. Amateurish or poorly done illustrations can detract from your book's quality and turn off potential readers.

Investing in professional artwork is about more than just aesthetics; it's about enhancing your book's value and ensuring it resonates with your audience. High-quality illustrations show that you're serious about your work and respect your readers enough to give them the best possible experience.

Making the Decision

When deciding how much to invest in illustrations, consider your book's genre and target audience. For example, children's books and graphic novels will require a larger budget for artwork, while a novel might only need a stunning cover design. Work with your illustrator to develop a budget that aligns with your needs and ensures high-quality results.

Conclusion

Investing in high-quality illustrations and graphics can elevate your book, making it more appealing and valuable to readers. By hiring a professional illustrator, you ensure that your visual elements are compelling and complementary to your text. Yes, it's an investment, but one that pays off in reader engagement and satisfaction.

So, don't skimp on this critical aspect of your book's presentation. Allocate the necessary funds, find a talented illustrator, and bring your book's visuals to life. Your readers will appreciate the effort, and your book will stand out in a crowded market. Let's make your book not just a read, but a visual delight!

5. ISBN and Distribution

Obtaining ISBNs (International Standard Book Numbers) and arranging for distribution are essential steps in making your book available to readers.

- **ISBNs:** Purchase ISBNs for both print and digital editions of your book. ISBNs are required for selling your book through major retailers and libraries.

- **Cost**: ISBNs can be purchased individually or in bulk from agencies like Bowker in the U.S., with prices ranging from $125 for a single ISBN to $295 for a block of ten.

- **Distribution Services**: Use print-on-demand services like Amazon KDP and IngramSpark to distribute your book. These platforms handle printing and shipping, reducing upfront costs and logistical challenges.

   - **Cost**: Distribution setup fees range from free (Amazon KDP) to around $49 for print setup (IngramSpark), plus a per-copy printing cost.

Hey, **self-publishing authors**! Let's talk about two essential steps in getting your book out to readers: obtaining ISBNs and arranging for distribution. These steps are critical for making your book available through major retailers and libraries, and ensuring it reaches your audience effectively. Trust me, handling this properly can make a huge difference in your book's accessibility and success.

ISBNs: Your Book's Unique Identifier

First off, let's discuss ISBNs (International Standard Book Numbers). These are unique identifiers required for selling your book through major retailers and libraries. Think of an ISBN as your book's social security number—it's essential for tracking and sales.

You need to purchase ISBNs for both print and digital editions of your book. In the U.S., you can buy ISBNs from agencies like Bowker. The cost can range from $125 for a single ISBN to $295 for a block of ten. While this might seem like an extra expense, it's crucial for ensuring your book is properly cataloged and easily found by readers and retailers alike.

Distribution Services: Getting Your Book Out There

Next, let's talk about distribution. Using print-on-demand services like Amazon KDP and IngramSpark is a smart move for self-publishing authors. These platforms handle printing and shipping, which reduces upfront costs and logistical challenges.

Amazon KDP offers free distribution setup, making it an accessible option for many authors. IngramSpark, on the other hand, charges around $49 for print setup, plus a per-copy printing cost. While IngramSpark's fees might be higher, they offer broader distribution options, including access to bookstores and libraries that might not order through Amazon.

The Wake-Up Call

Here's your wake-up call: as a self-publishing author, you can't afford to skip these steps. Traditional and hybrid publishers typically handle these details for you, but in self-publishing, it's all on you. Skimping on ISBNs or opting for limited distribution can severely restrict your book's reach and sales potential.

Investing in ISBNs ensures your book is correctly cataloged and available through major sales channels. Using reliable distribution services like Amazon KDP and IngramSpark makes your book accessible to a wider audience, increasing your chances of success.

Conclusion

For self-publishing authors, obtaining ISBNs and arranging for distribution are non-negotiable steps. Purchase ISBNs to ensure your book is properly identified and available through major retailers. Utilize print-on-demand services like Amazon KDP and IngramSpark to handle printing and shipping, reducing your upfront costs and logistical challenges.

Yes, there are costs involved—$125 to $295 for ISBNs and up to $49 for distribution setup—but these investments are crucial for your book's accessibility and success. So, don't cut corners on these essentials. Take the necessary steps to ensure your book reaches the readers who are waiting to discover it. Let's get your book out there and into the hands of your audience!

6. Marketing and Promotion

Effective marketing and promotion are essential for reaching your target audience and driving book sales.

- **Book Launch**: Plan a comprehensive book launch campaign to generate buzz and attract readers. This can include a launch event, social media promotion, and email marketing.

    - **Cost**: Book launch expenses can vary, but a well-executed campaign can cost between $500 and $2,000.

- **Paid Advertising**: Invest in paid advertising on platforms like Facebook, Amazon, and Google to increase visibility and drive traffic to your book's sales page.

    - **Cost**: Advertising budgets can range from $100 to $1,000 or more per month, depending on your goals and reach.

- **Public Relations**: Hire a publicist or PR firm to secure media coverage, book reviews, and interviews. Professional PR can significantly boost your book's visibility and credibility.

    - **Cost**: PR services can range from $500 to $5,000 or more, depending on the scope and duration of the campaign.

Let's dive into a critical aspect of your book's success: marketing and promotion. Effective marketing is essential for reaching your target audience and driving book sales. I've learned that skimping on marketing is not an option if you want your book to thrive. Let's break down the key components of a successful marketing strategy.

Book Launch

First, plan a comprehensive book launch campaign to generate buzz and attract readers. Your book launch is your first big splash, so make it count. This can include a launch event, social media promotion, and email marketing. A well-executed campaign can vary in cost but generally falls between $500 and $2,000. This investment is crucial for creating excitement and getting your book in front of as many potential readers as possible.

Paid Advertising

Next, consider investing in paid advertising. Platforms like Facebook, Amazon, and Google offer targeted advertising options that can significantly increase your book's visibility and drive traffic to your sales page. Depending on your goals and reach, advertising budgets can range from $100 to $1,000 or more per month. Paid ads are a powerful tool for reaching a larger audience and boosting sales, especially if you target the right demographics.

Public Relations

Public relations (PR) is another essential component of your marketing strategy. Hiring a publicist or PR firm can help secure media coverage, book reviews, and interviews. Professional PR can significantly boost your book's visibility and credibility. Costs for PR services can range from $500 to $5,000 or more, depending on the scope and duration of the campaign. While this might seem like a hefty investment, the credibility and exposure gained through PR can be invaluable.

A Special Plug for Trient Evolve

Speaking of effective marketing strategies, I highly recommend checking out [Trient Evolve](). They offer a range of services designed to help authors like you maximize your book's potential. From comprehensive marketing plans to targeted advertising and PR services, Trient Evolve can provide the support you need to succeed. Investing in professional marketing services can make a significant difference in your book's reach and sales, and Trient Evolve is an excellent resource to consider.

Conclusion

Investing in marketing and promotion is non-negotiable if you want your book to succeed. A comprehensive book launch, targeted paid advertising, and professional public relations are all critical components of an effective marketing strategy. Yes, these efforts come with costs—ranging from $500 to $5,000 or more—but they are essential for reaching your audience and driving sales.

Don't cut corners on marketing. Plan a robust book launch, invest in paid ads, and consider hiring a PR professional to secure the coverage your book deserves. And remember, resources like Trient Evolve can provide invaluable support to help you navigate the complexities of book marketing. Let's get your book the attention it deserves and reach those readers who are waiting to discover your story!

7. Author Website

A professional author website serves as your online hub, providing information about you and your books, and facilitating direct communication with readers.

- **Website Design and Hosting**: Invest in a professionally designed website that is visually appealing, user-friendly, and optimized for search engines.
    - **Cost**: Website design services typically range from $500 to $3,000, with additional costs for domain registration and hosting (around $100 per year).

Let's talk about one of the most important tools in your marketing arsenal: your author website. A professional author website serves as your online hub, providing information about you and your books, and facilitating direct communication with your readers. Trust me, having a polished, user-friendly website is essential for establishing your online presence and building your brand. Here's why investing in a professional website is a must.

Write It. Publish It. Sell It.

Website Design and Hosting

First, let's focus on the design and hosting of your website. Investing in a professionally designed website ensures that it is visually appealing, user-friendly, and optimized for search engines. Your website is often the first place potential readers will visit to learn more about you and your books, so it needs to make a great first impression.

A professional web designer can create a site that reflects your unique brand and meets industry standards. This includes responsive design (so it looks great on all devices), easy navigation, and SEO optimization to help people find you online. Costs for website design services typically range from $500 to $3,000. Additionally, you'll need to budget for domain registration and hosting, which are usually around $100 per year.

The Value of a Professional Website

So why is this investment so important? Your author website is the central hub for all your online activities. It's where readers can find detailed information about your books, sign up for your newsletter, read your blog, and contact you directly. A professional, well-maintained website builds credibility and trust with your audience. It shows that you're serious about your writing career and provides a platform for you to engage with your readers on a deeper level.

What to Include on Your Website

Here are some key elements to include on your author website:

1. **About Page:** Share your story, your writing journey, and what inspires you. Let readers get to know the person behind the books.
2. **Books Page:** Showcase your books with detailed descriptions, cover images, purchase links, and reviews.
3. **Blog:** Regularly update your blog with posts about your writing process, book updates, and other relevant topics to engage your audience.

4. **Newsletter Sign-Up:** Encourage visitors to join your mailing list for exclusive updates and content.
5. **Contact Information:** Make it easy for readers, media, and other professionals to reach you.

Conclusion

Investing in a professional author website is non-negotiable if you want to establish a strong online presence and connect with your readers effectively. The cost of website design and hosting might seem like a significant expense, ranging from $500 to $3,000 for design and about $100 per year for domain and hosting. However, the return on this investment is invaluable.

A well-designed, user-friendly website not only enhances your credibility but also provides a central hub for all your promotional activities. It's a space where you can share your journey, showcase your books, and engage with your audience in meaningful ways.

So, don't skimp on this essential tool. Invest in a professional website and create an online presence that truly represents you and your work. Let's build a digital home that your readers will love to visit and explore!

8. Book Reviews and Endorsements

Positive reviews and endorsements can enhance your book's credibility and attract new readers.

- **Review Copies**: Send out review copies to bloggers, reviewers, and influencers in your genre. This can lead to valuable reviews and endorsements.
    - **Cost**: The cost of review copies can vary depending on the number of copies sent and whether they are print or digital editions.

9. Professional Associations and Memberships

Joining professional associations can provide valuable resources, networking opportunities, and credibility.

- **Membership Fees**: Consider joining organizations like the Authors Guild, Romance Writers of America (RWA), or the Society of Children's Book Writers and Illustrators (SCBWI).
  - **Cost**: Membership fees typically range from $50 to $150 per year.

By investing in these essential areas, you can significantly enhance your book's quality and reach, ensuring a professional and successful publication. In the next section, we will explore cost-effective solutions for various publishing expenses, helping you make the most of your budget while maintaining high standards.

Hey, fellow authors! Let's discuss the benefits of joining professional associations and memberships. These organizations provide valuable resources, networking opportunities, and an added layer of credibility to your author brand. Trust me, being part of a professional community can significantly enhance your career and open up new opportunities. Here's why investing in memberships is worth it.

The Value of Professional Associations

Joining professional associations like the Authors Guild, Romance Writers of America (RWA), or the Society of Children's Book Writers and Illustrators (SCBWI) can be incredibly beneficial. These organizations offer a wealth of resources tailored to your genre and writing needs. From legal advice and contract reviews to writing workshops and marketing tips, the support you receive can be invaluable.

Networking is another significant advantage. Being part of a professional community allows you to connect with fellow authors, industry experts, and potential collaborators. Attending conferences, participating in webinars, and joining online forums can lead to meaningful connections and opportunities that you might not find on your own.

Credibility is also enhanced when you're a member of a reputable association. Readers, publishers, and other industry professionals recognize these memberships as a mark of professionalism and commitment to your craft. It shows that you're serious about your writing career and are continually striving to improve and grow.

Membership Fees

Of course, there's a cost involved. Membership fees for these organizations typically range from $50 to $150 per year. While this is an additional expense, the benefits far outweigh the costs. The resources, networking opportunities, and credibility you gain can significantly boost your career and help you achieve your publishing goals.

Conclusion

Investing in professional associations and memberships is a smart move for any serious author. The resources, networking opportunities, and credibility these organizations provide are invaluable. Membership fees, ranging from $50 to $150 per year, are a small price to pay for the potential benefits.

By joining organizations like the Authors Guild, Romance Writers of America (RWA), or the Society of Children's Book Writers and Illustrators (SCBWI), you're investing in your career and positioning yourself for success. These memberships provide the support and connections needed to navigate the complex world of publishing.

Write It. Publish It. Sell It.

Next Steps: Cost-Effective Solutions

In the next section, we will explore cost-effective solutions for various publishing expenses, helping you make the most of your budget while maintaining high standards. Stay tuned to learn how you can strategically manage your funds without compromising on quality. Let's ensure your book shines brightly in a competitive market!

Cost-Effective Solutions: Finding affordable alternatives for various publishing expenses.

While investing in essential areas is crucial for a successful book launch, it's also important to manage your budget wisely. Finding cost-effective solutions for various publishing expenses can help you maintain high standards without overspending. Here are some strategies and alternatives to keep your publishing journey affordable.

1. Freelance Services

Hiring freelancers can be a budget-friendly way to access professional services without the overhead costs of larger companies.

- **Editing**: Platforms like Upwork, Fiverr, and Reedsy offer access to freelance editors at competitive rates. Look for editors with good reviews and experience in your genre.
  - **Cost**: Freelance editing rates can be lower than those of established editing firms, typically ranging from $0.01 to $0.03 per word.
- **Cover Design**: Freelance designers can provide high-quality cover designs at a fraction of the cost of larger design firms. Websites like 99designs and DeviantArt can help you find talented designers.
  - **Cost**: Freelance cover design can range from $100 to $500.

Let's talk about a fantastic way to access professional services without breaking the bank: hiring freelancers. Utilizing freelance services can be a budget-friendly method to get high-quality support for your book. Whether you need editing or cover design, freelancers offer competitive rates and personalized service. Here's why and how you should consider hiring freelancers for your book project.

Editing

First up, let's discuss editing. Platforms like Upwork, Fiverr, and Reedsy are excellent places to find freelance editors. These platforms allow you to browse through profiles, read reviews, and see past work to ensure you're hiring someone with the right experience and skills for your genre. Freelance editors often charge lower rates than established editing firms, typically ranging from $0.01 to $0.03 per word. This can be a cost-effective way to get professional editing services without sacrificing quality.

When choosing a freelance editor, look for those with good reviews and specific experience in your genre. A well-matched editor can make a significant difference in polishing your manuscript and making it the best it can be.

Cover Design

Next, let's talk about cover design. Freelance designers can provide high-quality cover designs at a fraction of the cost of larger design firms. Websites like 99designs and DeviantArt are great resources for finding talented designers who can create a compelling cover that captures the essence of your book.

Freelance cover design costs typically range from $100 to $500. By hiring a freelancer, you can get a unique, professional cover that stands out in the market without spending a fortune. Look for designers with a portfolio that resonates with your vision and check their reviews to ensure reliability and quality.

Write It. Publish It. Sell It.

The Wake-Up Call

Here's the wake-up call: don't underestimate the value of professional services just because they come at a lower cost. Freelancers can offer personalized, high-quality work tailored to your needs. However, it's crucial to do your due diligence—review their portfolios, read client testimonials, and communicate your expectations clearly.

Freelancers provide a flexible and budget-friendly option for accessing the professional support you need to make your book shine. With the right freelancer, you can achieve excellent results without the overhead costs of larger companies.

Conclusion

Hiring freelancers for editing and cover design can be a smart, budget-friendly choice. Platforms like Upwork, Fiverr, Reedsy, 99designs, and DeviantArt offer access to skilled professionals at competitive rates. Freelance editing typically costs between $0.01 and $0.03 per word, while freelance cover design ranges from $100 to $500.

By carefully selecting freelancers with good reviews and relevant experience, you can get high-quality services that enhance your book's quality and appeal. This approach allows you to allocate your budget more efficiently while still ensuring professional results.

In the next section, we'll continue exploring cost-effective solutions for various publishing expenses, helping you make the most of your budget without compromising on quality. Let's keep your book project on track and within budget, while still aiming for excellence!

2. DIY Options

If you have the skills and time, doing some tasks yourself can save money.

- **Formatting**: Use software like Scrivener, Vellum, or Adobe InDesign to format your book for print and digital editions. These tools are user-friendly and offer professional-quality results.
    - **Cost**: Software like Scrivener ($49), Vellum ($199 for ebooks, $249 for print+ebook), and Adobe InDesign (monthly subscription around $20) can be cost-effective compared to hiring a formatter.
- **Cover Design**: If you have a knack for design, use tools like Canva or Adobe Photoshop to create your book cover. Canva offers templates that can help you create a professional-looking cover.
    - **Cost**: Canva is free with premium options available, while Photoshop requires a monthly subscription (~$20/month).

If you have the skills and the time, doing some tasks yourself can save money. However, seeking professional help is always the better route to ensure top-notch quality. Let's explore when and how you might consider taking the DIY approach for formatting and cover design.

Formatting

First, let's discuss formatting. If you're tech-savvy and enjoy learning new tools, formatting your book yourself can be a viable option. Software like Scrivener, Vellum, and Adobe InDesign are designed to help authors format their books for both print and digital editions.

- **Scrivener**: Priced at $49, Scrivener is a versatile writing tool that also offers robust formatting features. It's user-friendly and particularly helpful for organizing and structuring your manuscript.
- **Vellum**: At $199 for ebooks and $249 for print+ebook, Vellum is an excellent tool for creating professional-quality book formats. It's highly intuitive, making it a favorite among indie authors.
- **Adobe InDesign**: With a monthly subscription of around $20, Adobe InDesign is a powerful tool for those familiar with graphic design. It offers advanced formatting options and professional-quality results.

If you're comfortable with these tools and have the time to learn and execute the formatting process, DIY formatting can be cost-effective. However, if you're unsure or pressed for time, hiring a professional formatter might be the wiser choice to ensure your book meets industry standards.

Cover Design

Next, let's talk about cover design. If you have a knack for design and a good eye for aesthetics, creating your own book cover can be an option. Tools like Canva and Adobe Photoshop are popular among DIY designers.

- **Canva**: Canva is free with premium options available. It offers numerous templates that can help you create a professional-looking cover without extensive design skills.
- **Adobe Photoshop**: With a monthly subscription of around $20, Photoshop provides advanced design capabilities for those who are proficient in graphic design.

Designing your own cover can save money, but remember, your book cover is the first thing potential readers will see. If you're confident in your design skills, go for it. However, if there's any doubt, investing in a professional cover designer is a safer bet to ensure your book makes a great first impression.

The Wake-Up Call

Here's the wake-up call: DIY options can save money, but they require a significant investment of time and skill. If you're up for the challenge and feel confident in your abilities, DIY can be a great way to cut costs. However, if you're uncertain or time-constrained, seeking professional help is always the better option. Professionals bring expertise and experience that can make a significant difference in the quality and success of your book.

Conclusion

DIY options are a cost-effective way to manage some aspects of your book project, provided you have the necessary skills and time. Tools like Scrivener, Vellum, and Adobe InDesign can help you format your book professionally, while Canva and Adobe Photoshop can assist with cover design.

However, the decision to go DIY should be made with careful consideration of your capabilities and time availability. While DIY can save money, the quality of your book should never be compromised. If in doubt, hiring a professional is always a better choice to ensure your book meets high standards and appeals to your audience.

In the next section, we'll continue exploring cost-effective solutions for various publishing expenses, helping you make the most of your budget while maintaining high standards. Let's keep your book project on track and within budget, aiming for excellence at every step!

3. Barter and Trade

Exchanging services with other authors or creatives can be a mutually beneficial way to reduce costs.

- **Editing and Beta Reading**: Trade editing or beta reading services with fellow authors. This can provide valuable feedback and improve your manuscript without additional costs.
- **Design and Marketing**: If you have skills in design, marketing, or another area, offer your services in exchange for professional editing or other needed services.

Let's explore a smart and budget-friendly way to manage your book's production costs: bartering and trading services. Exchanging services with other authors or creatives can be a mutually beneficial way to reduce costs while still maintaining high quality. Here's how you can effectively use bartering to enhance your book project.

Write It. Publish It. Sell It.

Editing and Beta Reading

One of the most straightforward ways to barter is by trading editing or beta reading services with fellow authors. This can provide valuable feedback and improve your manuscript without any additional cost. Here's how you can make it work:

- **Join Writing Groups**: Engage with writing communities, either online or locally, to find authors willing to trade services. Platforms like Scribophile, Wattpad, and local writing clubs are great places to start.
- **Set Clear Expectations**: When trading editing or beta reading services, be clear about what each party will provide. Define the scope, deadlines, and specific areas of focus to ensure a fair and productive exchange.
- **Provide Constructive Feedback**: Treat the process professionally. Offer detailed, constructive feedback, and be open to receiving the same. This mutual support can significantly enhance both parties' manuscripts.

Design and Marketing

If you have skills in design, marketing, or another valuable area, consider offering your services in exchange for professional editing or other needed services. Here's how to leverage your talents:

- **Identify Your Strengths**: Determine what skills you can offer. Whether it's graphic design, website creation, social media marketing, or copywriting, there's likely another author or creative who needs your expertise.
- **Network with Creatives**: Connect with other authors, designers, and marketers through professional networks like LinkedIn, creative communities like DeviantArt, or social media groups focused on writing and publishing.
- **Propose a Trade**: Reach out to potential collaborators with a clear proposal. For example, you might offer to design a book cover or manage a marketing campaign in exchange for developmental editing or proofreading services. Ensure that both parties feel the trade is fair and beneficial.

The Wake-Up Call

Here's your wake-up call: bartering and trading services can be an excellent way to manage costs, but it requires professionalism and clear communication. Treat these exchanges with the same seriousness as paid services to ensure high-quality results and maintain good relationships.

Bartering can be especially useful if you're just starting out and need to stretch your budget. By exchanging skills with others in the community, you can access professional-quality services without the financial outlay, while also helping others achieve their goals.

Conclusion

Bartering and trading services with fellow authors and creatives is a cost-effective strategy that can help you reduce expenses and maintain high standards for your book project. Whether you're trading editing and beta reading or leveraging your design and marketing skills, these exchanges can provide mutual benefits.

Engage with writing communities, identify your strengths, and propose fair trades to enhance your book without stretching your budget. Remember, clear communication and professionalism are key to successful bartering.

In the next section, we'll continue exploring additional cost-effective solutions for various publishing expenses, helping you make the most of your budget while maintaining high standards. Let's keep finding innovative ways to ensure your book's success without breaking the bank!

4. Pre-made Covers

Purchasing pre-made book covers can be a cost-effective alternative to custom designs.

- **Online Marketplaces**: Websites like The Book Cover Designer, SelfPubBookCovers, and GoOnWrite offer a wide selection of pre-made covers at affordable prices.

    - **Cost**: Pre-made covers typically range from $50 to $150.

5. Print-on-Demand Services

Using print-on-demand (POD) services can significantly reduce upfront printing costs.

- **Amazon KDP and IngramSpark**: These platforms offer POD services that allow you to print copies of your book as they are ordered. This eliminates the need for large print runs and reduces financial risk.

    - **Cost**: Amazon KDP has no upfront costs, while IngramSpark charges a setup fee (~$49) plus printing costs.

6. Affordable Marketing and Promotion

Effective marketing doesn't have to break the bank. There are many affordable strategies to promote your book.

- **Social Media Marketing**: Utilize free social media platforms to build your author brand and engage with readers. Consistent posting, engaging content, and interactions can create a strong online presence.

    - **Cost**: Free, with optional paid advertising to boost reach.

- **Email Marketing**: Use affordable email marketing services like Mailchimp or MailerLite to build and maintain an email list. Offer incentives like free chapters or exclusive content to encourage sign-ups.

    - **Cost**: Free plans are available for small lists, with paid options starting at around $10 per month.

- **Book Review Services**: Sites like BookSirens and NetGalley offer affordable packages to get your book in front of reviewers.

- **Cost**: Packages can range from $50 to $400 depending on the level of service.

7. Libraries and Community Resources

Leverage local resources for cost-effective promotion and support.

- **Library Programs**: Many libraries offer author talks, book signings, and local author showcases. These events can provide valuable exposure at no cost.
- **Community Centers**: Partner with community centers to host events, workshops, or readings. These venues often welcome local authors and can help with promotion.

8. Crowdfunding

Crowdfunding can help cover your publishing expenses and generate early interest in your book.

- **Platforms**: Use platforms like Kickstarter, Indiegogo, or GoFundMe to raise funds for your book. Offer backers exclusive rewards such as signed copies, special editions, or early access.
  - **Cost**: Crowdfunding platforms typically take a small percentage of the funds raised (around 5%).

9. Grants and Contests

Look for grants and contests that provide funding or other resources for authors.

- **Writing Grants**: Organizations like the National Endowment for the Arts and local arts councils offer grants for writers. Research and apply for grants that align with your project.
  - **Cost**: Free to apply, with potential funding if awarded.

- **Writing Contests**: Enter writing contests that offer cash prizes, publishing contracts, or promotional support. Winning or placing in contests can provide valuable recognition and resources.
    - **Cost**: Entry fees vary, typically ranging from $10 to $50.

By utilizing these cost-effective solutions, you can maintain high standards for your book while managing your budget efficiently. In the next section, we will explore common financial pitfalls and provide strategies for avoiding them, ensuring a smooth and successful publishing journey.

Financial Pitfalls: Common money mistakes and how to avoid them.

Navigating the financial aspects of publishing can be challenging, especially for first-time authors. Avoiding common financial pitfalls is crucial to ensuring your publishing journey is smooth and successful. Here are some typical money mistakes authors make and strategies to avoid them.

1. Overestimating Sales

One of the most common pitfalls is overestimating how many books you will sell, leading to overspending on inventory and marketing.

- **Realistic Sales Projections**: Be conservative in your sales estimates. Research similar books in your genre to gauge realistic sales numbers.
- **Start Small**: Initially print a smaller batch of books if you're using a traditional printer, or use print-on-demand services to avoid large upfront printing costs.
- **Monitor Sales Trends**: Regularly track your sales data and adjust your marketing strategies accordingly. Be prepared to scale up or down based on actual performance.

Let's have an honest conversation about a common mistake that can derail your book publishing efforts: overestimating sales. It's easy to get caught up in the excitement and optimism of launching your book, but overestimating how many copies you'll sell can lead to overspending on inventory and marketing. Let's discuss how to set realistic expectations and manage your resources wisely.

Realistic Sales Projections

First and foremost, be conservative in your sales estimates. It's essential to ground your projections in reality rather than hope. Research similar books in your genre to gauge what kind of sales numbers are realistic. Look at how debut authors in your category are performing and use that data to inform your estimates. This approach helps you avoid the trap of assuming your book will immediately be a bestseller, which, while possible, is not a guarantee.

Start Small

If you're using a traditional printer, consider printing a smaller batch of books initially. This reduces the risk of ending up with unsold inventory and high storage costs. Alternatively, use print-on-demand services like Amazon KDP or IngramSpark. Print-on-demand allows you to print copies as they're ordered, eliminating the need for a large upfront investment in printing and reducing financial risk.

By starting small, you can gauge the initial market response and decide whether it makes sense to print more copies. This approach keeps your investment manageable and allows for flexibility.

Monitor Sales Trends

Regularly track your sales data and adjust your marketing strategies accordingly. Tools like Amazon's Author Central, Google Analytics, and social media insights can provide valuable information about how your book is performing. Be prepared to scale up or down based on actual performance. If your book starts gaining traction, you can invest more in marketing and inventory. If sales are slower than expected, you can adjust your strategies without having already spent too much.

The Wake-Up Call

Here's the wake-up call: overestimating sales can lead to significant financial losses. It's easy to get swept up in enthusiasm, but it's crucial to approach your sales projections with a clear-eyed realism. By being conservative in your estimates, starting small, and monitoring sales trends, you can manage your resources more effectively and avoid unnecessary expenses.

Conclusion

Overestimating sales is a common pitfall that can lead to overspending and financial strain. Set realistic sales projections by researching similar books in your genre. Start with a smaller batch of printed books or use print-on-demand services to minimize upfront costs. Regularly monitor your sales data and be prepared to adjust your marketing strategies based on actual performance.

By taking these steps, you can manage your expectations and resources wisely, ensuring a more sustainable and successful book launch. In the next section, we will explore additional cost-effective solutions for various publishing expenses, helping you make the most of your budget while maintaining high standards. Let's keep your book project on track and within budget, all while aiming for excellence!

2. Skipping Professional Services

Cutting corners on essential services like editing, cover design, and formatting can severely impact the quality and success of your book.

- **Prioritize Quality**: Allocate a significant portion of your budget to professional editing and cover design. These elements are crucial for making a good first impression and ensuring reader satisfaction.

- **Research Providers**: Take the time to find reputable service providers with good reviews and proven track records. Don't simply go for the cheapest option.
- **Get Multiple Quotes**: Obtain quotes from several professionals to ensure you're getting a fair price for quality work.

Let's tackle a critical topic that can make or break your book's success: skipping professional services. Cutting corners on essential services like editing, cover design, and formatting can severely impact your book's quality and reception. I've seen this mistake too many times, and it's one you'll want to avoid. Here's why prioritizing these services is vital and how to do it wisely.

Prioritize Quality

First and foremost, allocate a significant portion of your budget to professional editing and cover design. These elements are not just nice-to-haves—they're crucial for making a good first impression and ensuring reader satisfaction. A well-edited book reads smoothly and keeps readers engaged, while a professionally designed cover attracts attention and conveys the book's genre and tone. Investing in these areas shows readers that you take your work seriously and respect their time and money.

Research Providers

Don't just go for the cheapest option when selecting service providers. Take the time to find reputable professionals with good reviews and proven track records. Look for editors and designers who have experience in your genre and a portfolio of successful projects. Websites like Reedsy, Upwork, and even author forums can be great places to find vetted professionals. Remember, quality work often comes at a higher price, but it's an investment in your book's success.

Get Multiple Quotes

To ensure you're getting a fair price for quality work, obtain quotes from several professionals. This not only gives you a range of prices but also helps you compare the scope of services offered. When requesting quotes, be clear about your project's requirements and deadlines. This clarity will help professionals provide accurate estimates and ensure there are no surprises later on.

The Wake-Up Call

Here's your wake-up call: skipping professional services to save money can end up costing you more in the long run. A poorly edited book or an amateurish cover can turn readers away and result in negative reviews, which are hard to recover from. Investing in professional editing, cover design, and formatting is not just about making your book look good—it's about ensuring it meets industry standards and provides a high-quality reading experience.

Conclusion

Skipping professional services is a costly mistake that can severely impact your book's quality and success. Prioritize quality by allocating a significant portion of your budget to professional editing and cover design. Take the time to research and find reputable service providers with good reviews and proven track records. Obtain multiple quotes to ensure you're getting a fair price for quality work.

By investing in these essential services, you ensure your book makes a strong first impression, keeps readers engaged, and stands out in the competitive market. In the next section, we'll continue exploring cost-effective solutions for various publishing expenses, helping you make the most of your budget while maintaining high standards. Let's keep your book project on track and within budget, while aiming for excellence!

3. Ignoring Marketing

Failing to invest in marketing can result in poor sales, regardless of the quality of your book.

- **Allocate a Marketing Budget**: Set aside funds specifically for marketing activities. A good rule of thumb is to allocate 10-20% of your overall budget to marketing.
- **Use Free and Low-Cost Marketing Channels**: Leverage social media, email marketing, and blogging to promote your book without significant financial investment.
- **Measure ROI**: Track the return on investment (ROI) of your marketing efforts. Focus on strategies that provide the best results and be willing to adjust your approach based on performance data.

Let's talk about a critical mistake that can sabotage your book's success: ignoring marketing. No matter how great your book is, if you don't invest in marketing, it can languish unnoticed on virtual shelves. Let's dive into why marketing is essential and how to approach it effectively, even on a tight budget.

Allocate a Marketing Budget

First and foremost, allocate a specific portion of your budget to marketing activities. A good rule of thumb is to set aside 10-20% of your overall budget for marketing. This ensures that you have dedicated funds to promote your book and reach your target audience. Remember, writing a great book is only half the battle; getting it into readers' hands is the other half. By allocating a marketing budget, you're investing in your book's visibility and sales potential.

Use Free and Low-Cost Marketing Channels

Next, leverage free and low-cost marketing channels to maximize your reach without breaking the bank. Social media platforms like Facebook, Twitter, and Instagram are excellent for connecting with readers and building a community around your book. Regularly post updates, share behind-the-scenes content, and engage with your followers to keep them interested.

Email marketing is another powerful tool. Build an email list of interested readers and send them newsletters with updates, exclusive content, and promotions. Platforms like Mailchimp offer free plans that are perfect for getting started.

Blogging can also be an effective way to attract readers. Write blog posts related to your book's themes, your writing process, or industry insights. This not only drives traffic to your website but also establishes you as an authority in your genre.

Measure ROI

Finally, it's crucial to track the return on investment (ROI) of your marketing efforts. Use analytics tools to monitor the performance of your campaigns. For instance, social media platforms provide insights into engagement rates, while email marketing services track open and click-through rates. Google Analytics can help you understand your website traffic and user behavior.

Focus on strategies that provide the best results and be willing to adjust your approach based on performance data. If a particular social media platform is driving more sales, consider allocating more resources to it. Conversely, if a strategy isn't yielding the desired results, don't hesitate to pivot and try something new.

The Wake-Up Call

Here's your wake-up call: failing to invest in marketing can result in poor sales, regardless of your book's quality. Marketing is not an optional extra—it's a fundamental part of your book's success strategy. By setting a dedicated marketing budget, using cost-effective channels, and measuring your ROI, you can effectively promote your book and reach your audience.

Conclusion

Ignoring marketing is a costly oversight that can significantly impact your book's success. Ensure you allocate 10-20% of your overall budget specifically for marketing activities. Utilize free and low-cost marketing channels like social media, email marketing, and blogging to promote your book without significant financial investment. Track the ROI of your marketing efforts to focus on strategies that provide the best results and adjust your approach as needed.

Investing in marketing is essential to ensure your book gets the attention it deserves. In the next section, we'll explore more cost-effective solutions for various publishing expenses, helping you make the most of your budget while maintaining high standards. Let's keep your book project on track and within budget, aiming for excellence in every aspect!

4. Not Tracking Expenses

Failing to keep detailed records of your expenses can lead to overspending and budget mismanagement.

- **Expense Tracking Tools**: Use budgeting tools, spreadsheets, or financial software to track every expense related to your book. Regularly update and review your records.
- **Set Limits**: Establish spending limits for each category of your budget (e.g., editing, design, marketing) and stick to them.
- **Regular Reviews**: Schedule monthly or quarterly reviews of your financial status to ensure you're staying within budget and on track to meet your goals.

Let's have a heart-to-heart about something that can easily derail your publishing journey: not tracking your expenses. Failing to keep detailed records of your spending can lead to overspending and budget mismanagement, which is a surefire way to stress and financial strain. Here's why meticulous expense tracking is essential and how to do it effectively.

Write It. Publish It. Sell It.

First off, let's talk about the tools you can use to keep track of your expenses. Budgeting tools, spreadsheets, or financial software can be your best friends here. Use these tools to record every expense related to your book—from editing and design to marketing and distribution. Make it a habit to regularly update and review your records. This will give you a clear picture of where your money is going and help you avoid unexpected financial surprises.

Next, it's crucial to set spending limits for each category of your budget. Whether it's editing, cover design, or marketing, establish clear limits and stick to them. This discipline ensures that you allocate your funds wisely and avoid blowing your budget on one aspect of your project while neglecting others.

Regular reviews of your financial status are also vital. Schedule monthly or quarterly check-ins to go over your expenses and see how you're doing against your budget. These reviews help you stay on track and make any necessary adjustments before small issues turn into big problems. It's all about maintaining control over your finances and making informed decisions based on accurate data.

Here's the wake-up call: not tracking your expenses can lead to overspending and budget mismanagement, putting your entire project at risk. By using expense tracking tools, setting clear spending limits, and conducting regular financial reviews, you can manage your budget effectively and ensure your book's success.

In conclusion, meticulous expense tracking is not just a good practice—it's essential for staying within budget and achieving your publishing goals. Use tools to track every expense, set spending limits for each budget category, and review your financial status regularly. This approach will keep you on track and help you avoid the pitfalls of overspending. Let's make sure your book project stays financially healthy and successful!

5. Underpricing Your Book

Setting your book's price too low can undermine its perceived value and limit your profit margins.

- **Competitive Pricing**: Research the pricing of comparable books in your genre. Set a price that reflects the value of your book while remaining competitive.
- **Test Price Points**: Consider testing different price points to see what resonates best with your audience. Use promotional pricing for limited periods to attract new readers without permanently lowering the perceived value.
- **Factor in Costs**: Ensure your pricing covers all production, distribution, and marketing costs while providing a reasonable profit margin.

Let's talk about a pitfall that many new authors face: underpricing your book. Setting your book's price too low can undermine its perceived value and limit your profit margins. Here's how to price your book effectively and ensure it reflects its true worth.

First, engage in competitive pricing. Research the pricing of comparable books in your genre to understand the market. Set a price that reflects the value of your book while remaining competitive. You want to position your book as a high-quality option that's worth the investment, not just another bargain buy.

Consider testing different price points to see what resonates best with your audience. Use promotional pricing for limited periods to attract new readers without permanently lowering the perceived value of your book. This strategy can help you find the optimal price point that balances accessibility and profitability.

Always factor in your costs. Ensure your pricing covers all production, distribution, and marketing costs while providing a reasonable profit margin. Remember, your goal is to make a profit, not just break even.

6. Overcommitting Financially

Spending beyond your means or taking on debt to finance your book can lead to financial strain.

- **Set a Realistic Budget**: Create a budget based on what you can afford without compromising your financial stability. Avoid taking on debt to finance your publishing efforts.
- **Plan for Unexpected Expenses**: Set aside a contingency fund to cover unforeseen costs. This can help prevent financial stress and ensure you have the resources to handle any surprises.
- **Stick to Your Budget**: Once you've established your budget, commit to sticking to it. Avoid impulse spending and carefully consider each expense.

Spending beyond your means or taking on debt to finance your book can lead to financial strain. Here's how to avoid overcommitting financially.

Set a realistic budget based on what you can afford without compromising your financial stability. Avoid taking on debt to finance your publishing efforts. Debt can add unnecessary stress and risk to your project.

Plan for unexpected expenses by setting aside a contingency fund. This can help prevent financial stress and ensure you have the resources to handle any surprises. A good rule of thumb is to set aside 10-15% of your budget for contingencies.

Once you've established your budget, commit to sticking to it. Avoid impulse spending and carefully consider each expense. Discipline is key to maintaining financial health throughout your publishing journey.

7. Not Planning for Long-Term Financial Health

Focusing solely on short-term expenses without considering long-term financial health can jeopardize your career.

- **Revenue Streams**: Explore multiple revenue streams, such as audiobooks, foreign rights, and merchandise, to diversify your income and increase financial stability.
- **Continuous Learning**: Invest in ongoing education about the publishing industry and marketing strategies to stay informed and make better financial decisions.
- **Savings and Investments**: Set aside a portion of your earnings for future projects and personal savings. Building a financial cushion can provide security and flexibility for your career.

Focusing solely on short-term expenses without considering long-term financial health can jeopardize your career. Here's how to plan for long-term financial success.

Explore multiple revenue streams to diversify your income and increase financial stability. Consider options like audiobooks, foreign rights, and merchandise to create additional income sources.

Invest in continuous learning about the publishing industry and marketing strategies. Staying informed helps you make better financial decisions and adapt to changes in the market.

Set aside a portion of your earnings for future projects and personal savings. Building a financial cushion can provide security and flexibility for your career, allowing you to take risks and pursue new opportunities without financial worry.

8. Failing to Seek Professional Financial Advice

Many authors overlook the value of professional financial advice, leading to poor financial management.

- **Consult a Financial Advisor**: If you're unsure about managing your finances, consider consulting a financial advisor who can help you create a solid financial plan and offer advice on budgeting, investing, and tax planning.
- **Use Accounting Services**: For comprehensive financial management, consider hiring an accountant or using accounting services. They can help with tracking expenses, filing taxes, and ensuring compliance with financial regulations.

Many authors overlook the value of professional financial advice, leading to poor financial management. Here's why seeking professional help can be beneficial.

Consider consulting a financial advisor if you're unsure about managing your finances. A financial advisor can help you create a solid financial plan and offer advice on budgeting, investing, and tax planning. Their expertise can save you money in the long run and provide peace of mind.

For comprehensive financial management, consider hiring an accountant or using accounting services. They can help with tracking expenses, filing taxes, and ensuring compliance with financial regulations. Proper financial management is crucial for long-term success.

9. Overlooking the Cost of Time

Time is a valuable resource, and failing to account for the time spent on various tasks can lead to inefficiencies and lost opportunities.

- **Time Management**: Track how much time you spend on different aspects of your publishing process. Use this information to optimize your workflow and delegate tasks when necessary.
- **Value Your Time**: Recognize the value of your time and consider outsourcing tasks that are time-consuming and outside your expertise. This can free up time for writing and other high-priority activities.

Time is a valuable resource, and failing to account for the time spent on various tasks can lead to inefficiencies and lost opportunities. Here's how to value and manage your time effectively.

Track how much time you spend on different aspects of your publishing process. Use this information to optimize your workflow and delegate tasks when necessary. Efficient time management can increase productivity and reduce stress.

Recognize the value of your time and consider outsourcing tasks that are time-consuming and outside your expertise. This can free up time for writing and other high-priority activities. Investing in help can pay off by allowing you to focus on what you do best.

Conclusion

Avoiding common financial mistakes is crucial for the success of your book and your career as an author. Set realistic sales projections, invest in professional services, track your expenses meticulously, and plan for both short-term and long-term financial health. Seek professional financial advice when needed and value your time as an important resource.

By managing your finances wisely, you can navigate the publishing process with confidence and set your book up for success. Stay disciplined, informed, and proactive in your financial planning, and you'll be well on your way to achieving your publishing goals. Let's make smart financial decisions that support your journey and help your book thrive in the competitive market!

Chapter 5: Craft a Compelling Query Letter

Securing a traditional publishing deal often begins with crafting a compelling query letter. This single-page letter serves as your introduction to literary agents and publishers, and it must capture their attention and interest in your manuscript. A strong query letter can open doors and set the stage for your publishing success. In this chapter, we will explore the essential components of a query letter, common mistakes to avoid, strategies for personalization, and examples of successful queries. We will also discuss effective follow-up strategies to use after sending your query letter.

Query Letter Basics: Understanding the Components of a Strong Query Letter

A query letter is a concise, professional letter that introduces your manuscript to agents and publishers. It typically includes:

- **The Hook**: A captivating opening that grabs the reader's attention and succinctly conveys the essence of your book.
- **Book Summary**: A brief overview of your manuscript, highlighting the main plot points, characters, and themes.
- **Author Bio**: A short biography that includes relevant writing experience, publications, and credentials.
- **Closing**: A polite and professional closing that invites the agent or publisher to request more material.

Understanding these components and how to present them effectively is crucial for making a strong first impression.

Do's and Don'ts: Common Mistakes to Avoid When Writing a Query Letter

Writing a query letter can be challenging, and it's easy to make mistakes that could hinder your chances of success. Common pitfalls include:

- **Do**: Keep it concise and focused. Agents and publishers receive countless queries and appreciate brevity.
- **Don't**: Oversell your book or make unrealistic claims about its potential success.
- **Do**: Follow submission guidelines precisely. Each agent or publisher may have specific requirements.
- **Don't**: Be informal or overly familiar. Maintain a professional tone throughout your letter.

Avoiding these mistakes can help ensure your query letter is taken seriously and receives the attention it deserves.

Personalization: Tailoring Your Query Letter to Different Agents and Publishers

Personalizing your query letter shows agents and publishers that you have done your homework and are genuinely interested in working with them. Strategies for personalization include:

- **Research**: Learn about the agents or publishers you're querying. Understand their preferences, recent acquisitions, and submission guidelines.
- **Specific References**: Mention why you are querying them specifically. Highlight any connections to their current authors or projects.
- **Customization**: Tailor the tone and content of your query letter to align with the interests and preferences of each agent or publisher.

Personalized query letters are more likely to stand out and resonate with their recipients.

Write It. Publish It. Sell It.

Sample Query Letters: Examples of Successful Query Letters and Breakdowns of Why They Work

Studying successful query letters can provide valuable insights into what works and why. In this section, we will provide examples of query letters that led to representation or publishing deals, breaking down their components to illustrate key strengths and techniques.

- **Effective Hooks**: Analyzing how the hook immediately engages the reader.
- **Compelling Summaries**: Understanding how a concise, intriguing summary can convey the essence of the manuscript.
- **Professional Bios**: Learning how to present your writing credentials and relevant experience effectively.

These examples will serve as templates and inspiration for crafting your own query letters.

Follow-Up Strategies: What to Do After You've Sent Your Query Letter

After sending your query letter, it's important to know how to follow up appropriately. Follow-up strategies include:

- **Patience**: Understanding typical response times and waiting an appropriate period before following up.
- **Polite Inquiries**: How to craft polite follow-up emails to check on the status of your query.
- **Handling Rejections**: Strategies for dealing with rejections professionally and using feedback to improve your query.
- **Tracking Submissions**: Keeping detailed records of your submissions, responses, and follow-ups to stay organized and informed.

Effective follow-up can help you navigate the querying process smoothly and increase your chances of finding the right agent or publisher for your book.

By mastering the art of the query letter, you can significantly enhance your chances of securing representation and achieving your publishing goals. In the following sections, we will delve deeper into each of these topics, providing practical advice, detailed examples, and actionable strategies to help you craft compelling query letters and navigate the submission process with confidence.

Query Letter Basics: Understanding the components of a strong query letter.

A query letter is your first opportunity to make an impression on literary agents and publishers. It serves as a concise introduction to you and your manuscript, and it must be engaging, professional, and compelling. A strong query letter typically consists of four main components: the hook, the book summary, the author bio, and the closing. Understanding how to effectively present each of these elements can significantly enhance your chances of attracting the interest of an agent or publisher.

1. The Hook

The hook is the opening of your query letter, designed to grab the reader's attention and make them want to read more. It should be intriguing, concise, and reflective of the tone and style of your book.

- **Purpose**: To captivate the agent or publisher and pique their curiosity about your manuscript.
- **Length**: Typically 1-2 sentences.
- **Content**: A compelling statement, a provocative question, or a vivid description that encapsulates the essence of your book.

Examples:

- *For a mystery novel*: "When renowned detective Jane Doe discovers a cryptic message in a murder victim's diary, she embarks on a dangerous quest to unravel a conspiracy that could shake the city's foundations."

- *For a romance novel*: "In a small coastal town, two former high school sweethearts reunite after a decade apart, only to discover that the spark between them has never truly died."

2. The Book Summary

The book summary is a brief overview of your manuscript, highlighting the main plot points, characters, and themes. It should provide enough information to give a clear picture of your book while leaving the reader wanting more.

- **Purpose**: To summarize your book in a way that showcases its unique elements and market potential.
- **Length**: Generally 1-2 paragraphs (about 150-200 words).
- **Content**: Key plot points, main characters, central conflict, and themes. Avoid giving away the entire plot or ending.

Structure:

- **Introduction**: Introduce the main character(s) and the initial situation.
- **Conflict**: Present the central conflict or challenge the characters face.
- **Stakes**: Highlight what's at stake and why it matters.

Example: "In 'Whispers in the Wind,' young archaeologist Emma Collins discovers an ancient artifact that holds the key to a forgotten civilization. As she delves deeper into its mysteries, she must navigate treacherous terrain, rival treasure hunters, and a looming threat that endangers everything she holds dear. With the help of enigmatic historian Jack Reynolds, Emma uncovers secrets that could rewrite history—but only if they can survive long enough to reveal the truth."

3. Author Bio

The author bio provides a brief overview of your writing background, relevant experience, and any notable achievements. It should establish your credibility and give the agent or publisher confidence in your ability to complete and promote the book.

- **Purpose**: To introduce yourself as an author and highlight your qualifications.
- **Length**: Generally 1-2 short paragraphs.
- **Content**: Writing experience, previous publications, awards, relevant credentials, and personal information that relates to your book or its themes.

Tips:

- Focus on relevant experience and achievements.
- Mention any writing groups, workshops, or conferences you've attended.
- Include a personal touch that connects you to the book's subject matter or genre.

Example: "I am a graduate of the Iowa Writers' Workshop, where I honed my skills in literary fiction. My short stories have been published in 'The New Yorker' and 'The Atlantic,' and I am a recipient of the Pushcart Prize. Currently, I teach creative writing at the University of Washington. 'Whispers in the Wind' is inspired by my own adventures in archaeology and my passion for uncovering hidden histories."

4. The Closing

The closing wraps up your query letter with a professional and courteous sign-off, inviting the agent or publisher to request additional material. It should reinforce your enthusiasm for the project and your interest in working with them.

- **Purpose**: To conclude your letter politely and professionally, encouraging further communication.
- **Length**: 1-2 sentences.
- **Content**: A thank-you note, a mention of enclosed materials (if any), and an invitation to request more.

Tips:

- Keep it brief and polite.
- Express your willingness to provide additional materials (e.g., a full manuscript, a synopsis).

- Thank the reader for their time and consideration.

Example: "Thank you for considering 'Whispers in the Wind.' I am happy to provide the full manuscript, a detailed synopsis, or any additional information upon request. I look forward to the possibility of working with you. Sincerely, [Your Name]"

Putting It All Together

Here's how a complete query letter might look:

[Your Name]
[Your Address]
[City, State, ZIP Code]
[Email Address]
[Phone Number]
[Date]

[Agent's Name]
[Agency's Name]
[Agency's Address]
[City, State, ZIP Code]

Dear [Agent's Name],

Hook: When renowned detective Jane Doe discovers a cryptic message in a murder victim's diary, she embarks on a dangerous quest to unravel a conspiracy that could shake the city's foundations.

Book Summary: In 'Whispers in the Wind,' young archaeologist Emma Collins discovers an ancient artifact that holds the key to a forgotten civilization. As she delves deeper into its mysteries, she must navigate treacherous terrain, rival treasure hunters, and a looming threat that endangers everything she holds dear. With the help of enigmatic historian

Jack Reynolds, Emma uncovers secrets that could rewrite history—but only if they can survive long enough to reveal the truth.

Author Bio: I am a graduate of the Iowa Writers' Workshop, where I honed my skills in literary fiction. My short stories have been published in 'The New Yorker' and 'The Atlantic,' and I am a recipient of the Pushcart Prize. Currently, I teach creative writing at the University of Washington. 'Whispers in the Wind' is inspired by my own adventures in archaeology and my passion for uncovering hidden histories.

Closing: Thank you for considering 'Whispers in the Wind.' I am happy to provide the full manuscript, a detailed synopsis, or any additional information upon request. I look forward to the possibility of working with you.

Sincerely,
[Your Name]

By carefully crafting each component of your query letter, you can create a compelling and professional introduction to your manuscript that captures the interest of agents and publishers. In the next section, we will explore common mistakes to avoid when writing a query letter, helping you refine your approach and increase your chances of success.

Do's and Don'ts: Common mistakes to avoid when writing a query letter.

Writing a query letter is an art that requires careful attention to detail, professionalism, and an understanding of what agents and publishers are looking for. Avoiding common mistakes can significantly enhance the effectiveness of your query letter. Here are some crucial do's and don'ts to keep in mind:

Do's

1. Do Keep It Concise and Focused

- **Keep It Short**: A query letter should ideally be no longer than one page. Agents and publishers receive numerous queries, so brevity is appreciated.
- **Stay Relevant**: Stick to the essential elements—hook, book summary, author bio, and closing. Avoid extraneous details that do not directly support your pitch.

2. Do Follow Submission Guidelines

- **Research Requirements**: Each agent or publisher may have specific submission guidelines. These can include preferred formats, word count limits, and required materials.
- **Adhere Strictly**: Always follow these guidelines meticulously. Ignoring them can lead to immediate rejection.

3. Do Personalize Your Query

- **Address by Name**: Use the agent's or publisher's name in your salutation. Avoid generic greetings like "Dear Sir/Madam."
- **Tailor Content**: Customize your letter to reflect your understanding of the agent's or publisher's preferences and interests. Mention why you chose to query them specifically.

4. Do Showcase Your Book's Unique Selling Points

- **Highlight Uniqueness**: Clearly articulate what makes your book stand out. Focus on unique aspects of the plot, characters, or themes.
- **Be Specific**: Provide concrete details that illustrate the distinctiveness of your manuscript.

5. Do Maintain a Professional Tone

- **Professional Language**: Use formal, polite language. Avoid slang, overly casual expressions, or humor that might not translate well.
- **Proper Formatting**: Ensure your letter is neatly formatted, with appropriate font size (usually 12-point), standard font (Times New Roman or Arial), and proper spacing.

6. Do Proofread and Edit

- **Check for Errors**: Typos, grammatical mistakes, and awkward phrasing can detract from your professionalism. Carefully proofread your letter before sending it.
- **Seek Feedback**: Consider having someone else review your query letter. Fresh eyes can catch mistakes you might have overlooked.

Don'ts

1. Don't Oversell or Exaggerate

- **Avoid Hyperbole**: Statements like "This book will be a bestseller" or "This is the next Harry Potter" can come across as overconfident and unrealistic.
- **Stay Honest**: Be truthful about your book's strengths and your achievements.

2. Don't Be Too Informal or Familiar

- **Professional Salutation**: Avoid casual greetings like "Hey" or "Hi." Use "Dear [Agent's Name]" or "Dear [Mr./Ms. Last Name]."
- **Respect Boundaries**: Refrain from making jokes or personal comments that could be perceived as unprofessional.

3. Don't Include Irrelevant Personal Information

- **Focus on Relevant Experience**: Only include personal details that are pertinent to your writing credentials or the subject matter of your book.
- **Avoid TMI**: Sharing personal anecdotes or life stories unrelated to your manuscript can distract from the main message.

4. Don't Query Multiple Agents/Publishers in a Single Email

- **Individual Queries**: Send personalized, individual queries to each agent or publisher. Mass emailing comes across as impersonal and unprofessional.
- **Tailored Approach**: Customize each letter to address the specific interests and preferences of the recipient.

5. Don't Neglect Your Opening and Closing

- **Engaging Hook**: Avoid starting with generic or dull statements. Your opening should grab attention immediately.
- **Polite Closing**: Don't forget to thank the agent or publisher for their time and consideration. A courteous sign-off leaves a positive impression.

6. Don't Forget to Include Contact Information

- **Complete Contact Details**: Ensure your email address, phone number, and any other relevant contact information are included. This makes it easy for the agent or publisher to reach you.

Examples of Common Mistakes to Avoid

Overly Long and Detailed Summary

- **Mistake**: Including a multi-paragraph summary that delves into every subplot and character arc.
- **Solution**: Focus on the main plot points and central conflict. Keep your summary concise and engaging.

Using Unprofessional Language

- **Mistake**: Starting your letter with "Hey [Agent's Name]," or using colloquial phrases like "You're gonna love this book."
- **Solution**: Maintain a formal tone with a salutation like "Dear [Agent's Name]," and use professional language throughout.

Generic Query

- **Mistake**: Sending a one-size-fits-all query letter without personalization.
- **Solution**: Research each agent or publisher and tailor your letter to show why your book is a good fit for them specifically.

Lack of Focus on the Book

- **Mistake**: Spending too much time discussing your personal life or unrelated experiences.
- **Solution**: Keep the focus on your book and your relevant writing credentials.

By adhering to these do's and don'ts, you can craft a query letter that is professional, engaging, and tailored to capture the attention of agents and publishers. In the next section, we will discuss how to personalize your query letter for different agents and publishers, further enhancing your chances of a positive response.

Personalization: Tailoring your query letter to different agents and publishers.

Personalizing your query letter is a crucial step in making a strong impression on literary agents and publishers. A personalized query letter demonstrates that you have done your homework, understand the recipient's preferences and interests, and are genuinely interested in working with them. Here's how to effectively tailor your query letter to different agents and publishers.

1. Research Each Agent or Publisher

Before personalizing your query letter, you need to gather information about each agent or publisher you plan to contact. This research will help you understand their interests, preferences, and submission guidelines.

- **Read Their Profiles**: Start by reading the agent's or publisher's profile on their website or on industry sites like Publisher's Marketplace. Look for information about the genres they represent, their recent sales, and their professional background.
- **Follow Their Work**: Read books they have represented or published, especially those similar to yours. This can give you a sense of their tastes and what they are looking for.
- **Check Interviews and Articles**: Look for interviews, articles, or blog posts by the agent or publisher. These can provide valuable insights into their preferences and what they find compelling in a query letter.
- **Engage on Social Media**: Follow the agent or publisher on social media platforms like Twitter and LinkedIn. Engage with their posts to understand their interests and professional approach.

2. Personalize the Salutation

A personalized salutation sets the tone for your query letter and shows that you have addressed it specifically to the recipient.

- **Use Their Name**: Always address the agent or publisher by their full name (e.g., "Dear Ms. Smith," "Dear Mr. Johnson"). Avoid generic greetings like "Dear Agent" or "To Whom It May Concern."
- **Correct Spelling**: Ensure that you spell their name correctly. Double-check if necessary, as a misspelled name can create a negative impression.

3. Mention Why You're Querying Them

In the opening paragraph or early in the letter, mention why you chose to query this particular agent or publisher. Highlight any connections or reasons why you believe your book is a good fit for their list.

- **Specific References**: Mention specific books or authors they have represented that are similar to yours. This shows that you have done your research and understand their preferences.
- **Professional Fit**: Explain how your book aligns with their stated interests or recent acquisitions. For example, "I noticed you represent [Author Name], whose work in [Genre] resonates with the themes in my manuscript."

Example: "Dear Ms. Smith, I am writing to you because of your interest in contemporary romance with strong, independent female protagonists. Given your successful representation of [Author Name] and your enthusiasm for stories set in small-town settings, I believe my novel 'Love in the Lakeside' would be a great addition to your list."

4. Highlight Relevant Experience

Tailor your author bio to include any experience or credentials that are particularly relevant to the agent or publisher you are querying.

- **Relevant Background**: Mention any professional or personal experiences that connect you to the agent's or publisher's interests. For example, if you're querying an agent who specializes in historical fiction, highlight your background in history or related research.
- **Previous Work**: If you have published works similar to the genres they represent, make sure to include this information.

Example: "As a member of the Historical Novel Society and a contributor to 'Historical Fiction Review,' I have a deep passion for bringing the past to life through compelling narratives. My previous novel, 'Echoes of the Past,' was well-received and nominated for the Historical Novel Award."

5. Tailor the Book Summary

Adjust your book summary to emphasize elements that align with the agent's or publisher's interests. Focus on themes, characters, or plot points that are likely to resonate with them.

- **Emphasize Relevant Themes**: Highlight themes or elements that the agent or publisher has expressed interest in. For instance, if they enjoy stories with strong environmental themes, make sure to bring that aspect of your book to the forefront.
- **Connect with Their Preferences**: If the agent has shown a preference for certain types of characters or settings, tailor your summary to reflect these elements.

Example: "'Love in the Lakeside' is a contemporary romance set in a charming small town, focusing on the journey of Emma, a fiercely independent woman who returns to her hometown to save her family's inn. The novel explores themes of community, resilience, and the rediscovery of love, which align with your interest in heartwarming, character-driven stories."

6. Follow Their Submission Guidelines

Each agent or publisher may have specific submission guidelines that you need to follow. Adhering to these guidelines demonstrates your professionalism and respect for their process.

- **Specific Requirements**: Check if they require certain materials, such as the first three chapters, a synopsis, or a specific file format.
- **Submission Method**: Follow their preferred method of submission, whether it's via email, an online form, or postal mail.

Example: "Per your submission guidelines, I have attached the first three chapters and a one-page synopsis of 'Love in the Lakeside' for your review."

7. Express Genuine Interest

Convey your enthusiasm for working with the agent or publisher. A genuine expression of interest can make a positive impression and show that you are serious about your writing career.

- **Professional Enthusiasm**: Express your admiration for their work and your excitement about the possibility of collaborating with them.
- **Mutual Benefits**: Highlight how you believe the partnership can be mutually beneficial.

Example: "I admire your dedication to nurturing new voices in contemporary romance, and I am excited about the possibility of collaborating with you to bring 'Love in the Lakeside' to readers who appreciate heartfelt, character-driven stories."

By following these personalization strategies, you can create query letters that stand out and resonate with the specific agents and publishers you are targeting. Personalization shows that you are professional, diligent, and genuinely interested in building a productive working relationship. In the next section, we will provide examples of successful query letters and breakdowns of why they work, giving you practical insights and inspiration for crafting your own queries.

Sample Query Letters: Examples of successful query letters and breakdowns of why they work.

Studying successful query letters can provide valuable insights into what captures the attention of literary agents and publishers. Below are examples of query letters that led to representation or publishing deals, along with detailed breakdowns of why they work.

Example 1: Contemporary Romance

Query Letter:

[Your Name]
[Your Address]
[City, State, ZIP Code]
[Email Address]
[Phone Number]
[Date]

[Agent's Name]
[Agency's Name]
[Agency's Address]
[City, State, ZIP Code]

Dear Ms. Smith,

Write It. Publish It. Sell It.

I am writing to you because of your interest in contemporary romance with strong, independent female protagonists. Given your successful representation of [Author Name] and your enthusiasm for stories set in small-town settings, I believe my novel 'Love in the Lakeside' would be a great addition to your list.

Hook: When Emma Collins returns to her hometown of Lakeside to save her family's inn, she expects to face financial struggles—not to rediscover the love she left behind.

Book Summary: In 'Love in the Lakeside,' Emma Collins, a fiercely independent woman, returns to the small town of Lakeside to prevent her family's inn from closing. Facing financial difficulties and community opposition, Emma reluctantly teams up with Jack Harper, her high school sweetheart and the town's most eligible bachelor. As they work together to save the inn, old sparks reignite, and Emma must decide whether to embrace the love she once ran from or continue her life of independence. The novel explores themes of community, resilience, and the rediscovery of love, which align with your interest in heartwarming, character-driven stories.

Author Bio: I am a graduate of the Iowa Writers' Workshop, where I honed my skills in crafting contemporary romance. My short stories have been published in 'The New Yorker' and 'The Atlantic,' and I am a recipient of the Pushcart Prize. Currently, I teach creative writing at the University of Washington. 'Love in the Lakeside' is inspired by my own experiences growing up in a small town and my passion for stories that celebrate love and community.

Thank you for considering 'Love in the Lakeside.' I am happy to provide the full manuscript, a detailed synopsis, or any additional information upon request. I look forward to the possibility of working with you.

Sincerely,
[Your Name]

Breakdown:

- **Personalization**: The query is addressed specifically to the agent and references their interest in contemporary romance and small-town settings.
- **Hook**: The hook is engaging and sets up the central conflict and romance in a concise manner.
- **Book Summary**: The summary provides a clear overview of the plot, characters, and themes, highlighting elements that align with the agent's interests.
- **Author Bio**: The bio is relevant and showcases the author's credentials and writing experience.
- **Closing**: The closing is polite and professional, inviting the agent to request more material.

Example 2: Mystery/Thriller

Query Letter:

[Your Name]
[Your Address]
[City, State, ZIP Code]
[Email Address]
[Phone Number]
[Date]

[Agent's Name]
[Agency's Name]
[Agency's Address]
[City, State, ZIP Code]

Dear Mr. Johnson,

I am thrilled to query you because of your enthusiasm for fast-paced thrillers with intricate plots and strong female leads. Your representation of [Author Name] and your success with recent mystery titles convinced me that you would be the perfect advocate for my novel, 'Shadows of Deceit.'

Write It. Publish It. Sell It.

Hook: When Detective Sarah Blake uncovers a series of cryptic messages in a murder victim's diary, she is thrust into a deadly game of cat and mouse with a cunning serial killer.

Book Summary: 'Shadows of Deceit' follows Detective Sarah Blake as she investigates a string of brutal murders that have left the city of Seattle in fear. Each victim's diary contains a cryptic message that leads Sarah deeper into a web of deceit and danger. As she races against time to decode the messages, she discovers a chilling connection to her own past. With the help of forensic expert Dr. Jake Williams, Sarah must confront her deepest fears and outsmart a killer who is always one step ahead. This novel combines high-stakes action with psychological depth, making it a perfect fit for your list.

Author Bio: I have a background in criminal psychology and have worked closely with law enforcement agencies on criminal profiling. My short fiction has appeared in 'Ellery Queen's Mystery Magazine,' and I am a member of the Mystery Writers of America. 'Shadows of Deceit' draws on my professional experience and passion for creating suspenseful, character-driven stories.

Thank you for considering 'Shadows of Deceit.' I am excited to provide the full manuscript, a detailed synopsis, or any additional information upon your request. I look forward to the possibility of collaborating with you.

Best regards,
[Your Name]

Breakdown:
- **Personalization**: The query references the agent's interest in thrillers and their success with similar titles.
- **Hook**: The hook is intriguing and immediately sets up the high-stakes conflict.
- **Book Summary**: The summary effectively outlines the plot and central conflict while highlighting the novel's psychological depth and action.

- **Author Bio**: The bio emphasizes the author's relevant background in criminal psychology and previous publications.
- **Closing**: The closing is professional and invites the agent to request more material.

Example 3: Science Fiction

Query Letter:

[Your Name]
[Your Address]
[City, State, ZIP Code]
[Email Address]
[Phone Number]
[Date]

[Agent's Name]
[Agency's Name]
[Agency's Address]
[City, State, ZIP Code]

Dear Ms. Brown,

I am writing to you because of your passion for science fiction that explores complex themes and futuristic worlds. Your representation of [Author Name] and your keen interest in speculative fiction inspired me to query you with my novel, 'Eclipse of the Mind.'

Hook: In a future where memories can be erased and rewritten, one woman must uncover the truth about her past to save humanity's future.

Book Summary: 'Eclipse of the Mind' is set in a dystopian future where the government controls the population by manipulating memories. Elena Morgan, a former memory technician, discovers that her own memories have been tampered with, hiding a secret that could topple the regime. As she delves into the forbidden world of memory hacking, she joins forces with a group of rebels determined to restore freedom. Together, they must navigate a treacherous landscape of deceit, betrayal, and hidden truths. The novel explores themes of identity, freedom, and the ethical implications of memory manipulation.

Author Bio: I hold a degree in cognitive science and have published articles on memory and consciousness in scientific journals. My short stories have appeared in 'Asimov's Science Fiction' and 'Clarkesworld Magazine.' 'Eclipse of the Mind' combines my academic background with my love for speculative fiction, creating a thought-provoking and action-packed narrative.

Thank you for considering 'Eclipse of the Mind.' I am eager to provide the full manuscript, a detailed synopsis, or any additional information upon request. I look forward to the opportunity to work with you.

Sincerely,
[Your Name]

Breakdown:

- **Personalization**: The query is personalized to the agent's interest in science fiction and speculative fiction.
- **Hook**: The hook is compelling and sets up a high-concept premise.
- **Book Summary**: The summary provides a clear and engaging overview of the plot, characters, and themes, highlighting the novel's speculative elements and ethical questions.
- **Author Bio**: The bio emphasizes the author's relevant academic background and previous publications in the genre.
- **Closing**: The closing is polite and professional, inviting the agent to request more material.

By analyzing these examples, you can see how successful query letters are personalized, concise, and focused on showcasing the unique elements of the manuscript. Each letter effectively captures the agent's attention with a compelling hook, provides a clear and engaging summary, highlights relevant author credentials, and concludes with a professional invitation for further communication. In the next section, we will discuss follow-up strategies, detailing what to do after you've sent your query letter to maximize your chances of success.

Follow-Up Strategies: What to do after you've sent your query letter.

Sending out query letters to agents and publishers is just the beginning of your journey to getting published. Knowing how to follow up appropriately can enhance your chances of receiving a response and securing representation. Here are some effective follow-up strategies to keep in mind after you've sent your query letter.

1. Be Patient

Patience is crucial when waiting for responses to your query letters. Agents and publishers often receive hundreds of queries and need time to review them.

- **Typical Response Times**: Most agents and publishers specify their typical response times in their submission guidelines. These can range from a few weeks to several months.
- **No Early Follow-Ups**: Respect the stated response time before following up. Premature follow-ups can be seen as impatience and may work against you.

2. Track Your Submissions

Keeping organized records of your submissions helps you stay on top of your follow-up strategy and avoid duplicate submissions.

- **Create a Spreadsheet**: Use a spreadsheet or a dedicated tracking tool to record each submission. Include details such as the agent's name, agency, submission date, expected response time, and any responses received.
- **Note Key Dates**: Mark the expected response dates and set reminders for when it's appropriate to follow up.

3. Follow Up Politely

If the stated response time has passed and you haven't heard back, a polite follow-up email can prompt a response.

- **Keep It Brief**: Your follow-up email should be short and to the point. Reiterate your query and inquire about its status.
- **Be Professional**: Maintain a professional and courteous tone. Avoid expressing frustration or impatience.

Example Follow-Up Email:

Subject: Follow-Up on Query Submission: 'Love in the Lakeside'

Dear Ms. Smith,

I hope this email finds you well. I am writing to follow up on my query submission for my contemporary romance novel, 'Love in the Lakeside,' which I sent to you on [date]. I understand you receive many submissions and appreciate your time and consideration.
If you need any further information or materials, please let me know. I look forward to hearing from you.

Thank you again for your time and attention.

Best regards,
[Your Name]

4. Handling Rejections

Rejections are a natural part of the querying process. Knowing how to handle them professionally and constructively can help you move forward.

- **Stay Positive**: Remember that rejection is not a reflection of your worth as a writer. Agents and publishers reject manuscripts for many reasons, including personal taste and market trends.
- **Learn from Feedback**: If you receive personalized feedback, take it as constructive criticism. Use it to improve your manuscript or query letter.
- **Don't Burn Bridges**: Respond to rejections with professionalism and gratitude, especially if feedback is provided. Maintain a positive relationship for potential future submissions.

Example Response to a Rejection:

Dear Ms. Smith,

Thank you for taking the time to consider my query for 'Love in the Lakeside.' I appreciate your feedback and the insights you provided. I hope to have the opportunity to submit future projects to you.

Best regards, [Your Name]

5. Continue Querying

While waiting for responses, continue sending out query letters to other agents and publishers. This increases your chances of finding the right fit.

- **Keep a Steady Pace**: Aim to send out a set number of queries each week. This keeps your momentum going and ensures continuous progress.
- **Adapt and Improve**: Use any feedback received to refine your query letter and manuscript. Continuous improvement can enhance your chances of success.

6. Stay Informed and Engaged

Engage with the writing and publishing community to stay informed about industry trends and opportunities.

- **Join Writing Groups**: Participate in writing groups and forums where you can share experiences, seek advice, and support other writers.
- **Attend Conferences and Workshops**: Attend literary conferences, workshops, and webinars to network with industry professionals and learn from their insights.

7. Consider Alternative Paths

If traditional querying does not yield the desired results, consider alternative paths to publication.

- **Small Presses**: Small and independent presses may have different submission processes and be more open to new authors.
- **Self-Publishing**: With the rise of self-publishing platforms, many authors have successfully published and marketed their books independently.
- **Hybrid Publishing**: Hybrid publishers combine aspects of traditional and self-publishing, offering professional services while allowing authors more control.

Final Thoughts

Following up on your query letters with patience, professionalism, and persistence is key to navigating the submission process. By staying organized, handling rejections constructively, and continually improving your approach, you can enhance your chances of securing representation and achieving your publishing goals. In the next chapter, we will delve into building and engaging your audience, providing strategies to connect with readers and create a loyal fan base.

Chapter 6: Build and Engage Your Audience

Having a well-written and professionally published book is just the beginning. The true measure of success lies in how effectively you can connect with your readers and build a loyal audience. Engaging your readers not only boosts your book's visibility and sales but also creates a dedicated community that supports your ongoing writing career. In this chapter, we will explore strategies for identifying your target audience, building a loyal reader base, leveraging content marketing, creating a community around your book, and encouraging reader feedback.

Identifying Your Target Audience: Understanding Who Your Readers Are and Where to Find Them

Understanding your target audience is the foundation of successful reader engagement. Knowing who your readers are helps you tailor your marketing efforts and connect with them more effectively.

- **Demographics**: Identify key demographic characteristics such as age, gender, location, and occupation. This information can help you craft messages that resonate with your audience.
- **Psychographics**: Explore the interests, values, attitudes, and lifestyles of your potential readers. What do they care about? What motivates them?
- **Reading Preferences**: Determine the genres, themes, and styles your target audience prefers. What other books do they enjoy? Who are their favorite authors?
- **Where to Find Them**: Identify the platforms and places where your audience spends their time. Are they active on social media, frequent certain forums, or attend specific events?

By clearly defining your target audience, you can create more effective marketing strategies and foster deeper connections with your readers.

Audience Engagement: Techniques for Building a Loyal Reader Base

Building a loyal reader base involves consistently engaging with your audience and providing value that keeps them coming back.

- **Consistency**: Regularly update your audience with new content, whether through blog posts, social media updates, newsletters, or new books. Consistency builds trust and keeps your readers engaged.
- **Personal Connection**: Share personal stories, behind-the-scenes insights, and your writing journey. Let your readers get to know you as a person and as an author.
- **Interactive Content**: Encourage interaction through Q&A sessions, polls, contests, and discussions. Make your readers feel involved and valued.
- **Exclusive Content**: Offer exclusive content such as bonus chapters, early access to new releases, or special discounts to your loyal readers. Rewarding their loyalty fosters a stronger connection.

Content Marketing: Creating Content That Attracts and Retains Readers

Content marketing involves creating valuable and relevant content to attract and retain your audience. Effective content marketing can drive engagement and establish you as a trusted voice in your genre.

- **Blogging**: Maintain a blog where you share writing tips, book reviews, personal experiences, and industry insights. Blogging can attract new readers and keep existing ones engaged.
- **Social Media**: Use social media platforms to share updates, interact with readers, and promote your work. Visual content like images and videos can be particularly effective.
- **Newsletters**: Regular newsletters can keep your audience informed about your latest projects, upcoming events, and exclusive offers. Personalize your newsletters to make them more engaging.
- **Guest Posts and Collaborations**: Write guest posts for popular blogs or collaborate with other authors and influencers. This can expand your reach and introduce your work to new audiences.

Community Building: Using Online and Offline Methods to Create a Community Around Your Book

Creating a sense of community around your book can lead to a more engaged and supportive reader base. Both online and offline methods can be effective in building this community.

- **Online Communities**: Create or participate in online groups and forums where readers can discuss your books and related topics. Platforms like Facebook Groups, Goodreads, and Reddit are excellent for this purpose.
- **Events and Meetups**: Host or attend book signings, readings, workshops, and literary festivals. These events provide opportunities for personal interaction and can strengthen reader loyalty.
- **Book Clubs**: Encourage and support book clubs that choose to read your books. Offer to participate in their discussions, either in person or virtually.
- **Engage with Influencers**: Collaborate with bloggers, bookstagrammers, and booktubers who can help promote your work and engage their followers.

Feedback and Interaction: Encouraging and Managing Reader Feedback to Improve Your Work

Reader feedback is invaluable for improving your writing and deepening your connection with your audience. Encouraging and managing this feedback effectively can lead to better books and a more loyal reader base.

- **Solicit Feedback**: Actively seek feedback from your readers through surveys, reviews, and direct messages. Ask specific questions to get detailed insights.
- **Engage with Reviews**: Respond to reviews and comments professionally and gratefully. Acknowledge positive feedback and consider constructive criticism for future improvements.
- **Incorporate Feedback**: Use the feedback to refine your current projects and inform your future writing. Showing readers that you value their input can enhance their loyalty.
- **Beta Readers**: Establish a group of beta readers who can provide early feedback on your manuscripts. This can help you identify strengths and weaknesses before publication.

By identifying your target audience, engaging with them consistently, leveraging content marketing, building a community, and encouraging feedback, you can create a loyal and supportive reader base. In the next sections, we will delve deeper into each of these strategies, providing practical tips and actionable advice to help you connect with your readers and grow your audience effectively.

Identifying Your Target Audience: Understanding who your readers are and where to find them.

Identifying your target audience is a fundamental step in building and engaging a loyal reader base. Knowing who your readers are allows you to tailor your marketing efforts, create content that resonates with them, and find the best platforms to reach them. Here's how to understand and identify your target audience effectively.

1. Define Demographic Characteristics

Demographic characteristics provide a basic profile of your ideal readers, including their age, gender, location, occupation, and education level.

- **Age**: Determine the age range of your target audience. Are they teenagers, young adults, middle-aged, or seniors?
- **Gender**: Consider whether your book appeals more to a particular gender or if it has a broad appeal.
- **Location**: Identify where your readers are located. Are they primarily in a specific country, region, or city?
- **Occupation and Education**: Understand their professional backgrounds and education levels. Are they students, professionals, retirees, etc.?

Let's have a chat about a crucial aspect of marketing your book: understanding your ideal reader through demographic characteristics. Knowing who your readers are helps you tailor your marketing efforts effectively and ensures your book reaches the right audience. Let's break it down together.

Age

First, think about the age range of your target audience. Are you writing for teenagers, young adults, middle-aged individuals, or seniors? Understanding the age group helps you craft a message that resonates with their experiences and interests. For example, a young adult novel will have a different tone and style compared to a book aimed at retirees.

Gender

Next, consider whether your book appeals more to a particular gender or if it has broad appeal. Some genres or themes might naturally attract more male or female readers. Knowing this can help you tailor your marketing messages and choose the right platforms for promotion.

Location

Identify where your readers are located. Are they primarily in a specific country, region, or city? This information is vital for both your marketing and distribution strategies. If your book is set in a particular locale or deals with regional issues, focusing on readers from that area can be particularly effective.

Occupation and Education

Lastly, understand the professional backgrounds and education levels of your readers. Are they students, professionals, or retirees? What is their education level? Knowing this can help you decide where to market your book and what kind of language to use. For instance, a book aimed at professionals might benefit from LinkedIn promotions, while a novel for students could be promoted through social media and campus events.

Bringing It All Together

By defining these demographic characteristics, you can create a clear profile of your ideal reader. This profile guides your marketing efforts, helping you choose the right channels and craft messages that speak directly to your audience's interests and needs. It's like having a roadmap for your promotional activities, making them more focused and effective.

So, take some time to really think about who your readers are. The more you understand them, the better you can connect with them and make your book a success. Let's ensure your book reaches the right people and makes a lasting impact!

2. Explore Psychographic Profiles

Psychographics go beyond basic demographics to explore the interests, values, attitudes, and lifestyles of your readers.

- **Interests**: What hobbies, activities, and interests do your readers have? What do they enjoy doing in their free time?
- **Values and Beliefs**: Consider the core values and beliefs that resonate with your audience. Do they prioritize family, adventure, social justice, etc.?
- **Attitudes and Preferences**: Understand their attitudes towards certain subjects and their preferences in terms of book genres, themes, and writing styles.

Let's delve deeper into understanding your readers by exploring their psychographic profiles. While demographics give us the basic outline of who our readers are, psychographics help us paint a richer picture by examining their interests, values, attitudes, and lifestyles. This deeper understanding can significantly enhance your marketing strategies and connect you more closely with your audience. Let's explore how to define these elements together.

Interests

First, think about the hobbies, activities, and interests of your readers. What do they enjoy doing in their free time? Are they avid travelers, passionate about cooking, or maybe they love outdoor activities like hiking and camping? Knowing their interests can help you create marketing content that resonates with them and draws them in. For instance, if your readers are travel enthusiasts, you might share stories or tips related to travel that tie into your book's themes.

Values and Beliefs

Next, consider the core values and beliefs that resonate with your audience. Do they prioritize family, adventure, social justice, or personal growth? Understanding these values can guide how you position your book and craft your messaging. If your book deals with themes of social justice, for example, highlighting these aspects in your marketing can attract readers who are passionate about these issues.

Attitudes and Preferences

It's also important to understand your readers' attitudes towards certain subjects and their preferences in terms of book genres, themes, and writing styles. Are they looking for escapism through fantasy novels, or do they prefer hard-hitting, realistic fiction? Do they enjoy books with a fast-paced narrative, or are they drawn to deep, character-driven stories? Tailoring your content to match these preferences can make your book more appealing to your target audience.

Bringing It All Together

By exploring these psychographic elements, you gain a more nuanced understanding of your readers. This helps you craft marketing messages that truly resonate with their lifestyles and beliefs. For example, if your readers value adventure and personal growth, you can highlight these themes in your book promotions and social media posts, making your content more engaging and relevant.

So, take the time to get to know your readers on a deeper level. The more you understand their interests, values, and attitudes, the better you can connect with them and make your book a part of their world. Let's make your marketing efforts not just effective, but truly meaningful to your audience. Happy connecting!

3. Analyze Reading Preferences

Understanding your audience's reading habits and preferences is crucial for tailoring your content and marketing strategies.

- **Genre Preferences**: Identify the genres your target audience enjoys. Are they fans of romance, mystery, fantasy, sci-fi, non-fiction, etc.?
- **Reading Frequency**: How often do they read? Are they avid readers who consume books frequently, or more occasional readers?
- **Format Preferences**: Determine whether they prefer physical books, e-books, or audiobooks. This can influence how you distribute and market your work.

Let's dive into an important aspect of connecting with your readers: understanding their reading preferences. Knowing what your audience likes to read, how often they read, and their preferred formats can help you tailor your content and marketing strategies more effectively. Let's break down these elements together.

Genre Preferences

First, identify the genres your target audience enjoys. Are they fans of romance, mystery, fantasy, sci-fi, non-fiction, or perhaps a mix of several genres? Understanding their genre preferences helps you craft your book and marketing messages to align with their tastes. If your readers love mystery novels, for instance, emphasize the suspenseful and intriguing elements of your story in your promotions.

Reading Frequency

Next, consider how often your audience reads. Are they avid readers who consume books frequently, or are they more occasional readers? Avid readers might be more receptive to regular updates, new releases, and additional content like newsletters and blog posts. Occasional readers, on the other hand, might prefer concise and impactful communication that quickly captures their interest.

Format Preferences

Determine whether your readers prefer physical books, e-books, or audiobooks. This preference can significantly influence how you distribute and market your work. If your audience leans towards e-books, ensure your digital marketing is strong and consider exclusive online promotions. If they prefer audiobooks, investing in a high-quality audiobook version can be a worthwhile addition to your offerings.

Bringing It All Together

By analyzing your audience's reading preferences, you can tailor your content and marketing strategies to better meet their needs and interests. Here's how you can put this knowledge into practice:

- **Genre Alignment**: Ensure your book's genre is prominently highlighted in your marketing materials. Use genre-specific language and imagery that resonate with your audience.
- **Reading Frequency Engagement**: For avid readers, provide frequent updates and additional content to keep them engaged. For occasional readers, focus on high-impact messages that quickly convey the value of your book.
- **Format Focus**: Tailor your distribution strategies based on your audience's format preferences. If physical books are popular, consider partnering with local bookstores for events and signings. If e-books or audiobooks are preferred, focus on digital marketing and online sales platforms.

Conclusion

Understanding your audience's reading habits and preferences is crucial for tailoring your content and marketing strategies. By identifying their preferred genres, reading frequency, and format choices, you can craft a more personalized and effective approach to connecting with your readers.

Take the time to analyze these preferences and adjust your strategies accordingly. Doing so will not only help you reach your target audience more effectively but also enhance their overall reading experience. Let's make sure your book finds its way into the hands (or devices) of the readers who will love and appreciate it the most. Happy marketing!

4. Conduct Market Research

Market research helps you gather data and insights about your potential readers through various methods.

- **Surveys and Polls**: Create and distribute surveys to gather information about your readers' preferences, habits, and demographics. Use platforms like SurveyMonkey or Google Forms.
- **Social Media Insights**: Analyze data from your social media profiles to understand who follows you and engages with your content. Platforms like Facebook, Instagram, and Twitter offer detailed insights into your audience.
- **Industry Reports and Studies**: Review industry reports and studies that provide data on book sales, reading trends, and audience demographics. Organizations like the Pew Research Center and Nielsen provide valuable insights.

Let's talk about an essential step in understanding your audience better: conducting market research. Gathering data and insights about your potential readers helps you tailor your content and marketing strategies to meet their needs and preferences. Here's how you can effectively conduct market research.

Surveys and Polls

One of the most direct ways to gather information is through surveys and polls. Create and distribute surveys to collect data on your readers' preferences, habits, and demographics. Platforms like SurveyMonkey and Google Forms make it easy to design and share your surveys. Ask questions about their favorite genres, reading frequency, preferred formats, and any other details that can help you understand their needs better. This feedback is invaluable in shaping your book and marketing strategies.

Social Media Insights

Your social media profiles are gold mines of data about your audience. Analyze the insights provided by platforms like Facebook, Instagram, and Twitter to understand who follows you and engages with your content. These insights often include age, gender, location, and interests of your followers. By examining this data, you can get a clearer picture of your audience's demographics and preferences, helping you tailor your content to better engage them.

Industry Reports and Studies

Don't forget to tap into the wealth of information available in industry reports and studies. Organizations like the Pew Research Center and Nielsen provide comprehensive data on book sales, reading trends, and audience demographics. Reviewing these reports can give you a broader understanding of the market and help you identify trends that could impact your book's success. These insights are particularly useful for understanding the larger context in which you're publishing and how your book fits into current trends.

Bringing It All Together

By combining these methods, you can gather a well-rounded set of data about your potential readers. Here's how to integrate this information into your strategy:

- **Survey Results**: Use the direct feedback from your surveys to make informed decisions about your book's content and marketing approach. Pay attention to common themes and preferences that emerge.
- **Social Media Insights**: Tailor your social media content to reflect the demographics and interests of your followers. Engage with your audience by sharing relevant posts, asking questions, and responding to comments.
- **Industry Reports**: Leverage the data from industry reports to position your book within current trends and market demands. Use these insights to refine your target audience and adjust your marketing strategies accordingly.

Conclusion

Conducting thorough market research is crucial for understanding your potential readers and tailoring your book and marketing strategies to their needs. By creating surveys, analyzing social media insights, and reviewing industry reports, you can gather valuable data that informs your decisions and increases your chances of success.

Take the time to gather and analyze this data, and use it to create a more targeted and effective approach to reaching your audience. Let's ensure your book resonates with the readers who will appreciate it the most. Happy researching!

5. Identify Where to Find Your Audience

Once you have a clear understanding of your target audience, the next step is to find out where they spend their time online and offline.

- **Online Platforms**: Determine which social media platforms, forums, and websites your audience frequents. Are they active on Facebook, Instagram, Twitter, Goodreads, Reddit, etc.?

- **Offline Locations**: Identify physical locations where your audience might gather, such as bookstores, libraries, coffee shops, and literary events.

6. Create Reader Personas

Reader personas are detailed profiles of fictional individuals who represent your target audience. These personas help you visualize and empathize with your readers.

- **Build Detailed Profiles**: Create 2-3 reader personas, each with a name, age, occupation, interests, and reading preferences. Include their goals, challenges, and motivations related to reading.
- **Use Personas in Planning**: Refer to these personas when creating content, planning marketing campaigns, and developing engagement strategies. This ensures that your efforts are aligned with your audience's needs and preferences.

Example Reader Persona:

- **Name**: Emily Johnson
- **Age**: 34
- **Occupation**: Marketing Manager
- **Location**: San Francisco, CA
- **Interests**: Enjoys hiking, yoga, and photography. Loves reading contemporary romance and women's fiction.
- **Reading Habits**: Reads 2-3 books per month, prefers e-books for convenience but enjoys physical books for favorite authors.
- **Values**: Prioritizes personal growth, environmental sustainability, and work-life balance.
- **Motivations**: Reads to relax and escape from daily stress, enjoys stories with strong, relatable female protagonists.

7. Engage with Your Audience Directly

Direct engagement with your audience provides firsthand insights and strengthens your connection with them.

- **Social Media Interaction**: Engage with your followers by responding to comments, messages, and participating in discussions. Ask questions and encourage them to share their thoughts.
- **Email Newsletters**: Use your email newsletter to solicit feedback and insights from your subscribers. Include polls or questions in your emails to gather information.
- **Book Clubs and Events**: Attend or organize book clubs, readings, and literary events where you can interact with readers face-to-face. These interactions can provide valuable feedback and deepen your understanding of your audience.

By identifying and understanding your target audience, you can tailor your marketing and engagement strategies to resonate with them more effectively. In the next section, we will explore techniques for building a loyal reader base, ensuring that your audience remains engaged and supportive throughout your writing career.

Audience Engagement: Techniques for building a loyal reader base.

Building a loyal reader base is essential for long-term success as an author. Engaging with your audience not only helps boost your book's visibility and sales but also fosters a community of readers who are excited about your work and eagerly anticipate your future projects. Here are some effective techniques for building and maintaining a loyal reader base.

1. Consistent Communication

Consistency in communication helps maintain reader interest and builds trust over time.

- **Regular Updates**: Keep your audience informed about your writing progress, upcoming releases, and personal milestones. Regular updates can be shared through newsletters, blog posts, and social media.
- **Content Schedule**: Establish a content schedule to ensure you post regularly. This could include weekly blog posts, monthly newsletters, or daily social media updates.

- **Engagement Cadence**: Develop a rhythm for engaging with your readers. For example, you might reply to comments daily, host a Q&A session weekly, and send out newsletters monthly.

Let's dive into the importance of consistent communication with your readers. Maintaining regular and meaningful contact with your audience helps keep their interest alive and builds trust over time. Here's how to establish a solid communication strategy that keeps your readers engaged and invested in your journey.

Regular Updates

First, keeping your audience informed is key. Share regular updates about your writing progress, upcoming releases, and personal milestones. These updates can be communicated through newsletters, blog posts, and social media. Letting your readers know what's happening behind the scenes not only keeps them excited about your work but also makes them feel like part of your journey. For example, you might share a sneak peek of a new chapter, announce a book launch date, or celebrate reaching a writing milestone.

Content Schedule

To ensure you post regularly and keep your content fresh, establish a content schedule. Consistency is crucial here. Decide on a rhythm that works for you and your audience. This could mean weekly blog posts, monthly newsletters, or daily social media updates. By sticking to a schedule, you create a reliable pattern that your readers can look forward to. For instance, you might decide to publish a new blog post every Monday, send out a newsletter on the first of every month, and share a social media update every day.

Engagement Cadence

Engagement is more than just posting content; it's about interacting with your readers and building relationships. Develop a rhythm for engaging with your audience that feels natural and manageable. For example, you might reply to comments daily, host a Q&A session weekly, and send out newsletters monthly. Regular interaction shows your readers that you value their input and enjoy connecting with them. This could involve answering questions on social media, responding to emails, or setting up live chat sessions where readers can interact with you directly.

Bringing It All Together

By combining regular updates, a structured content schedule, and a consistent engagement cadence, you create a robust communication strategy that keeps your readers engaged and builds trust. Here's how you can implement this:

1. **Regular Updates**: Share behind-the-scenes glimpses, progress reports, and personal milestones regularly through various channels like newsletters, blogs, and social media.
2. **Content Schedule**: Plan and stick to a content schedule that ensures regular updates. This helps keep your content fresh and your audience engaged.
3. **Engagement Cadence**: Interact with your readers consistently. Develop a rhythm for replying to comments, hosting Q&A sessions, and sending newsletters to foster a strong connection with your audience.

Conclusion

Consistent communication is key to maintaining reader interest and building trust over time. By providing regular updates, establishing a content schedule, and maintaining an engagement cadence, you keep your readers engaged and excited about your work. This not only strengthens your relationship with your audience but also helps build a loyal fan base that supports your journey.

Let's make sure your readers feel connected and valued every step of the way. Happy communicating!

2. Personal Connection

Creating a personal connection with your readers makes them feel valued and appreciated.

- **Share Personal Stories**: Share your personal experiences, writing journey, and behind-the-scenes glimpses of your life. This helps readers relate to you as a person.
- **Authenticity**: Be genuine and authentic in your interactions. Readers appreciate honesty and transparency.
- **Reader Recognition**: Acknowledge your readers' contributions and interactions. Mention them in your newsletters, reply to their comments, and thank them for their support.

Making your readers feel valued and appreciated goes a long way in building a loyal fan base. Here's how you can foster a genuine connection with your audience through personal stories, authenticity, and reader recognition.

Share Personal Stories

First, sharing your personal experiences and writing journey can significantly help readers relate to you as a person. Don't hesitate to give them a behind-the-scenes glimpse of your life. Talk about what inspired your book, the challenges you faced while writing, or even how you celebrate your milestones. Personal stories make your updates more engaging and relatable. For example, you might share a funny anecdote from your writing process or a heartfelt story about what motivated you to write your book.

Authenticity

Next, authenticity is key. Be genuine and transparent in your interactions with your readers. People can sense when someone is being sincere, and they appreciate honesty. Whether you're sharing successes or setbacks, be open about your journey. Authenticity builds trust and makes your readers feel more connected to you. For instance, if you hit a rough patch in your writing process, don't shy away from sharing it. Let your readers know how you're overcoming obstacles and what keeps you going.

Reader Recognition

Recognizing and acknowledging your readers' contributions and interactions is crucial. Mention them in your newsletters, reply to their comments, and thank them for their support. This not only shows that you value their engagement but also makes them feel special and appreciated. For example, you could include a section in your newsletter where you highlight a reader's review or share fan art. Or simply take the time to respond thoughtfully to comments on your social media posts.

Bringing It All Together

By combining personal stories, authenticity, and reader recognition, you can create a strong personal connection with your audience. Here's how you can put these elements into practice:

1. **Share Personal Stories**: Let your readers in on your writing journey and personal experiences. This makes your updates more engaging and relatable.
2. **Be Authentic**: Maintain honesty and transparency in your interactions. Share both the highs and the lows of your journey.
3. **Recognize Your Readers**: Show appreciation for your readers' contributions and interactions. Mention them in your communications, respond to their comments, and thank them for their support.

Conclusion

Creating a personal connection with your readers makes them feel valued and appreciated. By sharing personal stories, being authentic, and recognizing their contributions, you build a loyal and engaged community around your work.

Let's ensure your readers know how much you appreciate them and make them feel like they're an integral part of your journey.

3. Interactive Content

Interactive content keeps readers engaged and encourages them to participate actively in your community.

- **Polls and Surveys**: Use polls and surveys to gather feedback and opinions from your readers. Ask them about their favorite characters, preferred book genres, or what they'd like to see next.
- **Contests and Giveaways**: Host contests and giveaways to create excitement and reward your readers. These can be as simple as a book giveaway or as elaborate as a fan art contest.
- **Q&A Sessions**: Host regular Q&A sessions where readers can ask you questions about your books, writing process, or personal life. These can be done through live streams, social media posts, or email.

4. Exclusive Content

Offering exclusive content can make your readers feel special and appreciated, encouraging them to stay engaged with you and your work.

- **Bonus Chapters**: Provide bonus chapters or scenes that are only available to your most loyal readers. These can be distributed through your newsletter or a special section on your website.
- **Early Access**: Give your readers early access to new releases, cover reveals, and special announcements.
- **Behind-the-Scenes**: Share behind-the-scenes content such as drafts, character sketches, or insights into your writing process.

5. Community Building

Building a community around your books helps foster a sense of belonging among your readers.

- **Online Groups**: Create or join online groups where readers can discuss your books and related topics. Platforms like Facebook Groups, Goodreads, and Discord are great for building communities.
- **Book Clubs**: Encourage readers to form book clubs around your books. Offer to join their discussions, either in person or virtually, to enhance their experience.
- **Reader Events**: Host or participate in events such as book signings, readings, workshops, and literary festivals. These events provide opportunities for personal interaction and strengthen reader loyalty.

6. Personalized Engagement

Personalized engagement shows your readers that you see them as individuals, not just as part of a larger audience.

- **Personal Messages**: Send personalized thank-you messages to readers who leave reviews, share your content, or support you in other ways.
- **Birthday Greetings**: If possible, send birthday greetings or special messages to your readers on their special days.
- **Customized Content**: Create content based on reader feedback and preferences. If a particular topic or character is popular, consider expanding on it in your blog or newsletter.

7. Collaborations and Cross-Promotions

Collaborating with other authors and engaging in cross-promotions can help you reach new audiences and build a stronger reader base.

- **Author Collaborations**: Work with other authors on joint projects, such as anthologies, co-written books, or cross-promotional campaigns.
- **Guest Posts and Features**: Write guest posts for other authors' blogs or have them write for yours. Feature each other's work in your newsletters and social media.
- **Interviews and Podcasts**: Participate in interviews and podcasts with other authors or influencers in your genre. This can introduce you to their audience and vice versa.

8. Responding to Feedback

Actively seeking and responding to reader feedback can improve your work and show readers that you value their opinions.

- **Solicit Feedback**: Encourage readers to leave reviews, comment on your posts, and provide feedback on your work.
- **Acknowledge Criticism**: Respond to criticism professionally and thoughtfully. Use constructive feedback to improve your future projects.
- **Incorporate Suggestions**: If readers suggest ideas or express particular interests, consider incorporating their input into your work. This can make them feel more connected to your creative process.

By employing these techniques, you can build a loyal reader base that supports your work and eagerly anticipates your future projects. Engaged readers are more likely to spread the word about your books, leave positive reviews, and become lifelong fans. In the next section, we will delve into content marketing, exploring how to create content that attracts and retains readers, further enhancing your engagement efforts.

Content Marketing: Creating content that attracts and retains readers.

Content marketing is a powerful strategy for attracting and retaining readers by providing valuable, relevant, and consistent content. Through content marketing, you can build a deeper connection with your audience, establish yourself as an authority in your genre, and keep readers engaged between book releases. Here's how to create compelling content that resonates with your audience and fosters loyalty.

1. Blogging

Blogging is an excellent way to share your thoughts, insights, and experiences with your readers.

- **Writing Tips**: Share advice on writing techniques, overcoming writer's block, and tips for aspiring authors. This positions you as a knowledgeable resource and attracts fellow writers and avid readers.
- **Book Reviews**: Write reviews of books in your genre. This can attract readers with similar tastes and foster a sense of community around shared interests.
- **Behind-the-Scenes**: Offer behind-the-scenes glimpses of your writing process, research, and daily life. This helps readers feel more connected to you as an author.
- **Guest Posts**: Invite other authors, industry experts, or influencers to write guest posts on your blog. This brings fresh perspectives and can attract their followers to your site.

2. Social Media

Social media platforms are vital for building your author brand and engaging with readers on a daily basis.

- **Visual Content**: Share images and videos related to your books, such as cover reveals, character art, and book trailers. Visual content is highly engaging and easily shareable.
- **Interactive Posts**: Create polls, quizzes, and interactive posts that encourage readers to participate. Ask questions about their favorite characters, plot predictions, or what they'd like to see in future books.
- **Live Sessions**: Host live sessions on platforms like Facebook, Instagram, or YouTube. Use these sessions for Q&A, book readings, and discussions about your work.
- **Daily Updates**: Keep your audience updated with regular posts about your writing progress, personal anecdotes, and book-related news.

3. Email Newsletters

Email newsletters are a direct way to communicate with your readers and keep them informed about your latest activities.

- **Exclusive Content**: Provide your subscribers with exclusive content such as bonus chapters, sneak peeks, and early access to new releases.
- **Regular Updates**: Send out newsletters on a regular schedule, whether weekly, bi-weekly, or monthly. Consistent communication keeps your audience engaged.

- **Personal Touch**: Write your newsletters in a personal and conversational tone. Share stories, reflections, and updates that make your readers feel valued and connected.
- **Call to Action**: Include clear calls to action in your newsletters, such as links to purchase your books, sign up for events, or follow you on social media.

4. Guest Posts and Collaborations

Collaborating with other authors and influencers can expand your reach and introduce you to new audiences.

- **Guest Blogging**: Write guest posts for popular blogs in your genre. Share your expertise, insights, and personal stories to attract new readers.
- **Interviews and Features**: Participate in interviews and features on other websites, podcasts, and YouTube channels. This exposure can drive traffic to your own platforms.
- **Collaborative Projects**: Partner with other authors on joint projects, such as anthologies, writing challenges, or cross-promotional campaigns.

5. Video Content

Video content is highly engaging and can help you connect with your audience on a deeper level.

- **Book Trailers**: Create professional book trailers that capture the essence of your story and entice viewers to read your book.
- **Author Interviews**: Share video interviews where you discuss your books, writing process, and personal journey.
- **Writing Vlogs**: Document your writing process through vlogs. Share your daily routines, challenges, and breakthroughs.
- **Tutorials and Workshops**: Create tutorial videos and workshops on writing, publishing, and marketing. This positions you as an expert and attracts a dedicated following.

6. Podcasts

Starting a podcast or appearing as a guest on existing podcasts can help you reach new audiences and engage with your current readers.

- **Author Podcast**: Host your own podcast where you discuss topics related to writing, interview other authors, and share book recommendations.
- **Guest Appearances**: Participate as a guest on popular podcasts in your genre. Share your insights and experiences to attract listeners to your work.
- **Q&A Sessions**: Record Q&A sessions where you answer questions from your readers. This can be a great way to address common queries and engage with your audience.

7. Content Series

Creating a series of related content can keep your audience coming back for more.

- **Blog Series**: Write a series of blog posts on a specific topic, such as character development, world-building, or book marketing.
- **Video Series**: Produce a series of videos that cover different aspects of your writing journey or provide tips for aspiring authors.
- **Newsletter Series**: Develop a themed series of newsletters that delve deeper into specific subjects or provide serialized content.

8. Engagement and Interaction

Engaging with your audience directly through content helps build a loyal community.

- **Respond to Comments**: Take the time to reply to comments on your blog, social media posts, and videos. This shows your readers that you value their input.
- **Encourage Sharing**: Ask your readers to share your content with their friends and followers. Provide easy sharing options and incentives, such as giveaways or shout-outs.
- **Host Challenges**: Organize writing challenges, reading marathons, or fan art contests. These activities encourage participation and build excitement around your work.

Making your readers feel valued and appreciated goes a long way in building a loyal fan base, and consistent, compelling content is key to keeping them engaged. Blogging is an excellent way to share your thoughts, insights, and experiences with your readers. Share writing tips to position yourself as a knowledgeable resource, attract fellow writers, and engage avid readers. Writing book reviews of titles in your genre can foster a sense of community around shared interests. Offering behind-the-scenes glimpses of your writing process, research, and daily life helps readers feel more connected to you as an author. Additionally, inviting other authors, industry experts, or influencers to write guest posts brings fresh perspectives and can attract their followers to your site.

Social media platforms are vital for building your author brand and engaging with readers on a daily basis. Share visual content such as images and videos related to your books—cover reveals, character art, and book trailers are highly engaging and easily shareable. Create interactive posts like polls, quizzes, and questions that encourage reader participation. Host live sessions on platforms like Facebook, Instagram, or YouTube for Q&A, book readings, and discussions about your work. Keep your audience updated with daily posts about your writing progress, personal anecdotes, and book-related news.

Email newsletters are a direct way to communicate with your readers and keep them informed about your latest activities. Provide your subscribers with exclusive content such as bonus chapters, sneak peeks, and early access to new releases. Send out newsletters on a regular schedule—whether weekly, bi-weekly, or monthly—to keep your audience engaged. Write your newsletters in a personal and conversational tone, sharing stories, reflections, and updates that make your readers feel valued and connected. Include clear calls to action, like links to purchase your books, sign up for events, or follow you on social media.

Collaborating with other authors and influencers can expand your reach and introduce you to new audiences. Write guest posts for popular blogs in your genre, sharing your expertise, insights, and personal stories to attract new readers. Participate in interviews and features on other websites, podcasts, and YouTube channels to drive traffic to your own platforms. Partner with other authors on joint projects such as anthologies, writing challenges, or cross-promotional campaigns.

Video content is highly engaging and can help you connect with your audience on a deeper level. Create professional book trailers that capture the essence of your story and entice viewers to read your book. Share video interviews where you discuss your books, writing process, and personal journey. Document your writing process through vlogs, sharing your daily routines, challenges, and breakthroughs. Create tutorial videos and workshops on writing, publishing, and marketing to position yourself as an expert and attract a dedicated following.

Starting a podcast or appearing as a guest on existing podcasts can help you reach new audiences and engage with your current readers. Host your own podcast where you discuss topics related to writing, interview other authors, and share book recommendations. Participate as a guest on popular podcasts in your genre to share your insights and experiences and attract listeners to your work. Record Q&A sessions where you answer questions from your readers to address common queries and engage with your audience.

Creating a series of related content can keep your audience coming back for more. Write a series of blog posts on specific topics like character development, world-building, or book marketing. Produce a series of videos that cover different aspects of your writing journey or provide tips for aspiring authors. Develop a themed series of newsletters that delve deeper into specific subjects or provide serialized content.

Engaging with your audience directly through content helps build a loyal community. Respond to comments on your blog, social media posts, and videos to show your readers that you value their input. Encourage your readers to share your content with their friends and followers by providing easy sharing options and incentives such as giveaways or shout-outs. Host challenges like writing contests, reading marathons, or fan art contests to encourage participation and build excitement around your work.

By leveraging these content marketing strategies, you can attract new readers, retain existing ones, and build a strong, engaged community around your books. In the next section, we will explore community building in more detail, discussing both online and offline methods to create a vibrant, supportive community around your work. Let's ensure your readers feel connected and valued every step of the way.

Community Building: Using online and offline methods to create a community around your book.

Building a community around your book is essential for fostering a sense of belonging and loyalty among your readers. A strong community not only supports your current work but also eagerly anticipates your future projects. By using both online and offline methods, you can create a vibrant, engaged community that enhances your presence as an author. Here's how to effectively build and sustain a community around your book.

1. Online Communities

Online communities offer a convenient and powerful way to connect with readers from around the world. Here are some strategies to build and engage with an online community:

- **Social Media Groups**: Create dedicated groups on platforms like Facebook or LinkedIn where readers can discuss your books, share their thoughts, and connect with each other. Regularly participate in these groups to keep the conversation active and engaging.
    - **Example**: "The [Your Book] Fan Club" on Facebook where members can discuss plot twists, favorite characters, and theories about future books.
- **Forums and Discussion Boards**: Participate in or create forums and discussion boards on sites like Goodreads and Reddit. These platforms are great for in-depth discussions and building a sense of community among readers.

    - **Example**: A Goodreads group where you host monthly book discussions, Q&A sessions, and reader polls.

- **Email Lists**: Build and maintain an email list to keep your readers informed and engaged. Use newsletters to share exclusive content, updates, and invitations to special events.

  - Example: A monthly newsletter that includes behind-the-scenes looks at your writing process, upcoming events, and subscriber-only contests.

- **Live Events and Webinars**: Host live events such as Q&A sessions, book readings, and writing workshops using platforms like Zoom, Facebook Live, or Instagram Live. These events allow you to interact directly with your readers in real-time.

  - Example: A live Q&A session on Instagram where you answer reader questions and discuss the themes and characters in your latest book.

- **Author Website and Blog**: Maintain an author website and blog where readers can find information about your books, read your latest posts, and join your mailing list. A blog can be a central hub for your community-building efforts.

  - Example: A dedicated section on your website where readers can submit their fan art, participate in writing challenges, and read guest posts from other authors.

2. Offline Communities

While online communities are powerful, offline interactions can deepen the connection with your readers and create memorable experiences. Here are some offline strategies for community building:

- **Book Signings and Readings**: Organize book signings and readings at local bookstores, libraries, and literary festivals. These events provide an opportunity for personal interaction and can attract new readers.

  - Example: A book signing event at a local independent bookstore where you read a chapter from your book, answer questions, and sign copies for attendees.

- **Book Clubs**: Encourage and support book clubs that choose to read your books. Offer to attend their meetings, either in person or virtually, to discuss your work and engage with readers.

    - **Example**: Partner with local libraries to promote book clubs that read your work and offer to join their discussions via Zoom or in person.

- **Workshops and Panels**: Participate in or host workshops and panel discussions on writing, publishing, and related topics. These events can position you as an expert and attract readers who are interested in your insights.

    - **Example**: A writing workshop at a literary festival where you share tips on character development and plot structure.

- **Community Events**: Engage with your local community by participating in events such as charity fundraisers, school visits, and community fairs. These events help build your presence and connect with potential readers who share your values and interests.

    - **Example**: A school visit where you talk about your journey as an author, conduct a creative writing session, and donate copies of your books to the school library.

3. Collaborative Activities

Collaborating with other authors, influencers, and organizations can help expand your community and bring fresh perspectives to your work.

- **Co-Hosted Events**: Partner with other authors to co-host events such as book signings, readings, or online webinars. This collaboration can draw in fans from both authors' audiences.

    - **Example**: A joint book launch event with a fellow author where you both read excerpts from your new releases and discuss your writing processes.

- **Cross-Promotions**: Collaborate with other authors and influencers for cross-promotional campaigns. This can include social media takeovers, guest blog posts, and shared giveaways.

- **Example**: A social media campaign where you and another author take over each other's Instagram accounts for a day, sharing insights and engaging with each other's followers.

- **Anthologies and Joint Projects**: Contribute to anthologies or other joint projects with other authors. These collaborative efforts can introduce your work to new readers and strengthen your community ties.
  - **Example**: Contributing a short story to an anthology featuring multiple authors in your genre, with each author promoting the collection to their audience.

4. Encouraging Reader Participation

Involving your readers in your creative process and promotional activities can deepen their investment in your work and foster a stronger community.

- **Reader Polls and Votes**: Use polls and votes to let your readers have a say in certain aspects of your book, such as character names, cover designs, or plot decisions.
  - **Example**: A poll on your website where readers can vote on their favorite cover design for your upcoming book.

- **Fan Art and Writing Contests**: Host contests that encourage readers to create fan art, write short stories, or develop other creative works based on your books. Share the best submissions on your website and social media.
  - **Example**: A fan art contest where the winning artwork is featured in your newsletter and the artist receives a signed copy of your book.

- **Beta Reader Programs**: Invite your most dedicated readers to become beta readers, offering them early access to your manuscripts in exchange for feedback. This not only helps improve your book but also makes readers feel valued and involved.
  - **Example**: A beta reader program where selected readers receive an early draft of your book and provide feedback on the plot, characters, and pacing.

5. Building Long-Term Relationships

Building a community is not just about one-time interactions but creating long-term relationships with your readers.

- **Personalized Communication**: Personalize your communications whenever possible. Address readers by their names in emails, acknowledge their contributions in public posts, and show genuine appreciation for their support.
- **Follow-Up**: After events or significant interactions, follow up with attendees or participants to thank them and keep the connection alive.
    - **Example**: Sending a thank-you email to attendees of your book signing event, along with a recap and an invitation to join your newsletter.
- **Ongoing Engagement**: Continue to engage with your community even when you don't have a new book to promote. Share updates, interesting content, and personal stories to keep the relationship strong.
    - **Example**: Regularly updating your blog with posts about your writing process, favorite books, and life updates, even between book releases.

Building a community around your book is essential for fostering a sense of belonging and loyalty among your readers. A strong community not only supports your current work but also eagerly anticipates your future projects. By using both online and offline methods, you can create a vibrant, engaged community that enhances your presence as an author. Here's how to effectively build and sustain a community around your book.

Let's start with online communities. These offer a convenient and powerful way to connect with readers from around the world. One effective strategy is to create dedicated groups on platforms like Facebook or LinkedIn where readers can discuss your books, share their thoughts, and connect with each other. Regularly participate in these groups to keep the conversation active and engaging. For instance, imagine a "The [Your Book] Fan Club" on Facebook where members can discuss plot twists, favorite characters, and theories about future books. Another approach is

Write It. Publish It. Sell It.

to participate in or create forums and discussion boards on sites like Goodreads and Reddit. These platforms are great for in-depth discussions and building a sense of community among readers. You could host monthly book discussions, Q&A sessions, and reader polls in a dedicated Goodreads group.

Building and maintaining an email list is another crucial aspect of online community building. Use newsletters to share exclusive content, updates, and invitations to special events. A monthly newsletter that includes behind-the-scenes looks at your writing process, upcoming events, and subscriber-only contests can keep your readers engaged and excited about your work. Additionally, hosting live events such as Q&A sessions, book readings, and writing workshops using platforms like Zoom, Facebook Live, or Instagram Live allows you to interact directly with your readers in real-time. Imagine a live Q&A session on Instagram where you answer reader questions and discuss the themes and characters in your latest book. Don't forget about your author website and blog, which serve as the central hub for your community-building efforts. Maintain an engaging website where readers can find information about your books, read your latest posts, and join your mailing list. A dedicated section on your website where readers can submit their fan art, participate in writing challenges, and read guest posts from other authors can foster a strong sense of community.

Now, let's move to offline communities. While online communities are powerful, offline interactions can deepen the connection with your readers and create memorable experiences. Organize book signings and readings at local bookstores, libraries, and literary festivals. These events provide an opportunity for personal interaction and can attract new readers. Picture a book signing event at a local independent bookstore where you read a chapter from your book, answer questions, and sign copies for attendees. Encourage and support book clubs that choose to read your books. Offer to attend their meetings, either in person or virtually, to discuss your work and engage with readers. Partnering with local libraries to promote book clubs that read your work and joining their discussions via Zoom or in person can be very rewarding.

Participating in or hosting workshops and panel discussions on writing, publishing, and related topics can position you as an expert and attract readers interested in your insights. Imagine leading a writing workshop at a literary festival where you share tips on character development and plot structure. Engage with your local community by participating in events such as charity fundraisers, school visits, and community fairs. These events help build your presence and connect with potential readers who share your values and interests. Think about a school visit where you talk about your journey as an author, conduct a creative writing session, and donate copies of your books to the school library.

Collaborating with other authors, influencers, and organizations can help expand your community and bring fresh perspectives to your work. Partner with other authors to co-host events such as book signings, readings, or online webinars. This collaboration can draw in fans from both authors' audiences. Imagine a joint book launch event with a fellow author where you both read excerpts from your new releases and discuss your writing processes. Collaborate with other authors and influencers for cross-promotional campaigns, such as social media takeovers, guest blog posts, and shared giveaways. Picture a social media campaign where you and another author take over each other's Instagram accounts for a day, sharing insights and engaging with each other's followers. Contributing to anthologies or other joint projects with other authors can introduce your work to new readers and strengthen your community ties. Imagine contributing a short story to an anthology featuring multiple authors in your genre, with each author promoting the collection to their audience.

Involving your readers in your creative process and promotional activities can deepen their investment in your work and foster a stronger community. Use polls and votes to let your readers have a say in certain aspects of your book, such as character names, cover designs, or plot decisions. For example, you could run a poll on your website where readers can vote on their favorite cover design for your upcoming book. Host contests that encourage readers to create fan art, write short stories, or develop other creative works based on your books. Share the best submissions on your website and social media. Imagine a fan art contest where the winning artwork is featured in your newsletter and the artist receives a signed copy of your book. Invite your most dedicated readers to become beta readers, offering them early access to your manuscripts in exchange for feedback. This not only helps improve your book but also makes readers feel valued and involved. Picture a beta reader program where selected readers receive an early draft of your book and provide feedback on the plot, characters, and pacing.

Building a community is not just about one-time interactions but creating long-term relationships with your readers. Personalize your communications whenever possible. Address readers by their names in emails, acknowledge their contributions in public posts, and show genuine appreciation for their support. Follow up after events or significant interactions to thank attendees or participants and keep the connection alive. For example, you could send a thank-you email to attendees of your book signing event, along with a recap and an invitation to join your newsletter. Continue to engage with your community even when you don't have a new book to promote. Share updates, interesting content, and personal stories to keep the relationship strong. Regularly updating your blog with posts about your writing process, favorite books, and life updates, even between book releases, can maintain engagement.

By combining online and offline methods, collaborative activities, reader participation, and long-term relationship-building strategies, you can create a vibrant and supportive community around your books. In the next section, we will discuss how to encourage and manage reader feedback, using it to improve your work and strengthen your connection with your audience. Let's ensure your readers feel connected and valued every step of the way.

Feedback and Interaction: Encouraging and managing reader feedback to improve your work.

Encouraging and managing reader feedback is crucial for any author aiming to improve their work and strengthen their connection with their audience. Constructive feedback helps you understand your readers' perspectives, identify areas for improvement, and enhance your future projects. Here are strategies to effectively encourage, collect, and manage reader feedback.

1. Encouraging Feedback

Creating an environment where readers feel comfortable providing feedback is the first step in gathering valuable insights.

- **Solicit Reviews**: Ask your readers to leave reviews on platforms like Amazon, Goodreads, and your own website. Mention this at the end of your book, in your newsletters, and on social media.
    - **Example**: "If you enjoyed 'Love in the Lakeside,' please consider leaving a review on Amazon or Goodreads. Your feedback helps me improve and reach more readers!"
- **Engage on Social Media**: Use your social media platforms to ask for feedback. Post questions about your books, characters, and plots, and encourage readers to share their thoughts.

    - **Example**: "What did you think of Emma's decision at the end of 'Love in the Lakeside'? I'd love to hear your thoughts!"

- **Email Newsletters**: Include a call-to-action in your newsletters asking subscribers for feedback on your latest release or upcoming projects.

    - **Example**: "As I work on my next book, I'd love your input. What themes or characters would you like to see explored?"

- **Beta Readers**: Establish a beta reader program where selected readers can provide early feedback on your manuscripts. This not only improves your book but also creates a sense of involvement and loyalty.

    - **Example**: "Join my beta reader team and get an early look at my next novel! Your feedback will help shape the final version."

2. Collecting Feedback

Once you've encouraged feedback, it's important to have a system in place to collect and organize it.

- **Surveys and Questionnaires**: Use tools like Google Forms or SurveyMonkey to create surveys that gather detailed feedback. Ask specific questions about different aspects of your book.

    - **Example**: A post-release survey with questions about plot pacing, character development, and overall enjoyment.

- **Review Aggregation**: Monitor reviews on various platforms to identify common themes and areas for improvement. Use review aggregation tools or manually compile reviews into a spreadsheet.

    - **Example**: A spreadsheet that tracks reader ratings and comments on Amazon and Goodreads.

- **Direct Communication**: Encourage readers to email you directly with their feedback. This allows for more personalized and detailed responses.

    - **Example**: "Feel free to email me at [Your Email] with any thoughts or feedback. I appreciate your insights!"

3. Managing Feedback

Effectively managing feedback involves analyzing, responding to, and incorporating it into your work.

- **Analyze Patterns**: Look for recurring themes in the feedback you receive. Identify what readers consistently praise or criticize, and use this information to guide your revisions.

    - **Example**: If multiple readers mention that the pacing is slow in the middle chapters, consider revising those sections to increase engagement.

- **Prioritize Constructive Criticism**: Focus on actionable feedback that provides specific suggestions for improvement. While all feedback is valuable, not all of it will be useful or relevant.

    - **Example**: Constructive feedback might highlight a plot hole or suggest deeper character development, whereas vague comments like "I didn't like it" are less actionable.

- **Respond Professionally**: Acknowledge and thank readers for their feedback, especially if they took the time to write a detailed review or email. Professional and courteous responses can turn critical readers into loyal fans.

    - **Example**: "Thank you for your detailed review of 'Love in the Lakeside.' I appreciate your insights on the pacing and will consider them as I work on my next book."

- **Incorporate Feedback**: Use the constructive criticism you receive to improve your future work. Whether it's refining your writing style, addressing plot issues, or enhancing character arcs, incorporating feedback can make your books stronger and more appealing.

    - **Example**: If readers consistently mention that they want to see more backstory for a particular character, consider adding more depth to that character in your next book.

4. Engaging with Your Audience

Regular interaction with your readers helps build a supportive community and shows that you value their opinions.

- **Discussion Forums**: Participate in online forums and discussion boards related to your genre or books. Engage with readers by answering questions, discussing plot points, and sharing insights.

    o **Example**: A Goodreads discussion thread where you interact with readers about their favorite scenes and characters.

- **Live Chats and Q&A Sessions**: Host live chats or Q&A sessions on social media platforms or through webinars. This provides a direct way for readers to ask questions and share feedback.

    o **Example**: A Facebook Live Q&A where you discuss the themes of your latest book and answer reader questions in real-time.

- **Reader Appreciation**: Show appreciation for your readers' support and feedback through shout-outs, giveaways, and exclusive content. Recognizing their contributions helps build a loyal and engaged audience.

    o **Example**: A monthly "Reader of the Month" feature in your newsletter, highlighting a reader who has provided valuable feedback or support.

5. Adapting to Feedback

Adapting to feedback means being open to making changes based on reader insights and continually striving to improve your craft.

- **Flexible Mindset**: Be open to constructive criticism and willing to make changes to improve your work. Understand that feedback is a tool for growth, not a personal attack.

    o **Example**: If readers suggest that a subplot is confusing, be willing to revisit and clarify it in your next draft.

- **Iterative Process**: View writing as an iterative process where each piece of feedback helps you refine and enhance your work. Continuously seek out and incorporate feedback throughout your writing career.

    o **Example**: Regularly share drafts with beta readers and use their feedback to make iterative improvements before final publication.

- **Celebrate Progress**: Acknowledge and celebrate the improvements you make based on reader feedback. Share your growth journey with your readers to show how their input has positively impacted your work.
  - **Example**: Share a blog post detailing how reader feedback helped shape a particular character or plot twist in your book.

Let's talk about the importance of encouraging feedback from your readers and how it can significantly enhance your work. Creating an environment where readers feel comfortable providing feedback is the first step in gathering valuable insights. Ask your readers to leave reviews on platforms like Amazon, Goodreads, and your own website. Mention this at the end of your book, in your newsletters, and on social media. For example, you might say, "If you enjoyed 'Love in the Lakeside,' please consider leaving a review on Amazon or Goodreads. Your feedback helps me improve and reach more readers!" Engage with your audience on social media by posting questions about your books, characters, and plots, encouraging readers to share their thoughts. A question like, "What did you think of Emma's decision at the end of 'Love in the Lakeside'? I'd love to hear your thoughts!" can spark meaningful discussions. Include a call-to-action in your newsletters asking subscribers for feedback on your latest release or upcoming projects, such as, "As I work on my next book, I'd love your input. What themes or characters would you like to see explored?" Establish a beta reader program where selected readers can provide early feedback on your manuscripts. This not only improves your book but also creates a sense of involvement and loyalty. Invite readers with, "Join my beta reader team and get an early look at my next novel! Your feedback will help shape the final version."

Once you've encouraged feedback, it's important to have a system in place to collect and organize it. Use tools like Google Forms or SurveyMonkey to create surveys that gather detailed feedback. For instance, a post-release survey with questions about plot pacing, character development, and overall enjoyment can provide valuable insights. Monitor reviews on various platforms to identify common themes and areas for improvement, and consider using review aggregation tools or manually compiling reviews into a spreadsheet. This can help you track

Write It. Publish It. Sell It.

reader ratings and comments on Amazon and Goodreads. Encourage readers to email you directly with their feedback, offering a personal touch with, "Feel free to email me at [Your Email] with any thoughts or feedback. I appreciate your insights!"

Effectively managing feedback involves analyzing, responding to, and incorporating it into your work. Look for recurring themes in the feedback you receive. Identify what readers consistently praise or criticize, and use this information to guide your revisions. For example, if multiple readers mention that the pacing is slow in the middle chapters, consider revising those sections to increase engagement. Focus on actionable feedback that provides specific suggestions for improvement. While all feedback is valuable, not all of it will be useful or relevant. Constructive feedback might highlight a plot hole or suggest deeper character development, whereas vague comments like "I didn't like it" are less actionable. Acknowledge and thank readers for their feedback, especially if they took the time to write a detailed review or email. Professional and courteous responses can turn critical readers into loyal fans. For example, you might say, "Thank you for your detailed review of 'Love in the Lakeside.' I appreciate your insights on the pacing and will consider them as I work on my next book." Use the constructive criticism you receive to improve your future work. Whether it's refining your writing style, addressing plot issues, or enhancing character arcs, incorporating feedback can make your books stronger and more appealing. If readers consistently mention that they want to see more backstory for a particular character, consider adding more depth to that character in your next book.

Regular interaction with your readers helps build a supportive community and shows that you value their opinions. Participate in online forums and discussion boards related to your genre or books. Engage with readers by answering questions, discussing plot points, and sharing insights. For example, you might join a Goodreads discussion thread where you interact with readers about their favorite scenes and characters. Host live chats or Q&A sessions on social media platforms or through webinars. This provides a direct way for readers to ask questions and share feedback. Imagine a Facebook Live Q&A where you discuss the themes of your latest book and answer reader questions in real-time. Show appreciation for your readers' support and feedback through shout-outs, giveaways, and exclusive content. Recognizing their contributions helps build a loyal and engaged audience. For instance, you could feature a "Reader of the Month" in your newsletter, highlighting a reader who has provided valuable feedback or support.

Adapting to feedback means being open to making changes based on reader insights and continually striving to improve your craft. Be open to constructive criticism and willing to make changes to improve your work. Understand that feedback is a tool for growth, not a personal attack. If readers suggest that a subplot is confusing, be willing to revisit and clarify it in your next draft. View writing as an iterative process where each piece of feedback helps you refine and enhance your work. Regularly share drafts with beta readers and use their feedback to make iterative improvements before final publication. Acknowledge and celebrate the improvements you make based on reader feedback. Share your growth journey with your readers to show how their input has positively impacted your work. For instance, you could write a blog post detailing how reader feedback helped shape a particular character or plot twist in your book.

By encouraging, collecting, managing, and adapting to reader feedback, you can significantly enhance the quality of your work and build a strong, engaged community around your books. In the next chapter, we will explore the final steps to set real expectations for your author journey, ensuring you approach your writing career with a realistic and strategic mindset.

Chapter 7: Set Real Expectations for Your Author Journey

Embarking on an author journey is an exciting and rewarding endeavor, but it also comes with its own set of challenges and realities. Understanding what to expect can help you navigate this path more effectively and set yourself up for long-term success. In this chapter, we will explore the realities of publishing, the importance of setting achievable goals, how to measure your success, strategies for maintaining motivation, and the necessity of long-term planning for your writing career.

The Reality of Publishing: Understanding the Challenges and Rewards of Being an Author

The world of publishing is complex and ever-evolving. While the idea of seeing your book on shelves and in the hands of readers is exhilarating, the journey to get there can be filled with obstacles.

- **Industry Challenges**: Learn about the various challenges you might face in the publishing industry, including competition, market trends, and the intricacies of both traditional and self-publishing routes.
- **Rejections and Criticism**: Understand that rejections are part of the process. Even best-selling authors have faced numerous rejections before finding success.
- **Rewards**: Recognize the immense rewards of being an author—creative fulfillment, the joy of connecting with readers, and the impact your work can have on others.

By gaining a clear picture of both the challenges and rewards, you can approach your author journey with a balanced perspective.

Goal Setting: Setting Achievable Goals for Your Writing and Publishing Career

Setting realistic and achievable goals is essential for maintaining momentum and tracking your progress. These goals should be specific, measurable, and aligned with your broader vision for your career.

- **Short-Term Goals**: Focus on immediate objectives, such as completing a chapter, finishing a draft, or submitting query letters.
- **Medium-Term Goals**: Set goals for the next 1-2 years, like publishing your first book, building an online presence, or expanding your readership.
- **Long-Term Goals**: Think about where you want to be in 5-10 years. Consider goals like publishing multiple books, earning awards, or becoming a full-time author.

Effective goal setting helps you stay focused, motivated, and on track with your author journey.

Measuring Success: Defining What Success Looks Like for You and Your Book

Success as an author can be measured in various ways, and it's important to define what it looks like for you personally.

- **Personal Fulfillment**: For some, success means the satisfaction of finishing a book or sharing their story with the world.
- **Reader Impact**: Consider the impact your book has on readers. Success might mean receiving heartfelt letters from fans or knowing your book has made a difference in someone's life.
- **Financial Goals**: Financial success can range from covering your publishing costs to making a sustainable income from your writing.
- **Professional Recognition**: This might include awards, bestseller lists, or recognition from peers and industry professionals.

By setting clear metrics for success, you can better appreciate your achievements and identify areas for growth.

Maintaining Motivation: Staying Motivated Through the Ups and Downs of the Publishing Process

The publishing process is a journey with highs and lows. Maintaining motivation is crucial for overcoming obstacles and continuing to write and publish.

- **Find Your Why**: Keep your core motivations and passions at the forefront. Remember why you started writing and what you hope to achieve.
- **Celebrate Milestones**: Acknowledge and celebrate your accomplishments, no matter how small. Each step forward is progress.
- **Stay Connected**: Engage with a community of writers and readers who can offer support, encouragement, and accountability.
- **Take Breaks**: Allow yourself to rest and recharge. Breaks can prevent burnout and keep your creativity flowing.

Staying motivated requires a mix of self-awareness, community support, and self-care.

Long-Term Planning: Planning for the Future of Your Author Career Beyond Your First Book

Your first book is just the beginning of your author journey. Long-term planning ensures that you continue to grow and succeed as a writer.

- **Career Vision**: Define your long-term vision as an author. What kind of legacy do you want to leave? What themes or genres do you want to explore?
- **Skill Development**: Continuously improve your craft by attending workshops, reading widely, and seeking feedback.
- **Networking**: Build relationships with other authors, industry professionals, and your readers. Networking can open doors to new opportunities and collaborations.
- **Diversification**: Consider expanding your reach by exploring different genres, writing for various formats (like articles, short stories, or screenplays), or venturing into related fields (like teaching or public speaking).

By planning for the long term, you can create a sustainable and fulfilling career as an author.

In this chapter, we will delve deeper into each of these topics, providing practical advice and strategies to help you set realistic expectations, achieve your goals, measure your success, stay motivated, and plan for a thriving author career.

The Reality of Publishing: Understanding the challenges and rewards of being an author.

Embarking on the journey of becoming an author is thrilling, but it's also important to go in with your eyes wide open. The world of publishing is like a rollercoaster, full of ups and downs, twists and turns. Understanding the reality of this journey can help you navigate it more smoothly and enjoy the ride.

Industry Challenges

First things first: the publishing industry is highly competitive. There are thousands of new books published every day, so standing out can be tough. You'll encounter various challenges, whether you're going the traditional route or opting for self-publishing.

- **Traditional Publishing**: Securing a literary agent and a publishing deal is no small feat. It involves crafting the perfect query letter, dealing with rejections, and sometimes waiting months to hear back. Even once you've got a deal, you'll need to work on edits, marketing plans, and deadlines.
- **Self-Publishing**: While self-publishing gives you control, it also means you're wearing all the hats. You'll be responsible for everything from writing and editing to cover design and marketing. It's a lot to juggle, but it can be incredibly rewarding if done right.

Rejections and Criticism

Let's talk about rejections. They're part and parcel of the writing life. Even famous authors like J.K. Rowling and Stephen King faced numerous rejections before finding success. It's essential to remember that a rejection isn't a reflection of your worth or your talent. It's often about finding the right fit.

Criticism is another reality. Not everyone will love your work, and that's okay. Constructive criticism can be incredibly valuable, helping you grow as a writer. Learning to take feedback in stride and use it to improve is a crucial skill.

The Rewards

Now, let's get to the good stuff—the rewards of being an author. Despite the challenges, the joys of writing and publishing are plentiful.

- **Creative Fulfillment**: There's nothing quite like the feeling of bringing a story to life. The process of creating characters, building worlds, and crafting plots is deeply satisfying.
- **Connecting with Readers**: Hearing from readers who were moved by your work or found escape in your stories is incredibly rewarding. It's one of the best feelings in the world to know that your words have touched someone's life.
- **Personal Growth**: Writing a book is a journey of personal growth. You'll learn a lot about yourself, your discipline, and your creativity. Each project helps you grow and develop as a writer.
- **Financial Rewards**: While not every author strikes it rich, there are financial rewards to be had. Whether it's through book sales, speaking engagements, or related writing gigs, there's potential to earn money doing what you love.

Balancing the Challenges and Rewards

Balancing the challenges with the rewards is key. Understanding that both exist helps you stay grounded and persistent. Embrace the journey, celebrate the small victories, and learn from the setbacks. Every author's path is unique, and yours will be full of its own unique blend of challenges and triumphs.

By acknowledging the reality of publishing, you can approach your author journey with resilience and optimism, ready to tackle the hurdles and savor the rewards. In the next section, we'll dive into setting achievable goals for your writing and publishing career, helping you stay focused and motivated on your path to success.

Let's have a candid conversation about the realities of the publishing industry. First things first: the publishing industry is highly competitive. With thousands of new books published every day, standing out can be tough. Whether you're pursuing traditional publishing or opting for self-publishing, you'll encounter various challenges.

Securing a literary agent and a publishing deal is no small feat. It involves crafting the perfect query letter, dealing with rejections, and sometimes waiting months to hear back. Even once you've got a deal, you'll need to work on edits, marketing plans, and deadlines. The process is rigorous and can be daunting, but landing that deal can be incredibly rewarding. On the other hand, self-publishing gives you control, but it also means you're wearing all the hats. You'll be responsible for everything from writing and editing to cover design and marketing. It's a lot to juggle, but it can be incredibly rewarding if done right. The independence and direct connection with your readers are significant benefits, but the workload can be intense.

Now, let's talk about rejections. They're part and parcel of the writing life. Even famous authors like J.K. Rowling and Stephen King faced numerous rejections before finding success. It's essential to remember that a rejection isn't a reflection of your worth or your talent. It's often about finding the right fit. Criticism is another reality. Not everyone will love your work, and that's okay. Constructive criticism can be incredibly valuable, helping you grow as a writer. Learning to take feedback in stride and use it to improve is a crucial skill.

Despite these challenges, the rewards of being an author are plentiful. Creative fulfillment is one of the biggest rewards. There's nothing quite like the feeling of bringing a story to life. The process of creating characters, building worlds, and crafting plots is deeply satisfying. Connecting with readers is another immense joy. Hearing from readers who were moved by your work or found escape in your stories is incredibly rewarding. It's one of the best feelings in the world to know that your words have touched someone's life. Writing a book is also a journey of personal growth. You'll learn a lot about yourself, your discipline, and your creativity. Each project helps you grow and develop as a writer. And while not every author strikes it rich, there are financial rewards to be had. Whether it's through book sales, speaking engagements, or related writing gigs, there's potential to earn money doing what you love.

Balancing the challenges with the rewards is key. Understanding that both exist helps you stay grounded and persistent. Embrace the journey, celebrate the small victories, and learn from the setbacks. Every author's path is unique, and yours will be full of its own unique blend of challenges and triumphs. By acknowledging the reality of publishing, you can approach your author journey with resilience and optimism, ready to tackle the hurdles and savor the rewards.

In the next section, we'll dive into setting achievable goals for your writing and publishing career, helping you stay focused and motivated on your path to success. Embrace the journey, keep writing, and remember that every challenge you face brings you one step closer to your dreams.

Goal Setting: Setting achievable goals for your writing and publishing career.

Setting goals is a vital part of any successful author journey. Goals give you direction, motivation, and a clear sense of what you're working towards. But it's not just about setting any goals—it's about setting achievable ones that keep you moving forward without overwhelming you.

Let's explore how to set realistic and inspiring goals for your writing and publishing career.

1. Short-Term Goals

Short-term goals are your immediate targets. They are the small steps that will get you closer to your bigger dreams. Think of them as your day-to-day or week-to-week objectives.

- **Daily Writing Targets**: Set a daily word count goal. It could be as modest as 500 words a day or as ambitious as 2,000 words. The key is consistency.
    - **Example**: "I will write 1,000 words every day."
- **Chapter Milestones**: Break your book into manageable chunks by focusing on completing one chapter at a time.
    - **Example**: "I will finish writing Chapter 3 by the end of this week."
- **Research and Planning**: Set goals for your research and planning phases. This could involve outlining your plot or developing character backstories.
    - **Example**: "I will complete character sketches for all main characters this month."

2. Medium-Term Goals

Medium-term goals bridge the gap between your daily efforts and your long-term dreams. These are your 1-2 year goals that keep you moving steadily forward.

- **Finish Your Manuscript**: Aim to complete the first draft of your manuscript within a specific timeframe.
    - **Example**: "I will finish the first draft of my novel within six months."
- **Editing and Revisions**: Plan out the time needed for editing and revising your manuscript.
    - **Example**: "I will complete the first round of edits by December."

- **Build Your Platform**: Work on growing your author platform through social media, a blog, or a website.
  - **Example**: "I will gain 1,000 followers on my author Instagram account in one year."

3. Long-Term Goals

Long-term goals are your big-picture dreams. These are the 5-10 year goals that guide your career trajectory and help you visualize your ultimate achievements.

- **Publish Multiple Books**: Set a goal for the number of books you want to publish over the next decade.
  - **Example**: "I will publish five novels in the next ten years."

- **Achieve Financial Milestones**: Consider financial goals, such as earning a certain amount of income from your writing.
  - **Example**: "I will make a full-time income from my writing within five years."

- **Awards and Recognition**: Aim for specific awards, bestseller lists, or other forms of recognition.
  - **Example**: "I will win a major literary award within ten years."

4. SMART Goals

To ensure your goals are effective, use the SMART criteria. This approach ensures your goals are clear and reachable.

- **Specific**: Clearly define what you want to achieve.
  - **Example**: "I will write 1,000 words each day."

- **Measurable**: Make sure you can track your progress.

- Example: "I will track my daily word count in a writing journal."

- **Achievable**: Set goals that are challenging but possible.

  - Example: "I will finish my novel's first draft in six months."

- **Relevant**: Ensure your goals align with your overall career objectives.

  - Example: "Building my social media presence will help me engage with my readers."

- **Time-Bound**: Set deadlines to create a sense of urgency.

  - Example: "I will complete my manuscript by June 30th."

5. Adjust and Reflect

Goals are not set in stone. It's essential to regularly review and adjust them based on your progress and changing circumstances.

- **Regular Check-Ins**: Set aside time each month or quarter to review your goals and assess your progress.

  - Example: "I will review my writing goals at the end of each month."

- **Celebrate Achievements**: Acknowledge and celebrate when you hit your milestones. This keeps you motivated and reminds you of your progress.

  - Example: "When I finish my manuscript, I will treat myself to a weekend getaway."

- **Adjust as Needed**: Be flexible and willing to adjust your goals if you encounter obstacles or if your priorities change.

  - Example: "If I find my daily word count goal too high, I'll adjust it to something more manageable."

6. Stay Motivated

Staying motivated is crucial for achieving your goals. Find ways to keep your passion for writing alive.

- **Join Writing Communities**: Engage with other writers for support, encouragement, and accountability.
  - **Example**: "I will join a local writers' group and attend monthly meetings."
- **Reward Yourself**: Set up a reward system for meeting your goals.
  - **Example**: "After completing each chapter, I'll reward myself with a favorite treat."
- **Visualize Success**: Regularly visualize your long-term goals and the success you aspire to achieve.
  - **Example**: "I will create a vision board with images and quotes that inspire my writing journey."

By setting achievable goals, you can stay focused, motivated, and on track with your writing and publishing career. In the next section, we'll discuss how to measure success, helping you define what success looks like for you and your book.

- **Measuring Success**: Defining what success looks like for you and your book.

Success in the world of writing and publishing can take many forms. It's not just about bestseller lists or blockbuster sales—success is personal and can be defined in numerous ways. Understanding what success means to you will help you stay focused, motivated, and satisfied with your progress. Let's explore various dimensions of success and how you can measure them.

1. Personal Fulfillment

For many authors, personal fulfillment is the most important measure of success. This involves the joy of creation, the satisfaction of completing a project, and the personal growth that comes with the writing process.

- **Creative Satisfaction**: Reflect on whether you're happy with the story you've told and the quality of your writing.
    - **Example**: "I feel proud of the characters I've developed and the plot I've crafted."
- **Completion**: Celebrate the accomplishment of finishing a manuscript, regardless of the outcome.

    - **Example**: "I've completed my novel, which is a huge personal milestone for me."

- **Growth**: Consider how much you've learned and grown as a writer through the process.

    - **Example**: "Writing this book has improved my storytelling skills and deepened my understanding of the craft."

2. Reader Impact

Impacting readers' lives is a profound measure of success. Knowing that your words have touched someone or made a difference can be incredibly rewarding.

- **Reader Feedback**: Look at the feedback and reviews from your readers. Positive reviews, heartfelt messages, and fan interactions can be indicators of your book's impact.

    - **Example**: "I've received emails from readers saying my book helped them through a tough time."

- **Engagement**: Measure the level of engagement from your readers, such as comments on social media, participation in discussions, and attendance at your events.

    o **Example**: "Readers are actively discussing my book in online forums and book clubs."

- **Word of Mouth**: Consider how often readers recommend your book to others.

    o **Example**: "I've noticed my book being recommended in various reading groups and social media platforms."

3. Financial Goals

Financial success can vary widely depending on your personal goals and needs. Whether you aim to make a full-time living from your writing or simply cover your publishing costs, financial metrics are a clear way to measure success.

- **Sales Figures**: Track your book sales over time. Set realistic targets based on your marketing efforts and the size of your audience.

    o **Example**: "I aim to sell 1,000 copies of my book in the first year."

- **Income**: Monitor the income generated from your writing, including book sales, speaking engagements, and other related activities.

    o **Example**: "I want to earn enough from my writing to supplement my income by $500 per month."

- **ROI**: Calculate the return on investment (ROI) for your publishing expenses, such as editing, cover design, and marketing.

    o **Example**: "I've recouped my initial investment in publishing within six months."

4. Professional Recognition

Professional recognition can validate your hard work and open doors to new opportunities. This can come in many forms, from awards and accolades to positive reviews from respected critics.

- **Awards and Nominations**: Winning or being nominated for literary awards can be a significant marker of success.
    - **Example**: "My book was nominated for the Best Debut Novel at the literary awards."
- **Critical Acclaim**: Receiving positive reviews from respected critics, publications, or industry professionals.
    - **Example**: "My book received a glowing review in a major literary magazine."
- **Peer Recognition**: Being acknowledged and respected by fellow authors and industry professionals.
    - **Example**: "Other authors in my genre have praised my work and recommended it to their readers."

5. Market Presence

Establishing a strong presence in the market is another way to measure success. This includes building a loyal reader base, maintaining a visible author brand, and achieving recognition in your genre.

- **Brand Recognition**: Assess how well-known your author brand is within your target audience and genre.
    - **Example**: "Readers immediately recognize my name and my books at conventions and online."
- **Loyal Following**: Measure the size and engagement level of your reader base.

- o **Example**: "I have a dedicated mailing list of 5,000 subscribers who regularly engage with my content."
- **Genre Influence**: Consider your influence and standing within your specific genre or niche.
  - o **Example**: "I'm frequently invited to speak at genre-specific conferences and events."

6. Personal Milestones

Personal milestones are unique to each author and can include a variety of achievements that resonate personally with you.

- **Publishing Milestones**: These might include signing your first book deal, completing a trilogy, or reaching a specific number of published works.
  - o **Example**: "I've published my first book with a major publisher."
- **Writing Achievements**: Completing a particularly challenging project, mastering a new writing technique, or receiving mentorship from a respected author.
  - o **Example**: "I've finished writing a book in a new genre I've never explored before."
- **Life Goals**: Achieving a balance between writing and other aspects of your life, such as family, travel, or hobbies.
  - o **Example**: "I've managed to write consistently while also spending quality time with my family."

7. Setting Realistic Expectations

Balancing ambition with realism is crucial. Understand that success doesn't happen overnight and that setbacks are part of the journey.

- **Patience**: Recognize that building a successful writing career takes time and persistence.

    - **Example**: "I'm committed to writing and improving, even if it takes years to achieve my goals."

- **Adaptability**: Be willing to adapt your goals based on your experiences and the feedback you receive.

    - **Example**: "I've adjusted my marketing strategy based on the results of my first book launch."

- **Continuous Improvement**: Focus on continuous learning and improvement, both in your writing craft and in your approach to publishing.

    - **Example**: "I'm taking writing courses and attending workshops to enhance my skills."

By defining what success looks like for you, you can create a clear and personalized roadmap for your writing career. Remember, this is your journey, and success can only be determined by you. No list, no journey of another can overshadow what **you** see as success. For some, success might mean simply writing the book and holding the printed copy in their hands. For others, it could mean landing on the New York Times bestseller list. Your vision of success is unique to you, and it's important to honor and pursue that vision. This personalized approach helps you stay focused, motivated, and fulfilled, regardless of how you choose to measure your achievements. In the next section, we'll discuss how to maintain motivation throughout the ups and downs of the publishing process, ensuring you stay on track and inspired.

Write It. Publish It. Sell It.

Building a community around your book is essential for fostering a sense of belonging and loyalty among your readers. A strong community not only supports your current work but also eagerly anticipates your future projects. By using both online and offline methods, you can create a vibrant, engaged community that enhances your presence as an author. Here's how to effectively build and sustain a community around your book.

Online communities offer a convenient and powerful way to connect with readers from around the world. Create dedicated groups on platforms like Facebook or LinkedIn where readers can discuss your books, share their thoughts, and connect with each other. Regularly participate in these groups to keep the conversation active and engaging. For example, start "The [Your Book] Fan Club" on Facebook where members can discuss plot twists, favorite characters, and theories about future books. Participate in or create forums and discussion boards on sites like Goodreads and Reddit. These platforms are great for in-depth discussions and building a sense of community among readers. You might host monthly book discussions, Q&A sessions, and reader polls in a dedicated Goodreads group.

Building and maintaining an email list is crucial. Use newsletters to share exclusive content, updates, and invitations to special events. For instance, a monthly newsletter can include behind-the-scenes looks at your writing process, upcoming events, and subscriber-only contests. Host live events such as Q&A sessions, book readings, and writing workshops using platforms like Zoom, Facebook Live, or Instagram Live. These events allow you to interact directly with your readers in real-time. Imagine hosting a live Q&A session on Instagram where you answer reader questions and discuss the themes and characters in your latest book.

An author website and blog are central to your community-building efforts. Maintain an author website where readers can find information about your books, read your latest posts, and join your mailing list. A blog can be a hub for your community-building efforts. For example, have a dedicated section on your website where readers can submit their fan art, participate in writing challenges, and read guest posts from other authors.

While online communities are powerful, offline interactions can deepen the connection with your readers and create memorable experiences. Organize book signings and readings at local bookstores, libraries, and literary festivals. These events provide an opportunity for personal interaction and can attract new readers. Picture a book signing event at a local independent bookstore where you read a chapter from your book, answer questions, and sign copies for attendees. Encourage and support book clubs that choose to read your books. Offer to attend their meetings, either in person or virtually, to discuss your work and engage with readers. Partner with local libraries to promote book clubs that read your work and offer to join their discussions via Zoom or in person.

Participate in or host workshops and panel discussions on writing, publishing, and related topics. These events can position you as an expert and attract readers who are interested in your insights. Imagine leading a writing workshop at a literary festival where you share tips on character development and plot structure. Engage with your local community by participating in events such as charity fundraisers, school visits, and community fairs. These events help build your presence and connect with potential readers who share your values and interests. Think about visiting a school where you talk about your journey as an author, conduct a creative writing session, and donate copies of your books to the school library.

Collaborating with other authors, influencers, and organizations can help expand your community and bring fresh perspectives to your work. Partner with other authors to co-host events such as book signings, readings, or online webinars. This collaboration can draw in fans from both authors' audiences. Imagine a joint book launch event with a fellow author where you both read excerpts from your new releases and discuss your writing processes. Collaborate with other authors and influencers for cross-promotional campaigns. This can include social media takeovers, guest blog posts, and shared giveaways. Picture a social media campaign where you and another author take over each other's Instagram accounts for a day, sharing insights and engaging with each other's followers. Contribute to anthologies or other joint projects with other authors. These collaborative efforts can introduce your work to new readers and strengthen your community ties. For example, contribute a short story to an anthology featuring multiple authors in your genre, with each author promoting the collection to their audience.

Involving your readers in your creative process and promotional activities can deepen their investment in your work and foster a stronger community. Use polls and votes to let your readers have a say in certain aspects of your book, such as character names, cover designs, or plot decisions. Host a poll on your website where readers can vote on their favorite cover design for your upcoming book. Host contests that encourage readers to create fan art, write short stories, or develop other creative works based on your books. Share the best submissions on your website and social media. Imagine a fan art contest where the winning artwork is featured in your newsletter and the artist receives a signed copy of your book. Invite your most dedicated readers to become beta readers, offering them early access to your manuscripts in exchange for feedback. This not only helps improve your book but also makes readers feel valued and involved. Consider a beta reader program where selected readers receive an early draft of your book and provide feedback on the plot, characters, and pacing.

Building a community is not just about one-time interactions but creating long-term relationships with your readers. Personalize your communications whenever possible. Address readers by their names in emails, acknowledge their contributions in public posts, and show genuine appreciation for their support. After events or significant interactions, follow up with attendees or participants to thank them and keep the connection alive. Imagine sending a thank-you email to attendees of your book signing event, along with a recap and an invitation to join your newsletter. Continue to engage with your community even when you don't have a new book to promote. Share updates, interesting content, and personal stories to keep the relationship strong. Regularly update your blog with posts about your writing process, favorite books, and life updates, even between book releases.

By combining online and offline methods, collaborative activities, reader participation, and long-term relationship-building strategies, you can create a vibrant and supportive community around your books. In the next section, we will discuss how to encourage and manage reader feedback, using it to improve your work and strengthen your connection with your audience.

Maintaining Motivation: Staying motivated through the ups and downs of the publishing process.

Staying motivated as an author can be challenging, especially when facing the inevitable ups and downs of the publishing process. However, maintaining motivation is crucial for your long-term success and personal fulfillment. Here are strategies to help you stay inspired and driven, no matter what obstacles you encounter.

1. Find Your Why

Understanding your core motivations for writing can help you stay focused and inspired. Reflect on why you started writing in the first place and what you hope to achieve.

- **Passion for Storytelling**: Remind yourself of your love for creating stories and characters.
    - **Example**: "I write because I love bringing imaginary worlds to life and sharing them with readers."
- **Personal Fulfillment**: Acknowledge the personal satisfaction and joy that writing brings you.

    - **Example**: "Writing helps me express myself and explore my creativity."

- **Impact on Readers**: Think about the potential impact your stories can have on readers' lives.
    - **Example**: "I want to inspire and entertain readers, providing them with an escape or new perspectives."

2. Set Manageable Goals

Breaking your larger writing and publishing goals into smaller, manageable tasks can make the process less overwhelming and more achievable.

- **Daily and Weekly Goals**: Set specific, short-term goals to keep you on track.
    - **Example**: "I will write 500 words every day this week."
- **Celebrate Small Wins**: Acknowledge and celebrate your achievements, no matter how small.
    - **Example**: "I finished a chapter today—time for a small celebration!"
- **Track Progress**: Keep a journal or use a tracking app to monitor your progress and stay motivated.
    - **Example**: "I've written consistently for 30 days—this streak is motivating me to keep going."

3. Connect with Other Writers

Engaging with a community of fellow writers can provide support, encouragement, and a sense of camaraderie.

- **Join Writing Groups**: Participate in local or online writing groups where you can share your work, receive feedback, and discuss challenges.
    - **Example**: "I'm part of a weekly writing group that offers valuable feedback and support."

- **Attend Workshops and Conferences**: Take part in writing workshops and literary conferences to learn from others and stay inspired.

    - **Example**: "Attending a writing workshop rejuvenated my enthusiasm for my current project."

- **Online Communities**: Engage with online writing communities and forums to connect with other authors.

    - **Example**: "I've found a supportive community on a writers' forum where we share tips and encouragement."

4. Reward Yourself

Incorporate a system of rewards to keep yourself motivated and celebrate your achievements.

- **Small Rewards**: Treat yourself for reaching small milestones, like completing a chapter or hitting a word count target.

    - **Example**: "After finishing this chapter, I'll reward myself with a movie night."

- **Larger Rewards**: Plan bigger rewards for major accomplishments, such as completing a manuscript or publishing your book.

    - **Example**: "When I finish my manuscript, I'll take a weekend getaway to relax and recharge."

5. Embrace Breaks and Self-Care

Taking regular breaks and practicing self-care are essential for maintaining long-term motivation and preventing burnout.

- **Scheduled Breaks**: Incorporate regular breaks into your writing routine to rest and recharge.

- - **Example**: "I take a short walk every afternoon to clear my mind and re-energize."

- **Self-Care Activities**: Engage in activities that nurture your well-being, such as exercise, meditation, or hobbies.

  - **Example**: "I practice yoga to stay physically and mentally balanced."

- **Avoid Overworking**: Recognize when you need to step back and take a break to avoid burnout.

  - **Example**: "If I'm feeling overwhelmed, I give myself permission to take a day off from writing."

6. Keep Learning and Growing

Continual learning and skill development can keep your passion for writing alive and fuel your motivation.

- **Writing Courses**: Enroll in writing courses to improve your craft and gain new insights.

  - **Example**: "I'm taking an online course on character development to enhance my skills."

- **Reading Widely**: Read books in various genres to stay inspired and learn from other authors.

  - **Example**: "Reading a diverse range of books helps me understand different writing styles and techniques."

- **Seek Feedback**: Regularly seek feedback from beta readers, critique partners, or writing mentors to improve your work.

  - **Example**: "Feedback from my writing mentor has been invaluable in refining my manuscript."

7. Visualize Your Success

Visualization techniques can help you stay focused on your goals and maintain a positive mindset.

- **Vision Board**: Create a vision board with images, quotes, and goals that inspire you.
    - **Example**: "My vision board includes my dream book cover, motivational quotes, and goals for my writing career."

- **Mental Visualization**: Regularly visualize your success and the achievement of your goals.
    - **Example**: "I spend a few minutes each day visualizing my book on the bestseller list."

- **Positive Affirmations**: Use positive affirmations to reinforce your belief in your abilities and potential.
    - **Example**: "I repeat affirmations like 'I am a successful author' to stay motivated."

8. Adapt and Stay Flexible

The publishing process can be unpredictable, and flexibility is key to staying motivated despite setbacks or changes.

- **Adjust Goals**: Be willing to adjust your goals based on your progress and circumstances.
    - **Example**: "I had to push back my manuscript deadline, but I adjusted my schedule to accommodate it."

- **Learn from Setbacks**: View setbacks as learning opportunities and stay resilient in the face of challenges.

- o **Example**: "A rejection letter is just a step closer to finding the right publisher."
- **Stay Open to New Ideas**: Embrace new ideas and approaches to keep your writing fresh and exciting.
  - o **Example**: "I'm exploring a new genre to challenge myself and keep my writing journey interesting."

Understanding your core motivations for writing can help you stay focused and inspired. Reflect on why you started writing in the first place and what you hope to achieve. Passion for storytelling is a powerful motivator; remind yourself of your love for creating stories and characters. Think about the joy of bringing imaginary worlds to life and sharing them with readers. Acknowledge the personal satisfaction and joy that writing brings you. Writing can be a profound form of self-expression and creativity, providing immense personal fulfillment. Consider the potential impact your stories can have on readers' lives. You might want to inspire, entertain, or provide an escape or new perspectives to your audience.

Breaking your larger writing and publishing goals into smaller, manageable tasks can make the process less overwhelming and more achievable. Set specific daily and weekly goals to keep yourself on track. For instance, you might aim to write 500 words every day this week. Celebrate your small wins along the way, like finishing a chapter, and take a moment to acknowledge these achievements. Keeping track of your progress can be incredibly motivating. Use a journal or a tracking app to monitor your consistency and see how far you've come.

Engaging with a community of fellow writers can provide support, encouragement, and a sense of camaraderie. Join local or online writing groups where you can share your work, receive feedback, and discuss challenges. Participating in workshops and conferences can also be invigorating, offering new insights and rekindling your enthusiasm for your projects. Online communities and forums are another excellent resource for connecting with other authors, sharing tips, and finding encouragement.

Incorporate a system of rewards to keep yourself motivated and celebrate your achievements. Treat yourself for reaching small milestones, like completing a chapter or hitting a word count target. Plan bigger rewards for major accomplishments, such as completing a manuscript or publishing your book. These rewards can keep you motivated and provide something to look forward to.

Taking regular breaks and practicing self-care are essential for maintaining long-term motivation and preventing burnout. Incorporate regular breaks into your writing routine to rest and recharge. Engage in activities that nurture your well-being, such as exercise, meditation, or hobbies. Recognize when you need to step back and take a break to avoid burnout, giving yourself permission to rest and rejuvenate.

Continual learning and skill development can keep your passion for writing alive and fuel your motivation. Enroll in writing courses to improve your craft and gain new insights. Read widely across various genres to stay inspired and learn from other authors. Regularly seek feedback from beta readers, critique partners, or writing mentors to improve your work. This continual growth can keep you excited about your writing journey.

Visualization techniques can help you stay focused on your goals and maintain a positive mindset. Create a vision board with images, quotes, and goals that inspire you. Spend a few minutes each day visualizing your success and the achievement of your goals. Use positive affirmations to reinforce your belief in your abilities and potential, helping to maintain your motivation.

The publishing process can be unpredictable, and flexibility is key to staying motivated despite setbacks or changes. Be willing to adjust your goals based on your progress and circumstances. View setbacks as learning opportunities and stay resilient in the face of challenges. Embrace new ideas and approaches to keep your writing fresh and exciting. Exploring new genres or techniques can reinvigorate your writing process and keep your journey interesting.

By implementing these strategies, you can maintain your motivation and enthusiasm throughout the publishing process. Remember, every author's journey is unique, and staying motivated is about finding what works best for you. In the next section, we'll discuss long-term planning for your author career, ensuring you're prepared for a sustainable and fulfilling writing journey beyond your first book.

Long-Term Planning: Planning for the future of your author career beyond your first book.

Writing and publishing your first book is a significant achievement, but it's just the beginning of your author journey. Long-term planning is essential to ensure that your career continues to grow and thrive beyond that initial success. By setting clear goals, continually developing your skills, and strategically managing your career, you can build a sustainable and fulfilling life as an author.

1. Career Vision

Start by defining your long-term vision as an author. This vision will guide your decisions and help you stay focused on what you want to achieve.

- **Legacy and Impact**: Think about the legacy you want to leave as an author. What messages or themes do you want your work to convey? How do you want your books to impact readers and the literary world?
    - **Example**: "I want to write stories that inspire and empower readers, leaving a lasting impact on their lives."
- **Genres and Themes**: Consider the genres and themes you want to explore over the course of your career. This can help you plan future projects and build a consistent author brand.
    - **Example**: "I aim to write a series of historical fiction novels that explore different eras and cultures."

2. Skill Development

Continually improving your writing skills is crucial for long-term success. Investing in your growth as a writer will help you produce higher-quality work and stay competitive in the industry.

- **Workshops and Courses**: Regularly attend writing workshops and take courses to learn new techniques and refine your craft.
    - **Example**: "I will enroll in an advanced writing workshop each year to continue developing my skills."
- **Reading Widely**: Read a diverse range of books to expose yourself to different styles, genres, and perspectives.
    - **Example**: "I will read at least one book outside my primary genre each month to broaden my literary horizons."
- **Feedback and Critique**: Seek feedback from beta readers, critique partners, and writing groups to identify areas for improvement.
    - **Example**: "I will participate in a critique group that meets monthly to get constructive feedback on my work."

3. Networking and Relationships

Building relationships with other authors, industry professionals, and readers is essential for a successful long-term career.

- **Industry Connections**: Network with agents, editors, publishers, and other industry professionals. Attend conferences, book fairs, and literary events to make connections.
    - **Example**: "I will attend at least two major literary conferences each year to network and stay informed about industry trends."

- **Author Community**: Engage with other authors through writing groups, social media, and collaborative projects. These relationships can provide support, inspiration, and opportunities for collaboration.

  - **Example**: "I will join an online writing community and actively participate in discussions and events."

- **Reader Engagement**: Foster a strong connection with your readers through social media, newsletters, and events. Building a loyal reader base is crucial for ongoing success.

  - **Example**: "I will send out a monthly newsletter to keep my readers updated and engaged."

4. Diversification

Exploring different writing opportunities and formats can help you diversify your income and reach new audiences.

- **Multiple Genres**: Consider writing in different genres to expand your audience and challenge yourself creatively.

  - **Example**: "I will write a mystery novel in addition to my ongoing historical fiction series."

- **Various Formats**: Experiment with different formats, such as short stories, novellas, screenplays, or articles.

  - **Example**: "I will write a series of short stories to submit to literary magazines."

- **Related Fields**: Explore opportunities in related fields, such as teaching writing workshops, speaking engagements, or freelance writing.

  - **Example**: "I will offer online writing workshops to share my expertise and generate additional income."

5. Financial Planning

Effective financial planning is essential for sustaining a long-term writing career. Managing your finances wisely ensures that you can continue writing without undue stress.

- **Budgeting**: Create a budget that accounts for your writing expenses, such as editing, cover design, marketing, and travel for events.
    - **Example**: "I will allocate a specific budget for each book project and track my expenses closely."
- **Income Streams**: Identify and develop multiple income streams related to your writing.
    - **Example**: "I will generate income from book sales, freelance writing, and speaking engagements."
- **Savings and Investments**: Set aside savings for future projects and consider investing in resources that can enhance your writing career.
    - **Example**: "I will save a portion of my writing income each month to fund future book projects."

6. Setting Milestones

Establishing long-term milestones helps you track your progress and stay motivated. These milestones should align with your overall career vision and goals.

- **Publishing Milestones**: Set specific targets for the number of books you want to publish and the timeline for achieving these goals.
    - **Example**: "I will publish a new book every 18 months."
- **Recognition and Awards**: Aim for specific awards, recognitions, or achievements that can validate your work and boost your career.

- - **Example**: "I will submit my work for consideration in major literary awards."
- **Growth and Expansion**: Plan for the growth and expansion of your author brand and platform.
  - **Example**: "I will grow my mailing list to 10,000 subscribers within the next three years."

7. Adapting to Change

The publishing industry is constantly evolving, and being adaptable is key to sustaining a long-term career. Stay informed about industry trends and be willing to adjust your strategies as needed.

- **Market Trends**: Keep up with changes in the publishing industry, such as new marketing strategies, technological advancements, and shifts in reader preferences.
  - **Example**: "I will regularly read industry publications and blogs to stay updated on market trends."
- **Flexibility**: Be open to exploring new opportunities and changing your approach based on what you learn.
  - **Example**: "I will adapt my marketing strategy based on the performance of my latest book launch."

By planning for the future and setting clear, achievable goals, you can build a sustainable and fulfilling author career. This long-term approach will help you navigate the challenges of the publishing industry and continue to grow and succeed as a writer.

Start by defining your long-term vision as an author. This vision will guide your decisions and help you stay focused on what you want to achieve. Think about the legacy you want to leave as an author—what messages or themes do you want your work to convey? How do you want your books to impact readers and the literary world? For instance, you might say, "I want to write stories that inspire and empower readers, leaving a lasting impact on their lives." Consider the genres and themes you want to explore over the course of your career. This can help you plan future projects and build a consistent author brand, such as aiming to write a series of historical fiction novels that explore different eras and cultures.

Continually improving your writing skills is crucial for long-term success. Investing in your growth as a writer will help you produce higher-quality work and stay competitive in the industry. Regularly attend writing workshops and take courses to learn new techniques and refine your craft. For example, you might enroll in an advanced writing workshop each year. Reading a diverse range of books can also expose you to different styles, genres, and perspectives, broadening your literary horizons. Seek feedback from beta readers, critique partners, and writing groups to identify areas for improvement. Participating in a monthly critique group can provide valuable insights.

Building relationships with other authors, industry professionals, and readers is essential for a successful long-term career. Network with agents, editors, publishers, and other industry professionals by attending conferences, book fairs, and literary events. For instance, attending at least two major literary conferences each year can help you stay informed about industry trends. Engage with other authors through writing groups, social media, and collaborative projects, which can offer support, inspiration, and collaboration opportunities. Additionally, foster a strong connection with your readers through social media, newsletters, and events. Sending out a monthly newsletter can keep your readers updated and engaged.

Exploring different writing opportunities and formats can help you diversify your income and reach new audiences. Consider writing in different genres to expand your audience and challenge yourself creatively. You might write a mystery novel in addition to your ongoing historical fiction series. Experiment with different formats, such as short stories, novellas, screenplays, or articles. Writing a series of short stories to submit to literary magazines can be a good start. Explore opportunities in related fields, such as teaching writing workshops, speaking engagements, or freelance writing. Offering online writing workshops can share your expertise and generate additional income.

Effective financial planning is essential for sustaining a long-term writing career. Managing your finances wisely ensures that you can continue writing without undue stress. Create a budget that accounts for your writing expenses, such as editing, cover design, marketing, and travel for events. Allocate a specific budget for each book project and track your expenses closely. Identify and develop multiple income streams related to your writing, such as generating income from book sales, freelance writing, and speaking engagements. Set aside savings for future projects and consider investing in resources that can enhance your writing career.

Establishing long-term milestones helps you track your progress and stay motivated. These milestones should align with your overall career vision and goals. Set specific targets for the number of books you want to publish and the timeline for achieving these goals. For instance, you might aim to publish a new book every 18 months. Aim for specific awards, recognitions, or achievements that can validate your work and boost your career, such as submitting your work for consideration in major literary awards. Plan for the growth and expansion of your author brand and platform, like growing your mailing list to 10,000 subscribers within the next three years.

The publishing industry is constantly evolving, and being adaptable is key to sustaining a long-term career. Stay informed about industry trends and be willing to adjust your strategies as needed. Keep up with changes in the publishing industry, such as new marketing strategies, technological advancements, and shifts in reader preferences. Regularly read industry publications and blogs to stay updated on market trends. Be open to exploring new opportunities and changing your approach based on what you learn. Adapt your marketing strategy based on the performance of your latest book launch.

By planning for the future and setting clear, achievable goals, you can build a sustainable and fulfilling author career. This long-term approach will help you navigate the challenges of the publishing industry and continue to grow and succeed as a writer.

Conclusion

Your Publishing Power Move: Recapping the Key Takeaways

Congratulations! You've reached the end of this journey, equipped with the knowledge and tools to make your publishing dreams a reality. Let's recap the key takeaways from this book and the accompanying course, ensuring you're ready to make your ultimate publishing power move.

- **Master the Writing Process**: You've learned how to find your unique voice, establish a consistent writing routine, overcome writer's block, and refine your manuscript through diligent editing and revising.
- **Explore Publishing Options**: With a clear understanding of self-publishing, traditional publishing, and hybrid models, you're equipped to make an informed decision that aligns with your goals and career aspirations.
- **Marketing and Promotion**: You now know the difference between marketing and promoting your book, with practical strategies to build your brand, engage your audience, and leverage social media and public relations.
- **Financial Insights**: Setting a budget, identifying essential investments, and avoiding financial pitfalls ensures you manage your resources wisely throughout the publishing process.
- **Crafting Query Letters**: With the tools to write compelling query letters, you can effectively pitch your manuscript to agents and publishers, increasing your chances of securing a deal.
- **Building and Engaging Your Audience**: You've learned the importance of identifying your target audience, creating engaging content, and fostering a community around your work.
- **Setting Real Expectations**: Understanding the realities of publishing, setting achievable goals, and defining what success looks like for you helps keep your journey fulfilling and grounded.
- **Maintaining Motivation**: Strategies to stay motivated through the highs and lows of the publishing process ensure you keep moving forward with resilience and passion.

- **Long-Term Planning**: Planning for the future of your author career, from skill development and networking to financial planning and adaptability, positions you for sustained success.

Next Steps: Practical Advice for Moving Forward

As you embark on the next phase of your publishing journey, here are some practical steps to keep you on track and moving forward:

Create a Detailed Plan: Outline your short-term and long-term goals, breaking them down into actionable steps. Use the SMART criteria to ensure your goals are Specific, Measurable, Achievable, Relevant, and Time-bound.

Stay Consistent: Maintain a regular writing schedule and stay disciplined in your approach. Consistency is key to making progress and achieving your milestones.

Build Your Network: Continue to engage with writing communities, attend events, and build relationships with industry professionals. Networking can open doors to new opportunities and provide valuable support.

Invest in Learning: Never stop learning. Take courses, read widely, and seek feedback to continually improve your craft and stay updated on industry trends.

Market Actively: Implement your marketing and promotion strategies consistently. Build your brand, engage with your audience, and leverage various channels to increase your book's visibility.

Adapt and Pivot: Be flexible and willing to adapt your plans based on feedback and changing circumstances. The ability to pivot is crucial in navigating the dynamic landscape of publishing.

Resources: Additional Resources and Reading for Continued Learning

To further support your journey, here are some valuable resources and recommended readings:

Writing Craft:

- "On Writing: A Memoir of the Craft" by Stephen King
- "Bird by Bird: Some Instructions on Writing and Life" by Anne Lamott
- "The Elements of Style" by William Strunk Jr. and E.B. White

Publishing and Marketing:

- "The Business of Being a Writer" by Jane Friedman
- "How to Market a Book" by Joanna Penn
- "The Creative Penn" blog and podcast by Joanna Penn

Industry Insights:

- "Writer's Market" by Writer's Digest Books
- "Publishers Weekly" and "The Writer" magazines
- "Jane Friedman" blog and resources by Jane Friedman

Community and Networking:

- Join writing organizations such as the Society of Children's Book Writers and Illustrators (SCBWI) or Romance Writers of America (RWA)
- Participate in online writing communities like Scribophile or Wattpad
- Attend literary festivals and writing conferences

Final Thoughts

Remember, this journey is uniquely yours. Celebrate every milestone, learn from every setback, and keep moving forward with passion and determination. Your voice matters, and your stories have the power to inspire, entertain, and transform lives. Embrace your publishing power move, and let your words create a lasting impact in the world. Here's to your success and the incredible journey ahead—happy writing and publishing!

Appendices

Templates and Worksheets

To help you apply the concepts and strategies discussed in each chapter, we have created a series of practical tools and worksheets. These resources are designed to assist you with planning, writing, marketing, and more. Please refer to our exclusive workbook for all worksheets, which include:

- **Writing Routine Planner**: Schedule and track your daily writing goals.
- **Character Development Sheet**: Outline and detail your characters' traits, backgrounds, and arcs.
- **Plot Structure Template**: Organize your story's structure and key plot points.
- **Query Letter Template**: Format and draft your query letters with ease.
- **Marketing Plan Outline**: Create a comprehensive marketing plan for your book.
- **Budgeting Worksheet**: Manage and plan your publishing expenses.
- **Goal Setting Tracker**: Set, track, and reflect on your short-term and long-term goals.
- **Reader Feedback Log**: Collect and organize feedback from beta readers and reviews.

Recommended Reading

To further expand your knowledge and understanding of the publishing process, here are some recommended books and articles:

Writing Craft

- *On Writing: A Memoir of the Craft* by Stephen King
- *Bird by Bird: Some Instructions on Writing and Life* by Anne Lamott
- *The Elements of Style* by William Strunk Jr. and E.B. White
- *Writing Down the Bones: Freeing the Writer Within* by Natalie Goldberg

Publishing and Marketing

- *The Business of Being a Writer* by Jane Friedman
- *How to Market a Book* by Joanna Penn
- *The Essential Guide to Getting Your Book Published* by Arielle Eckstut and David Henry Sterry
- *Ape: Author, Publisher, Entrepreneur—How to Publish a Book* by Guy Kawasaki and Shawn Welch

Industry Insights

- *Writer's Market* by Writer's Digest Books
- *Self-Publishing Boot Camp Guide for Authors* by Carla King
- *The Creative Penn* blog and podcast by Joanna Penn
- *Jane Friedman* blog and resources by Jane Friedman

Community and Networking

- Join writing organizations such as the Society of Children's Book Writers and Illustrators (SCBWI) or Romance Writers of America (RWA)
- Participate in online writing communities like Scribophile or Wattpad
- Attend literary festivals and writing conferences

Glossary

Below are definitions of key terms used throughout this book:

- **Beta Readers**: Early readers who provide feedback on a manuscript before it is published.
- **Book Proposal**: A document that authors use to pitch a nonfiction book to publishers, typically including an outline, sample chapters, and market analysis.

Write It. Publish It. Sell It.

- **Branding**: The process of creating a unique image and identity for an author and their work.
- **Copyediting**: The process of reviewing and correcting written material to improve accuracy, readability, and fitness for its purpose.
- **Hybrid Publishing**: A publishing model that combines elements of traditional publishing and self-publishing, often involving shared costs and royalties.
- **Imprint**: A trade name under which a work is published; an imprint can be part of a larger publishing house.
- **ISBN (International Standard Book Number)**: A unique identifier for books, allowing them to be easily cataloged and sold.
- **Literary Agent**: A professional who represents authors in dealings with publishers, often helping to negotiate contracts and secure publishing deals.
- **Marketing**: The activities involved in promoting and selling books, including advertising, public relations, and social media outreach.
- **Platform**: The combined reach and influence an author has, typically encompassing social media, blogs, public speaking, and other forms of audience engagement.
- **Query Letter**: A letter sent to literary agents or publishers to pitch a book manuscript, summarizing the story and the author's credentials.
- **Self-Publishing**: The process of publishing a book independently, without the involvement of a traditional publishing house.
- **Synopsis**: A brief summary of a book's plot, characters, and main themes, often used in query letters and book proposals.
- **Traditional Publishing**: A publishing model where an author signs a contract with a publisher who handles the production, distribution, and marketing of the book.
- **Vanity Press**: A type of publishing where authors pay to have their books published, often with limited distribution and marketing support.

By utilizing these templates, recommended readings, and understanding key terms, you'll be well-equipped to navigate the complex world of publishing and make your ultimate publishing power move. Best of luck on your author journey!

Business Plan Template for _____

1. Executive Summary

- **Book Title:** _____
- **Author:** _____
- **Mission Statement:** _____
  (e.g., "To inspire and empower writers to achieve their publishing dreams through comprehensive guidance and support.")
- **Vision Statement:** _____
  (e.g., "To become the leading resource for aspiring authors seeking to write, publish, and market their books successfully.")
- **Objectives:**
  - **Short-term Goals:**
    _____
  - **Long-term Goals:**
    _____

2. Market Analysis

- **Target Audience:**
  - **Primary Audience:**
    _____
  - **Secondary Audience:**
    _____
- **Market Need:** _____ (e.g., "There is a growing need for accessible, comprehensive resources for aspiring authors who want to navigate the complexities of writing, publishing, and marketing their books.")
- **Market Trends:** _____ (e.g., "Self-publishing is on the rise, and more authors are seeking direct-to-consumer sales channels.")

3. Competitive Analysis

- **Competitors:**
  - **Direct Competitors:**
    _____

Write It. Publish It. Sell It.

- o **Indirect Competitors:** _____
- **Competitive Advantage:** _____ (e.g., "Our book provides a unique, step-by-step approach combined with practical tools and templates.")
- **SWOT Analysis:**

    - o **Strengths:** _____
    - o **Weaknesses:** _____
    - o **Opportunities:** _____
    - o **Threats:** _____

4. Marketing Strategy

- **Brand Positioning:**

    - o **Brand Identity:** _____
    - o **Value Proposition:** _____

- **Marketing Channels:**

    - o **Social Media:** _____
    - o **Email Marketing:** _____
    - o **Content Marketing (Blogs, Podcasts, etc.):** _____
    - o **Advertising (Paid Ads, Influencer Collaborations, etc.):** _____

- **Promotional Activities:**

    - o **Book Launch Events:** _____

- Partnerships and Collaborations: _____

5. Sales Strategy

- **Sales Channels:**
    - Online Retailers (Amazon, etc.): _____
    - Author's Website: _____
    - Bookstores: _____
    - Events and Speaking Engagements: _____

- **Pricing Strategy:** _____
  (e.g., "Competitive pricing with periodic discounts and promotions to attract and retain customers.")
- **Sales Forecast:**
    - Year 1: _____
    - Year 2: _____
    - Year 3: _____

6. Operational Plan

- **Production Plan:**
    - Manuscript Completion: _____
    - Editing and Proofreading: _____
    - Design and Formatting: _____
    - Printing and Distribution: _____

Write It. Publish It. Sell It.

- **Key Milestones:**
    - Book Launch: _____
    - Marketing Campaigns: _____
    - Sales Reviews: _____

7. Financial Plan

    - **Budget:**
        - Initial Investment: _____
        - Ongoing Costs: _____

    - **Revenue Projections:**
        - Year 1: _____
        - Year 2: _____
        - Year 3: _____

    - **Break-even Analysis:** _____
    - **Funding Requirements:** _____

8. Appendix

    - **Supplementary Materials:**
        - Sample Marketing Materials: _____
        - Detailed Financial Projections: _____
        - Additional Resources: _____

This template is designed to help you think strategically about your book project and manage it like a thriving business. By filling in each section thoughtfully, you can create a robust plan that guides your efforts in writing, publishing, and selling your book.

www.ingramcontent.com/pod-product-compliance
Lightning Source LLC
LaVergne TN
LVHW030315070526
838199LV00069B/6473